Frank with Edmée
with love & pleasure.

WILLIE GAVIN, CROFTER MAN
Portrait of a Vanished Lifestyle

WILLIE GAVIN, CROFTER MAN

Portrait of a Vanished Lifestyle

by

DAVID KERR CAMERON

LONDON
VICTOR GOLLANCZ LTD
1980

© David Kerr Cameron 1980

ISBN 0 575 02816 5

Printed in Great Britain at
The Camelot Press Ltd, Southampton

AUTHOR'S NOTE

This is a portrait of crofting life in the bare and sometimes bitter landscape of Scotland's North-east Lowlands. It is, closely reconstructed, the life of one crofter man in particular and, beyond that, the wider story of a croft and its people. Their time is past and done with now but their days were typical of the crofting experience in that old countryside. It is a record assembled mainly from a family's folk memory and to avoid any undue embarrassment I have blurred Willie Gavin's real identity. To his folk, who gave so freely of their memories, I am deeply indebted.

ACKNOWLEDGEMENTS

For permission to quote and reproduce copyright material the author wishes to thank the following: Margaret, Marchioness of Aberdeen; the Bailies of Bennachie and Routledge and Kegan Paul.

Among those who so kindly helped to locate and identify photographs which reflect the life and work of the old landscape, he wishes particularly to thank the following: Gavin Sprott of the National Museum of Antiquities of Scotland; Ian Hardie and Tam Forsyth of *Aberdeen Journals*; Douglas M. Spence of D. C. Thomson; and *The Scots Magazine* for permitting the use of material from the Robert M. Adam collection.

CONTENTS

LIST OF ILLUSTRATIONS

A country rag-and-bone man, in the 1890s (*Aberdeen Journals*)

Old smith and smiddy at Dallachy, in Banffshire (*Albert Bodie, Banff*)

The lonely life (*Aberdeen Journals*)

A country kitchen in the 1880s (*Aberdeen Journals*)

Harvesting with the reaper (*E. W. Tattersall, St Albans*)

Harvesting with the scythe (*Glenesk Museum*)

A North-east poacher, early-1900s (*Robert M. Adam collection*)

An Oldmeldrum farmtoun horseman in 1904 (*Robert M. Adam collection*)

Day out for country folk about the turn of the century (*National Museum of Antiquities of Scotland*)

Unacknowledged photographs belong to the author

WILLIE GAVIN, CROFTER MAN
Portrait of a Vanished Lifestyle

I

The Old Crofter Man

WILLIE GAVIN INHERITED two things from his father: his new tile hat and the old Gavin croft. The one he wore long to funerals after that fashion had turned to the bowler; the other was a heartbreak to him, all of his days. Yet he would not leave it; the croft was in his blood, gripping him like a fever. He had been born into the dark recess of its box-bed and it had beckoned him from the cradle. He was never able to see past its old thatched dwelling and the rickle of its old *biggings*, or to lift his gaze beyond the immediate horizon of its small bare fields.

If ever a man should have sold his inheritance, it was Willie Gavin; and it is difficult now to know what possessed him, and drew him into the life. A love for the land perhaps, and its possession; a hunger certainly for that strong identity and continuity of family and race that passes down in an ancestral landscape—a hunger no less in the bare Lowlands of Scotland's North-east than in the wilder glens of the West, with their memory of the brutal Clearances. Whatever it was, in Willie Gavin it ran deep, and like most of his kind, and for most of his life, he ran in the double harness that was the curse of the old crofting existence: working away by day and coming home to do his croft work by night, often enough by the light of the wintry stars. The bitter irony of it was: he had no need to. Other men might take on crofts, with their ceaseless work and their treadmill slavery, to keep themselves and their families out of the chill charity of the parish poorhouse; Willie Gavin was a craftsman and a good one at that, a master stonemason in that now-distant time when *biggings* for both man and beast had been accorded the dignity of stone, and sometimes the grandeur of granite, and when the glint and sparkle of mica in the landscape had drawn the eye constantly to the old builders' skill. In that time before the fraudulence of the composition block and the instant obscenity of asbestos scarred the countryside, men like Willie Gavin had built their own memorials in the old stone *biggings* that would long outlast them and the sons who came after them. His skill in his prime, folk said, was proverbial and even now, in that bleak landscape that lies between the blue mound of the Grampians and the growl of the grey North Sea there are old men who will stop in the bygoing to take a look at the simple harmony of an old farmtoun or the plain lines of a stark grey kirk among the trees and say quietly: "Willie Gavin biggit it"—meaning not that his was the hand that chiselled its every stone but that his was the eye that gave it dour grace.

The tribute might have pleased the crofter man well enough had he heard it, for certainly, had he been minded to, he might have set himself up in a fine, stone-built house on the edge of the little quarrytoun that had taught him his trade. There he could have put past a winter of ease after the hard-building of summer. And had he, like so many of the old North-east masoning men, been tempted to the States for a season or two of work, there was no telling: he might have become a rich man with a trowel in his hand. It would have been a wonder, people said, for the folk over there to see the ease with which his eye could take the pure lineaments of the stone out of the grey granite lump. And surely there had been folk who would have been pleased to see the back of him for a while for other reasons, for all his life Willie Gavin had that awkward, unbending kind of integrity that made other folk uncomfortable. As a masoning boss he drove hard—punctilious about time-keeping, strict on the avoidance of oaths (even when the chisel slipped), demanding at times the kind of workmanship that was beyond the lesser-gifted. He was never an easy man to please, or to work with.

But it was the croft, not the masoning trade, that was his life: he cared little about the stone he could so easily master, much more for the soil he never could conquer. Folk said whiles that he cared more for his bit *grun*, his land, than he did for his wife and bairns and maybe he did; rotting fences would have to be replaced supposing they should all of them starve, which they often damned nearly did. He would have been a poor crofter man had it been otherwise. All the same, his creed was ironclad and he was as hard on himself as he was on everyone else: however sharp the hunger in his belly he would clean and oil his spade, or sharpen his scythe and set it away against the next day's work, before he stepped indoors for his own supper. For all that, his family found it difficult to forgive him. And the old croft betrayed him.

It took its toll slowly, consuming him, honing him with work, morning and night, year after year. By the time he came to put away his mason's white moleskins for the serviceable cords in a landsman's brown that would take him through his years of retirement, it had begun to drain him. That was the way of it with the old crofter men. His measured stride as he stepped round his *biggings* or through his small cornyard (tightening a thatch-rope here and there) after a bad night of storm or high wind, would falter a little now and then, and as the challenge of harvest or the rush of spring work drew on you could see him begin to gird himself mentally for the onslaught.

But his obsession with his small fields remained undimmed. And though his ladder legs had forsaken him, he still built his few ricks of *hairst* with his own hands. Now and then folk would tryst him away, putting the occasional job of masoning his way, mindful of the careful workman he still was. The old crofter man took the work, glad of the *siller* it would bring in, repointing the school playground wall maybe, or repairing the kirkyard dyke, and for a day or two the old magic would return as he handled simple stones with his old arrogance and the speed of the trowel awakened a memory of the man he had been. But maybe it all mattered little to him by then, for who was there to see him?: just the school bairns let out for their playtime, or the ghosts of earlier Gavins long into the kirkyard and finally at peace. Long before the end of the afternoon he would be away home, mindful of the load of turnips he had still to barrow in to the byre or the hay he might turn in the swath before the night air came down.

Always his fields drew him home, and his small *hairsts*, hard won though they were, were a delight to him; they put a lightness, a jauntiness almost, into his step as he took down the croft close in the morning to get his scythe, sharpened and waiting, and strode into the standing corn. For Willie Gavin that was a moment of fulfilment, of consummation, and maybe you had to be a crofter man yourself to understand it. By then, the young fresh-faced mason-man of the proud farmsteads and the stark kirks had himself grown gaunt: frail and grizzled, his tall sinewy frame stooped in the shoulders from the careless unconcern of too many wettings and damp clothes and the rheumatic rewards they could bring.

The heavy Kitchener that had been the manly adornment of his youth had for long seemed too heavy a burden on that austere face, and the skin had begun slowly to waxen and tighten over the cheekbones. Willie Gavin had come to look what he was: the old, archetypal crofter figure.

Near the end of his days, and as the clouds of war loomed dark over the countryside, his small holding and his few beasts became his entire life and he was never happy away from them, not even in his Sabbath pew. He would be anxious to be home, in case a *stirk* should sicken. Twice a year though he would willingly put on his best tweeds, his Sabbath patent boots and his bicycle clips and set off with the other crofter men for the estate office, his half-year's rent in the frayed wallet he kept closed with one of Grannie Gavin's old black-elastic garters. There, with the tenants of the farmtouns (some of them men of substance), the croft men would be given a bottle of ale, a token of the laird's esteem (or maybe to stifle complaint) as their *siller* was counted into his safe and entered upon the grand page of his ledger. That ale was like fine wine on Willie Gavin's lips, a sacrament almost as potent as the Communion he took regularly in his own plain kirk. That day, that conclave of farming men, gave him status as a holder of land. It gave him identity. Maybe that was important to Willie Gavin and to the old crofter men like him. It is difficult to say now, for they were a different breed entirely; and they spoke seldom of the hopes that drove them.

Folk said that Willie Gavin was a dour man and likely he was, for he had never had the facile gift for friendship and, God knows, he never had but little to smile about. His plight was the same as that of the other croft men: the silver that came in from one year's harvest was already bespoken for next year's seed. It was always so. Far away, in Edinburgh and London, there were kindly pin-striped men who worried about Willie Gavin and his kind. Masters of the careful form and the unshakeable statistic, they looked at the old crofting landscape with genuine concern, shaking their heads on the homeward trains and calling its way of life a finely-balanced economy. Theirs was a flight of the wildest fantasy. Its reality was a stark subsistence, often at its lowest ebb.

II

A Patch of the Lonely Moor

THE CROFTS CAME down in the generations like a good watch or a tinker's curse, sifting the men and imposing their own kind of suffering on their women; they preserved a close patriarchal society. They stood all round that cold countryside, singly and in the colonies that emerged and endured, though more sparsely, into the 1930s, anachronistic memorials to men with impossible dreams. They sat everywhere on the fringe of the good farming ground, in everybody's way, though nobody would have given you a thank-you for their sour bit parcels of land or their damp dwellings. They stitched the quilt of the landscape where the farmtouns lost interest, where the soil was thin or stony and, often enough, practically non-existent—on the edge of the moor, the side of the moss, the steep brae-face of the hillside where even the sure-footed Clydesdale was hard put to it to stand its ground and the plough came up from its down-furrow on its side, its draught beyond the power of any beast. It was a compromise that avoided the reproach of outright defeat, though it made for a poor, protracted agriculture.

But that had mattered little to the crofter men, for they existed always beyond the uttermost pale of respectable farming, their quaint ways at times almost an endorsement of the events that had placed them there. Gathered on the bare hillside, in the tucks and folds of the countryside, their small fields fought for a foothold with the whins and the broom, forever in danger of losing ground as they supported their inmates in that special thraldom of hope that distils slowly to the acuteness of despair. It was no wonder whiles if their folk went quietly mad with a strange lucidity of mind that knew itself to be at odds with the landscape. Yet they would not quit, though neighbour and laird were against them, for where else could they go? They faced both whiles for the land they had so hardily won, whether from the moor or the hill; blessed the rushes that sprouted as the ready material of thatch for their few ricks of harvest while knowing the warning they gave: they were there by nature's tolerance.

The crofts had been there for as long as most folk could mind, going back to that time of the land improvers and their harsh inexorable rule of change, when their first *biggings* had been little better than beggarly hovels. In that maelstrom the crofts had taken the poor ground and it is likely that their early tenants, those men and women who carved them from the hill and the moor, were often those shaken loose from the multi-tenanted farmtouns of the ancient landscape—the folk left sadly without affiliation as the new single-unit farmtouns of an improved agriculture rose over the ruins of their old dwellings and the time-hallowed pattern of their run-rigs.

Sometimes, it is true, the great farming improvements of the late-1700s and early-1800s were the work of lairds of integrity, men with a sense of compassion. But they, too, were caught in the fever of change as they geared their estates to the new high farming that would keep agriculture (and food production) apace with the Industrial Revolution. Just as surely, they marked out the ground, laying the good acres together to form their new farmtouns, thrusting the sub-tenants of the old communities overnight—and at best—into the rôle of hired hands and the indignity, twice-yearly, of the feeing fair. It would have been surprising if hardy men had not chosen, at times, to secede from that new order.

Often the crofts hugged the roadside as though they were afraid to leave it; sometimes they sat away at the back of the hills on the lonesome end of some stony track. Occasionally, even the track would peter out so that a man leaving the old holding in a hurry would put his bike on his back and strike over the fields for the nearest known road. A postman, to find some of them, would have to know the parish from childhood. Not that it mattered greatly: few of the croft folk took such a thing as a posted newspaper, weekly or daily, and most dwelt blissfully incommunicado and innocent of the world's affairs. And even when someone wrote them a letter (which was seldom), by the time it reached them the delay had smothered that immediacy which is the vital spark of communication. Only the seed catalogues were perused with any semblance of urgency and these at least were kept for a month or two—an indication of their importance—before being carefully quartered for the privvy nail. Packmen, though, called upon these lonely outposts, stumbling on them almost by accident as they crested a hill. Their very isolation, where no merchant called, in some cleft of the land where the silence was immortal, made them venues of fast trade, though doubtless their voracious, peat-reeked occupants scared the hell out of the packman. There were other places still, so far from the beaten paths of civilisation that they were as lost to the Word of God as to the Post Office. The track had long defeated the minister's bike. Their strange inhabitants dwelt there in the peace of all eternity and even the tinkers avoided them.

Of that rage for improvement, the birth of crofting was maybe the greatest betrayal of all; it deluded men, then trampled on their dreams. Folk took on crofts for the independence they thought they gave and doomed themselves to long disappointment. They believed they were perhaps putting a tentative first foot on the farming ladder and found instead that their position was untenably ambiguous in that new countryside and in a restructured society: they were neither masters nor hired men. Sometimes the croft's appeal lay in the deep-seated desire for a house that would be a home, settled and secure, in that new farming landscape of the tied house and the wandering cottar; the occupants found soon enough that the laird was sometimes as hard to please, and always to pay.

For all his sad past, the crofter was (and remains) a charismatic figure, a romantic one even. He stands in the grey gloam of history indistinguishable at times from the ancient cottar, a man whose alternative lifestyle still sheds its deep attraction for wearied city folk. He has begotten his own mythology. The poor cottar stands nowhere so richly robed in legend. Yet it was the crofter who was the new man on the landscape. We can speak of him safely only after the days of Improvement and the betrayal of the Clearances. Always he is a lonely figure.

Climate and temperament as well as terrain distanced men of Willie Gavin's kind from their crofting contemporaries of the West. One, with the sad Gaelic of his song, lived in the kind of pastoral tradition that Moses himself might not have found unfamiliar; Willie Gavin's world was rooted in the arable pattern of the bare eastern seaboard with its harder lifestyle and its hardier men. The Gael's holding was (and still is) the main form of settlement; in the East the crofter man's was the least-regarded. Willie

Gavin's neighbours were not the lonely and sometimes beautiful hills; they were the fields of his farmtoun neighbours where the ceaseless winter ploughs drew unending furrows and the spring harrows raised that vapour of dust that betokens good husbandry. Round him the ritual of work went on like an obsession, giving rest to neither man nor beast.

Unlike his Highland counterpart, Willie Gavin was a member of no community of crofts but a man on his own. Neighbourliness might bring a fellow-crofter along the road to feed and milk his beasts should a close relative be so inconsiderate as to die away from his own folk. And the visit of the threshing-mill might take one crofter man to the place of his neighbour with his barn fork under his arm. But there it ended; the Lowlands crofter man was concerned with no common pasture; no souming (that system of grazing calculation that balanced the crofting ecology of the old Highlands); no summer removal to the high shieling that took the women and girls out of the western crofting community for most of the summer. His primary implement was not the archaic foot-wielded *caschrom* (hallowed by history and somehow binding its user to the primordial past) but the iron plough, horse-drawn. His acres were his own and he engaged in no lottery of the run-rigs. If they were brothers at all under the skin—and even in the 1930s Willie Gavin still clung to a Hebridean *croman* to hoe between his turnip rows—there would have been little that they recognised in each other's crofting. The one, whatever his present hardship, bathed still at times in that aura of tragedy and romance that was the legacy of the Clearances. Living beyond that legend, Willie Gavin, crofter man, was an even lonelier figure, one of contempt when his crofting failed and he could not feed his wife and children. It was only the emblem of the sickle and the Free Kirk's psalms that united them. And maybe something else: the central place the croft took in each of their lives. In 1883—the year that the Gavin croft, coming near to the end of its first-recorded lease, was drawn in plan and carefully measured by the laird's surveyor— the Napier Commission, after a century of evictions in the Gaelic kingdom, was conducting its now-famous inquiry into crofting and the disintegration of a society. It would define the crofter man, and pin him to the landscape like a dead butterfly to the wall, as "a small tenant of land with or without a lease, who finds in the cultivation of his holding a material proportion of his occupation, earnings and sustenance, and who pays rent directly to the proprietor". As a definition it has rarely been bettered.

Despite the late emergence of the crofter class, however, "croft" had long been an honourable word in the language, feeding its long roots from an Anglo-Saxon past, enshrined in the litigious Latin of ancient charters and holy feus from at least as far back as the twelfth century. It has described the plots of bishops and saints (and sometimes of the Devil), bestowals on poets as well as the habitations of humbler men, giving the irony of its grand past to the patch on the inhospitable moor, its grace to the holy glebe. It is a vague and unlimiting term, irritatingly unquantitative. A croft could be as big as you cared to call it, so small as to be unworthy of the name (which many of them were). In the North-east Lowlands, where the cautious outlook ensures a landscape not given to extremes, there might be the occasional oddity that ran to all of twenty-five acres, though most (outside the early crofter-villages) fell between seven and fifteen. That, though, was on the estates in the prime farming areas; up-country where the heather encroached harder on the corn, they might be as small as three acres, divided into half-acre plots. At that, the least a man could hope for was a steady and fairly lucrative secondary occupation to keep him from the edge of starvation. Or failing that, charitable neighbours.

For all its hardships and its heartbreak, the spread of crofting continued in the North-east Lowlands well beyond the high tide of farmtoun improvement—indeed, for some time after the farm-touns had hit their peak of prosperity. Even into the 1880s there were hopeful men still breaking in ground from the moor and the hillside. Much of the early crofting settlement was planned, well-intentioned if not always successful; some of it, at first, was quietly behind the laird's back though it would not be long before he came to hear of it. Some of it, especially in that indeterminate time of pause while the landscape shrugged off the past, was contrived to bend the old countryside to the new, even to stimulate some form of local light industry, a visionary concept that owed more to the dreams of the planner than the hard realities of the northern landscape. It was in some ways a step into the past, for those inter-mediate crofting settlements were neither recognisably crofting nor acceptably new villages. They returned to an idea centuries old and one from which even the capital Edinburgh itself had grown when it could no longer huddle on its famous Rock: allotments of land, running down either side of a broad main street, on which the burgher kept his cow and his stock, with a back lane out to the common grazing of the burgh moor. Most were founded on a belief in the wrong industry at the wrong time.

Kincardine's Luthermuir, that old weaver toun, dates from 1771 and was more successful than most. Local landowners laid out the ground as feu crofts and the township's first *clay biggings* were raised by the croft-villagers themselves when they were not taking in their secondary income at the hand-loom or bringing the adjoining moor under cultivation. Their enterprise brought the start of the coarse-linen and Osnaburghs boom to the Mearns and neighbouring Angus.

There were subtler schemes. On Speyside at Rothes, already a settlement of sorts, the Earl of Seafield in 1776 gave leases of thirty-eight years on holdings or "tenements" of an eighth of an acre for ten shillings (50p) a year. The further two acres, optionally available though, were without the security of the lease, and if the earl was looking for some kind of wholly industrial development he died a disappointed man. It never materialised.

Some of the little lairds' touns were novel in their approach. Some twenty years earlier, the first Earl of Fife, who as Lord Braco, MP for Banffshire, had astonished the House with his piquant advice to "give our own fish guts to our own sea maws" (thus betraying his fishing concerns), laid out the new town of Newmill in Strathisla. Each settler would have five or six acres, but in scattered lots. In the main street of the town, each crofter (to anticipate the use of the term) had a quarter of an acre of land for his *clay hoose* and *biggings*. The dwellings were single-storey, thatched but-and-bens, and each barn would have two doors to create the through-draught so desirable for threshing by flail or for *sheelin'* the grain. The accompanying land for cultivation, however, would be in three strips, each numbered, so that every crofter would have an inbye strip, a "middle strip" and one at some distance—a more sophisticated version, when you come down to it, of the old run-rig with all its interminable squabbles and lack of cohesion. It would be easy enough to scoff at the plan but in all probability the countryside was not yet ready for more radical change. There was a further concession, typical of all such townships: each settler would have the right to cut peats on the moor behind the village. There were a hundred fues, and so fascinating is the whole idea that it seems sad to have to report its failure. But that, alas, was the case. Few of the new town's original 330 inhabitants were the weavers for whom the planners had hoped.

There was an even more charitable instance of new settlement by the same landed line, that briefly linked east with west. In the 1830s the fourth earl allotted another hundred plots, this time of ten acres each, on the Hills of Fisherie—at the centre of the region of experimental crofter-villages. They were for the dispossessed of the Highlands, victims of the Clearances. Though their folk had to break in the hill from the heather, that was better than being part of some laird's grandiose scheme. Most of the old crofter men must have preferred it, for it was where their dreams began: with a patch of the hill or the lonely moor.

III

The Crofter Folk

THE CROFT FOLK were sometimes less than welcome in genteel society and often unacceptable among their tenant neighbours of the farmtouns. Their antecedents might be questionable and, besides, they were guilty at times of not knowing when to defer to their betters. Their standing, indeed, in the subtle structure of country society was little better than that of the cottars who were usually their nearest neighbours and who married happily into croft families without feeling either that they were going up or going down in the world. There was just this one difference: the crofter's domicile was more permanent.

There was reason enough, if little excuse, for being uncivil about the crofter folk's past. Some, to be sure, would have come down in their generations from that time when men refashioned the landscape; that had left its sad débris, people without hope or a place on the land who might have drifted to the cities of a growing industrial age but had chosen instead to become the wanderers of the road: little better than tinkers many of them, hawking their respective trades round the countryside, taking the track between one farmtoun and the next, the road from one new village community to its neighbour to mend a berrypan here, sell a besom there. It is likely that some of these folk were the first occupants of the early scattered crofts, for there came always a time in a man's life when he had to forsake the road. He would put down his pack on a bit of the moor where fortune had taken him and start a new life—and sometimes a dynasty. If you were come of crofter folk it did not pay you to have a long memory, for sooner or later it would tell you something you had no wish to hear.

But not all the first squatters were folk of the road (though it is fairly certain that neither were they the cream of society) and the pattern of settlement and the kind of situation it created may also have had something to do with the lingering suspicions about the croft folk's past. Not infrequently, where the settlement was unplanned, there grew up enclaves of crofter men and their families. One such colony arose, in the early 1800s, on the flanks of Bennachie, that most modest of North-east mountains, and its story demonstrates not only their determination as frontiersmen but the kind of action that brought them legally to heel. It leaves its own taint of unsympathetic lairdship. Their historian was the Rev. N. L. A. Campbell: his account is reprinted in that fascinating portrait of the Lowlands landmark, *The Book of Bennachie*:

> In the colony there was no trouble about title deeds. As a man's family increased it was an easy matter to increase the number of rooms, and the even greater problem of building a new house for a new settler presented little difficulty. The materials were to hand in plenty and the story is told how once the neighbours completed a house for a new settler in a single day and celebrated the event by a supper that same evening in the newly erected home.

The Rev. Campbell goes on to give a picture that was probably true of other early crofting communities, far from the centres of local administration and their more sober inhabitants: "[they] were a law unto themselves. They had their private supply of whisky which paid no duty and as to other forms of private property, well, some of them had their own ideas—and these ideas rather vague concerning thine and mine. . . ."

There seems no reason to doubt the minister or to seek further reason for the retribution such free-wheeling behaviour brought on them. Such lawless freedom was unthinkable for poor squatters, and the local lairds could be relied on to make sure it did not last. In 1859, by legally encompassing the commonty, the no-man's-land on which the crofter families had settled, they acquired a crofting community, ready-made. That year, writes the Rev. Campbell, allowing himself the merest hint of irony, "John Esson signed a lease waiving all claim to compensation and agreeing to pay £2 10s. a year for the privilege of using the house his own hands had built and tilling the fields, five and a half acres, which by the sweat of his brow he had fenced and trenched from the hill."

By such means, through law or persuasion, were the early croft settlers given their status on the laird's rent-roll and a place, officially, on his land.

Whatever its short-comings, theirs was a society knit by

obligation and kinship (both the need of poor men) and as frequently rent by vendetta; where the lustre of forebears could be worn like a badge or a family misdemeanour tell against you unto the third and fourth generations, making plain at times a conspicuous lack of preferment. There was despotism, nepotism, and all kinds of favour (if a man did not look to his own, who would?). The ties were at once subtle and powerful; commitment at times painfully enduring.

There was this you could say for the croft folk, it grew out of their social isolation: they were a kittle crew, sensitive to every nuance of slight. If you were a friend, well and good (though that did not always save you); if you were not, their wrath could be scarifying and you might as well leave the parish. Persistent worshippers though many of them were, they could at times be damnably poor forgivers.

So what type of people were they, the later croft folk, settled in their sometimes insular communities? They were first the people whose small holding had long gone with their trade and sat near the road: the blacksmith, the *souter* (the shoemaker), the tailor, the saddler—a whole motley of men whose commercial interest made sure their croft work was always behind-hand and who grew schizoid and sometimes demented from balancing the urgency of one against the irreconcilable demands of the other. Because he was kept busy mending other men's reapers, the smith's *hairst* was always late. Besides these men, the succourers of any community, there were the men who, even late into the 1920s, still found their work at the great farmtouns of the Clydesdale era: bailies (stockmen) and orramen, horsemen and even grieves, those bailiffs of the big touns whose belief in hard work made them excellent candidates. There were the men who broke horses and brave men who travelled stallions round the countryside to the terror of all other road-users, their salacious beasts a constant reminder of the force that made the world go round, that fertility on which a dour countryside was founded. There were roadmen crofters who took time off every *hairst* (it was part of their agreement) to take a farmtoun *fee*, letting their wives shear their own few acres with the *heuk*; estate workers, masons and ditchers and dykers, foresters and carpenters (all those who did not have to dance close attendance), who kept the laird's domain by day and their own by night; postmen whose double life could delay the mail; and men now and then without other visible means of support and who were supposed to have *siller* in the bank. There were others, of course, who lived perilously between the poles of freedom and starvation, who had no regular, supplementary rôle and took casual work where and when they could find it. They might get seasonal jobs, the womenfolk, if they lived not too far from the coast, when the fish-curers came canvassing round the country communities for herring-gutters. And a croft man, if he had a cart and a beast fit enough to pull it, might get contract carting taking the fish from the boats to the curing yards from July to September. When the herring boom was at its height folk thronged to the little North-east ports from deep in the country, eager for the *siller* they could take home to help their poor, subsistence economy. Some of them were hard cases, unwilling to call any man master. They might be short of this world's gear but they were never short of an opinion whether or not it was asked for. Some were too awkward for their own good or anybody else's. Yet all shared the crofter's classic dilemma: their bit of ground could not keep them, yet it needed them most when they were needed elsewhere.

One of the North-east's most notable antiquarians and farmers, Willie Cook, a man who believed the past of that countryside should not be forgotten, at ninety recorded his early memories of the crofter folk whose small holdings ringed his father's farmtoun. His reminiscences, like the Rev. Campbell's in *The Book of Bennachie*, paint the portrait of a folk whose kindliness combined with some oddity of character and a determination not to pay duty on good whisky:

I knew many of the crofters of Auchleven. Three acres they rented, half an acre to the shift. As I grew older, and able to drive a pair of horses, I would be sent down to plough the crofts. The kindly crofter wives would bring me tea and jammy pieces. They were in the habit of putting a handful of cloves in the tea-caddy, and the tea tasted very clovy. Naturally there were some great characters, whose rough corners had not been polished off in a day when travel was slow and dear. One I remember was Lang Ross, a great tall streik of a man, who had been grieve at Overton of Premnay, and had the knack of breaking in the vicious young horses. When a lad he was fee'd at Overhall, where the best barley grew. He used to tell me about setting off with the foreman about four in the morning with two carts loaded with bags of barley. Their destination was the Cabrach, where the Highlanders had gathered from their crofts on their shelts. The barley bags were opened and the grain poured into the panniers, a bushel or two to each pony. Premnay barley properly malted and Cabrach water from the still, blended well together. Today in the little glens, from which folk have long vanished, they tell me you can still find the odd ruined stills, where no gauger came.

It was, and is, a lament for a lost landscape.

There were only two things the old croft folk had in plenty: bairns who ran the hills bare-footed all summer long, and dogs, and it wasn't easy to know which were the worst, except that you could threaten the child when its father's back was safely turned. Crofters' dogs though were deaf to all entreaty; they saw all good-will as a character weakness. They lolled with panting tongues by every croft gable all through the North-east Lowlands, awaiting the unwary cyclist or, latterly, the renegade car, for there was this you could say for croft dogs: they were not lacking in courage. They did not discriminate. Male or female, master or servant, it was all the same to them; they were as readily inflamed by the glimpse of an ankle in a lisle stocking as the sight of clerical cashmere demarcated by the minister's bicycle clips. The trick, when you knew it, was to pedal like the wind as you came up to some roadside croft and then, as you drew level, tuck your feet up (on the front-wheel forks), trusting to the momentum to carry you beyond the old dog's interest—or into the sight of his master working in some roadside field. He might see your plight (if you were a friend) and cry the beast to heel. Still and all, it was the kind of thing that could unbalance a stately matron and up-end her into the ditch. And again, the tactic could work only where the slope was with you. In the face of a gradient there was little you could do—except to keep pedalling, lifting your feet off the pedals only fractionally ahead of Old Spot's teeth and (preferably) with the kind of precision timing that brought the pedal up sharply under his salivating jaws. An old dog could learn something from that; in time you could get his respect and then you were somebody in the parish. He might *gurr* savagely and show you his teeth but your passing would be unmolested. Saddest of all though was the plight of the bairn on the school road: there was little he could do but sue for friendship.

The need to get along with the rest of the world was something a croft child had quickly to learn, for his was never a promising start in life and the future was generally heavily circumscribed. Indeed, it could be easily predicted: it was into the rough world of the farmtouns as a *fee*'d horseman; in some instances, into an apprenticeship with a local tradesman; sometimes into the police force in the southern industrial cities; into the ministry (with a background that made it easy to believe in the Devil); exceptionally, into an academic world that took him away from the life completely and often from all sympathy with it.

Such then was the old landscape of the crofting men: it made them hard where it did not break them entirely; even so, it sometimes twisted them, in time intolerably, and soured them of life. Its folk were poor without two sixpences most of them to rub together, and sometimes as shorn in spirit. Most went to the kirkyard leaving little behind them.

Willie Gavin's immediate neighbours, their crofts lying to either side of his own, were McPhee and McCaskill, unremarkable men whose destinies were as delicately poised and whose whole future, like his own, could be cast into jeopardy by a year of persistent rain and the bad *hairst* that followed it. The names of their holdings—Bogside, Whinfield and Hillbrae—were a reminder not only of the terrible lack of imagination in the Doric soul but of its propensity for facing dreadful truths squarely and at whatever the cost. Their emphasis on location, so typical of that hard landscape, was also a reminder of their fringe location and a warning to every mail-order clerk against the advisability of sending anything on credit to such an address. In some cases, perhaps, the crofter-holdings had been christened before their folk ever put a plough-point into the ground; but they had not been disappointed. As the years would prove, their beliefs had been well founded.

The men were not so much friends as bondsmen in a common predicament. Lang Andra McCaskill did work for the estate and was therefore suspect, for there was no telling what a man who was always falling in with the factor might let slip about a neighbour's affairs and there is no doubt that Lang Andra lost friends because of it. Besides which, there was the suspicion, quite unfounded, that he was sometimes looked on favourably when the rents had to rise. And he *was* known to be ambitious for a bit more ground and kept his crofting affairs very much to himself. For all that, he was not a bad man, willing enough to put in an appearance at the threshing mill and as pleased to have a day's work in return.

The McCaskills left nobody in doubt that they were superior kind of folk who were not able to call everybody their equal. Mistress McCaskill was come of farmtoun stock, a farmer's daughter. Modest though her father's toun was, she had been unwilling to leave it for the down-come of crofting life and Lang Andra, it was said, had a sore job getting her. They had superior bairns too, who made a success of life and were hardly out of the school before they were away to the city or to fine jobs in the south. And the McCaskills, seeing nothing for them at home, had not hindered them.

McPhee, on the other hand, was no threat to anybody and was always referred to (even by the croft children) as Puir Angus, in that homely kind of benediction that at once enlightened those with understanding of the speak to Angus's misfortune in life without in any way offending against him (which would have been unforgivable). For the truth of it was that Angus was a bit simple-minded, apt indeed to forget where he was going before he was halfway there whether it was the inn or the kirk, though generally he was more often to be found in the one than the other.

"Poor stock," folk said, sympathetic about the way the drink had taken hold of him, and wondering where in hell he got the *siller* to pay for it anyway. As a second livelihood Puir Angus did some shepherding; there was, after all, little damage you could do to a sheep short of hitting it over the head with an iron bar. His croft, Bogside, was always behind-hand: he lost his hay whiles through reluctance to put his hand to the scythe and his *stirks* never looked healthy enough to go anywhere near to a market, let alone attract the eye of the farmers who came looking for beasts to fatten for the mart. Even his *hairsts* were saved only in the nick of time by a son who hung up his grocer's apron in Arbroath and came north to labour under the September sun. He did it for his mother's sake, folk said, and sure enough, she was a dominating figure who treated Puir Angus badly but somehow managed to steer him from one staggering year to the next—and always to the estate office on rent days. Yet she had three children by him, a son and two daughters, all of them as sharp as thistles. You would wonder, folk said, how he had managed it. But that was just the rough speak of the croft folk. Willie Gavin would not have liked it, for he never made fun of his crofting neighbour. Late on a summer evening when his own croft work was done for the night, he might take a walk along the road to give Puir Angus a help with his hay or with his *stooking* for an hour before bedtime. Puir Angus would be grateful for that, a different man, sober and sensible and almost overcome by the gesture.

"God, but it is fine to have friends," he would say, in his own way as lonely a man.

IV

The Testimony of a Tombstone

GRACE WAS THE first of the Gavins, born into the 1800s before
they were barely begun. We know little of her now, though if her
son inherited her looks, she may have been a handsome woman
with features finer than the common clay of her class in that far
landscape. But the documentation of her days is brief: only the
words of a weathered headstone in a country kirkyard erected in
homage by her son John in his middle years and some time after
her death—the one single and determined act of a man who took
little in his own life seriously and whose action in this speaks
loudly of his love for his mother. In the Scots manner of such
things, it duly records his own passing.

It is a simple stone without the ostentatious decoration of its
Victorian time; a slab rounded on top to bear the ravages of the
northern rains and the years and gently lichened. It stands near
the dyke at the lower end of the kirkyard as though, after all, the
crofting Gavins had been admitted only to the fringe of the
respectable dead; its position and the hanging lie of the grassy
ground long made family burials difficult in all but the driest
weather. It is here that the Gavin story begins, and it is here that
it ends. The old stone, a little indistinctly now, makes the one bold
statement about Grace's existence; it says simply:

Erected by
John Gavin, Whinfield Croft,
In memory of His Mother,
Grace Connolly, who died
Feb. 20th, 1868 . . .

It goes on to record the croft-tree of the Gavins and the women
who married into them, the inhabitants of the croft house up from
the burnside; the tireless folk who ceaselessly worked the small
fields belonging to it. At the end of their hard-working years they

had been brought to lie where the manse trees overhung the wall, to fill the family lair and have their names in turn chiselled into its cold granite and maybe (in the case of later arrivals) embellished with gilt, their splendour in death almost greater than anything they had achieved in life.

There is no mention of a husband to Grace Connolly. Not on the stone; neither in the family's long memory. The past is silent on her relationships with men and with the one in particular who passed down the Gavin name; we do not know whether Grace Connolly was taken in marriage or in a moment of biblical adultery. But the lack of a proclaimed progenitor for her crofting dynasty is no proof that her union was unblessed. Nor is the absence of the Gavin name a condemnation for then, as now, in that northern countryside death returned the withered old woman to the bloom of her girlhood, to lie through eternity in the innocence of her maiden name.

Yet his lack is lamentable, an inconvenience perhaps, in a landscape where many families suffer similar affliction, more than an embarrassment, for it is in the kirkyard that a countryside seeks the roll of its past and it would have been fine (and seemly) if he had been able to put in an appearance. There is a persistent rumour, no more, of a seaman who could not leave the sea for a land-locked life; who sailed away and never came home. It is not possible now to say whether he existed other than as a romantic figment to cover family discomfiture in a straiter age; what is sure is that the Gavin croft did indeed lie only ten miles from the sea and but a little way off the Cadger's Road that led directly from it.

The association must have been brief, however it ended. For that there is some supporting evidence, threads at least that lead to that conclusion: John Gavin was an only son and never spoke of sisters, though he was born in a countryside where large families were the rule when Grace was only twenty-nine and with many more child-bearing years ahead of her. And fond though he had been of his mother, as an old man John Gavin was never heard to mention his father.

The truth of it all was something that only Grace Connolly knew, and alone by the dyke in her quiet grave she raised no scandals. And folk taking a turn round the kirkyard before going in to the Sabbath morning sermon, if they noted the lack of a male founder for the Gavins' line, would be kind to her. "Maybe," they would say one to another, "she lookit for the hats owre lang— and let all the bonnets gang bye." Silent Grace would remain, a mystery in life to all later Gavins.

Yet if the facts of her personal destiny are few it is not difficult, even now, to fill out the pattern of her days or to clothe the stark record of her existence from the folk memory of the region; or to set that against the grander tapestry of history. When she was born, Burns, Scotland's national poet, was only nine years dead, his name not nearly so resounding as it would yet become, and Waterloo was still twelve years away. It was a violent landscape, disease-ridden still, stalked at times by the kind of grinding want that would leave country folk, after a bad *hairst*, gaunt and hollow-eyed. Blind beggars wandered the old baulks and the drove roads tethered to the lean and slavering dogs that would wile a path for them by the lochside and through the bog; bands of vagrants, fearsome in their tatters, roamed unwashed to the terror of the lonely farmtouns, where their demands could be resisted only at the risk of grievous injury. The years that followed Waterloo would swell their numbers as men made redundant by the prospect of an enduring peace joined the ranks to wander from hamlet to hamlet. Often enough the new vagrants had vivid memories of the battle; the Duke of Wellington was a hero in the land, and in the ballads they sometimes sang. Some of them were Irish and they travelled their women with them. For all we know, Grace, with her Irish name, may have been one of them.

It was a landscape not yet tamed and largely unfenced, its fame as the future cradle of fine bulls and pedigree livestock as yet undreamed of. It was a countryside barely entered upon the maelstrom of farming improvement. In 1805, shortly after Grace's birth, there came home from Harrow and Cambridge—and more immediately from the grandeur of the Levant—the gilded youth who would transform much of that bare North-east Lowlands landscape. His inheritance was the Big House by the river—and a prospect so drear and forbidding that his first impulse was to remount and spur his horse back the way they had come. His second was quickly to sell it. It was a chill January day when the man who would soon be a statesman of note (and one day, prime minister) came home to the estate he had not seen since the days of childhood. What he saw was a house empty and long neglected, spectral in the winter-grey light. Fuel was stacked haphazardly round it, sheds filled with logs leaned against it, and from it ran its one brief avenue—all the way down to the peat moss. It was all but a ruin and unlike many a similar laird's dwelling it lacked even the quality of kindliness. All about him, as he entered upon laird-ship, lay a harsh, barren landscape, one without the softening out-line of trees, lacking dykes, hedges and fences, one in which his tenantry, at best, lived in two-roomed hovels and struggled to maintain themselves from subsistence farming on sour and stony ground.

Slowly the landscape would be reworked, the new single-unit farmtouns rise at the centre of their walled fields. And from the young laird's policy of improvement there would spring, too, many of the croft holdings that would come on to his rent-roll (935 by 1870), some of them where the plough had never reigned before, some on the fringe of what would one day be rich farming land, a few perhaps where some squatter had already scratched out a plot and a bare existence. Somehow, from somewhere, Grace Connolly became a statistic in that turmoil of change and (with her consort, if he existed) began to break in the ground along the burnside.

It is speculation, though not unlikely, that they were squatters at first, tethering their milk cow on the burn bank and clearing a patch of the boggy ground to grow poor-quality oats or bere (barley). Their harvest would be won with that abiding emblem of commissars and crofter men, the sickle, and would be easily gathered—a *hairst* that even at the best of times hardly sufficed to keep them beyond the reproach of other folks' charity and in a bad year reduced them to shameless beggary. Driven by need after a bad year, the young croft woman would have gone *thigging* round the countryside: begging the seed corn that would sow next season's harvest from the better-off farmtouns. A fine-looking woman, she may have had little trouble getting a small sackful of seed, and more keeping herself out of the farmer's hands, always supposing she had a mind to. In those bitter years the grain was for the folk and the beasts would want, the horses being put on a starvation diet and worked lightly through the winter in the hope that they would survive it. With hardly a cart in the parish the corn had gone to the miller in a bag strapped to the pony's back with *rushen* cords, the lime and dung for the fields, the peat from

the moss, panniered to where it was needed on the poor beast's
back, though like the women of her time Grace would have
carried the seed corn to the spring fields and the sowing hopper in
a small sack on her head. If she had time at all to herself, maybe in
the long winter evenings, she filled it with her factory *shank*,
knitting stockings for a manufacturer by the light of the *puirman*
(the rustic bog-fir candelabrum of the old countryside) for the
siller it would bring in, lighting her short clay pipe with an ember
of peat, like many another croft wife, before she sat down. If men
came her way, after John Gavin's father, we cannot know of it;
but if the merry, sociable son took the mother's temperament she
may well have given a man a bed whiles, and succoured him in
the bygoing.

If the portrait of Grace Connolly's past lacks hard confirmation,
it cannot be far from the truth, for the folk who knew her son
never heard him speak of territorial connection elsewhere—not
even the grandson who was the constant companion of his old age.
Besides that, there was the fact, accepted through the countryside,
that the Gavins had always been crofter folk and in Whinfield for
as long as anybody could mind. It is with the mid-1860s and the
knowledge of John Gavin's connection with the farmtoun on the
hill beyond the burn that all speculation finally ends. Grace's son,
by then, was in his mid-thirties, a dapperly good-looking man,
and the events of that time are etched firmly in his family's folk
history.

Like many of the later crofter men, John Gavin was a ploughman, a horseman, at the farmtoun on the hill, walking winter-long
behind the plough with a break now and then to cart turnips home
from the frost-rimed fields to the beasts in the byre; his favourite
grandson never heard him speak of any other employment. One
dull afternoon in the fall of the year when the *hairst* was well past
he stabled his pair early to marry Rachel Annand, one of four
sisters of the same parish, all of them with the kind of face far
stronger on character than in beauty. Only a short time before,
one of them had wed the master of John's farmtoun and with her
sister so comfortably ensconced in the master's bed it is just
possible that Rachel inadvertently succumbed to the wiles of the
jovial little man ten years older. The countryside would long
remember their union, for in the pithy recollection of its folk
memory: "The ane marriet the fairmer and the tither the fee'd

man." They also said the lass had maybe not had the best of the bargain.

In the circumstances of the time the event was almost certainly celebrated in the farmtoun's barn, and the lavish preparation for such an occasion has been delightfully recorded by Helen Beaton in her book *At the Back o' Benachie*, much of which is in the old Doric of its region:

There were many and great preparations at the bride's home before the wedding day and if it was a farm the barn was swept clean from roof to threshold. Tables were then placed in the middle of the floor; and planks of wood, resting on two bushels of oats or barley, acted as supports, thus providing strong seats for the guests.

The preparations for the wedding feast also constituted a large item. Large junks of beef were boiled or roasted in very large pots or ovens, which were hung over a fire of sticks and peat, the fire being usually built against a dykeside or other suitable place. When the beef was roasted for large parties or weddings, peat was piled on the top of the oven lid, and puddings were fired under an old tray or sheet iron in the same manner. To baste the beef and ascertain if the pudding was firing properly was usually hot and trying work for the cook.

Fowls were sent in large numbers to the bride, and as the fowls were not so large as they are now, it was not unusual for a man to eat a whole fowl! There were boiled puddings, and milk puddings with currants in them, and these, owing to their thickness, required a knife to cut them before a spoon could serve them out. At a wedding feast, knives, spoons and forks, and several other things, were turned out of drawer or press, where they rarely saw the light of day, except for such high occasions, and at Yule and Fastern's Even.

After the guests had eaten a *rimrax* of substantial food, large bowls of strong toddy were handed round, and after such rounds it was not uncommon for a number of the male guests to be found under the table.

The feast itself, however, was far from being the end of it. Mrs Beaton again:

> Fan they hae done wi' eatin' o't,
> Fan they hae done wi' drinkin' o't,
> For dancing they gae tae the green,
> An' ablins, to the beatin' o't.
> He dances best that dances fast

An' loups at ilka reesin' o't
An' claps his hands frae hough tae hough,
An' furls aboot the feezins o't.

Lamentably, Mrs Beaton reports, "The end of a wedding was frequently more boisterous than seemly." If there was a man who would have enjoyed such a day it was the convivial bridegroom; his new brother-in-law, they say, was less than pleased with the sudden degree of kinship.

Willie Gavin was the couple's first-born and his mother (in the way of mothers) favoured him. The sisters who followed him, resentful of that and of the endless croft chores, and maybe of being forced as children to carry squealing pigs on their backs to the market in the kirktoun, took away from the life or anything approaching it as fast as their feet and presentable suitors could carry them. Certainly, they did better for themselves than the young weaver's lass that their brother would bring into the croft, but what is interesting now is the strides a young crofter lass could make in society when she put her mind to it. One wed a fruit traveller who shortly came to rest in his own shop in Aberdeen's fishing community and did as well with the hard liquor which he was also licensed to sell as ever he did with his groceries. Another took on a policeman of that same city, a man of such impeccable character and integrity that retirement took him into the rôle of bank messenger and also man-of-mystery, for he spent most of his life riding the rails in a locked compartment and surrounded by *siller* between that northern city and the money-houses of London. With his croft lass he ended his days in a fine granite house in the doucely residential fringe of the city. The third and youngest stayed at home for a time till finally, with fine judgement, she married a mere farmtoun strapper whose career immediately took flight as the chauffeur of the first car in the parish.

Folk said old John Gavin's daughters had all done well for themselves and they did. In one generation they severed all connection with the old croft way of life and rose into the lower ranks of the middle classes; they sent their own children to good schools and if they returned whiles to the croft in the 1920s and '30s, it was in the motor cars they all ran and on a journey that was more a measure of the distance they had gone in life than any genuine pilgrimage. Their brother was pleased enough to welcome them;

he took their smart-suited men round his small croft fields on a Sunday afternoon with the same good grace he would have shown to any young farmtoun lad. But he was never sorry to see them go. He shut their car doors behind them without regrets. And he never envied them.

It was a family divided also by other tensions. Old John, when he had given up his ploughman's work in later years, had gone reluctantly out to his fields or the byre, driven by his wife. It was she who directed the croft work (and did much of it) and after her man's death she would give young Willie the same benefit of her advice, and was critical even of the wife he had brought home and not above hinting that had he tried harder he might have done better. Her son though had little need of her direction for he was a different kind of man from his father, a different man entirely, and their conflicting natures had long been a source of dissension. Old John, for example, was careless of his roadside fences—the only ones he had—so that his son, home at the weekend from his masoning work, would chide him over the broken paling wire or the rotting fenceposts that threatened to collapse at any moment and give the livestock their freedom.

"Ye'll need to mend the paling, man," the son would remonstrate, cross in his soul at such dereliction, contemptuous even and quite unable to understand the man who could allow it. "Gin ye dinna get it seen to, the beasts will be out on to the road."

"Maybe, maybe . . ." Old John was always a man to admit his faults freely (even some he didn't have, so amiable was he). "But where the devil would they gang tae, anyway, supposing they were free the morn? The girss is nae better ben at Bogside."

There was an irony in their exchanges for they would precipitate a pattern that divided the mason man from his own sons: the bickering between his father and grandfather stirred a deep resentment in the grandson who would become the companion of Old John's later years and who inherited much of his sociable nature. Many years later he would recall the conflict that had separated the Gavin generations:

My grandfather and I got along exceptionally well. My own father, however, was rather critical of my grandfather on many occasions. He would take issue with him about such and such a piece of fencing that needed attention—that would be toppling down. Or it might be something else that might be needing attending to. He was quite critical of my grandfather in many, many cases and I was rather resentful of him for that particular reason.

The voice now, like many another from the old crofting landscape, is transatlantic. It was a wound that never healed.

There is something else we know about the Gavins and that too with certainty: they lived long. The weathered tombstone in that quiet kirkyard that records their crofting years bears its bald testimony to that. Grace, the first of them, was sixty-five when she died. She had lived to see her first grandchild take his first faltering steps and maybe she had marked the dour set of him and known that life would not be easy on him. The son who had loved her so, and erected a stone to her memory poor ploughman-crofter though he was, lived to be eighty-one; the wife who had steered him so relentlessly between one day and the next, to be eighty-six. Willie Gavin himself died in his seventies tired out with work, but the up-country weaver's lass he had brought into the family, for all the hardship of her life, survived to the age of ninety-six. All the Gavins now are out of the crofting life or anything remotely like it. They were a dour breed mainly, not to be meddled with, respected rather than widely loved—folk, it was sometimes said, with a good conceit of themselves and more independent by far than they had any right to be.

V

The Croft "Biggings"

WILLIE GAVIN LOVED the old landscape: all the days of his masoning life he travelled its roads, first on foot, later on, when they became common, by bicycle. Pratt's *Buchan*, his favourite reading, gave the history of every ruin and farmtoun and castle of its region; it lay with the family Bible, unlocking the past of that far countryside. He loved its seasons, its sorrows and its several rejoicings: the sweet scent of clover hanging over the evening fields, the blaze of broom on the hill as it gathered the last of the sunlight, the ease of autumn in the soul as well as the melancholy of the winter parks lying still and bare. It was his landscape and he sought no other.

The old croft of his folk and his boyhood stood at the centre of that awareness, the thing that focused his life. It was strung with its near neighbours by the roadside, its sour ground stretching down to the burn. Beyond that the good farm land rose, gently at first, and then into the fine swell of the brae that set Laverockhill's fields up to the sun. The big farmtoun—where the young plough-man John Gavin had once driven a Clydesdale pair—sat smug with prosperity, its low sandstone steading and well-slated roofs claiming the ridge for their own, aloof from the croft ground below. Behind it lay the old castle, ruined and lichened now, a flawed jewel amid the farmtoun fields but like an old brooch on a bosom, gathering the green shawl of the countryside to it still. Past it on the ridge ran the old road to the sea, a dry highway in that time before drainage had let traveller and tink alike into the shelter of the howe and along by the burn-side. Away to the left it passed the door of the old milltoun, a farmstead now with steep, hill-hung fields, where once they had reaped the wind to mill the shorn corn and fill the girnals of the parish. But that day was gone, bye and done with now, the old mill-stones, if they had survived at all, long into the hidden heart of some dyke where the farming im-prover had thrust them, for they had not been strong on memorials, the folk of that old landscape. It was a lonely place, now that folk no longer brought their grain to it, up and away from the world; dreich among the huddled firs that ringed it, bent and wind-twisted—arthritic crones that walked the gloam skyline and gave the old place its aura of foreboding. Neither grocer nor baker's van could reach it and its folk, understandably, had a diminishing circle of friends. Bye it now and then, on the old road, came only the weird and travelling folk at one with its haunted past.

On the other side of Laverockhill the old road on its way to the sea came down the rump of the hill where it eased out to the flat-lands and the well-worked fields of more modest one-, two- and three-pair farmtouns where the tenor of life was taken slow-footed at the Clydesdale's pace—a strange dour world uneventful except for the occasional outbreak of murder; a world in which a sophis-ticated man might have felt himself menaced by the guttural speak of unshaven faces when all they were offering was the awkwardness of friendship.

From its lonely height the old road watched the path of its usurper: a beige, stone-metalled ribbon that ran through a land-scape so bare it had difficulty finding obstacles to put in its pro-gress. Along it went the same kind of folk, better-dressed now, more of them maybe with a place to call home. It carried still the scholar to his imprisonment, the cottar to his new farmtoun *fee*, servant maids to secret embraces, the bad case of fever and folk with diphtheria; it carried the bride to her bedding and the shaven corpse of the man who had never in his life worn anything but a five-day beard and known nothing but the sweet breath of the parks to the long rest of eternity. On that day at least they would clear the roads for him and keep the turnip carts about the farm-steading till his funeral had gone past.

It was a road, even at the turn of the century, hardly adequate for the job it had taken on; only the early cyclists of the era could meet without confrontation and with anything wider came a need for prolonged negotiation. A heavy run of traffic or the slow progress of the traction engine shifting its threshing mill on from one place to the next could put the work of the farmtouns back half a day. But slow though its commerce was, it was the only road the croft folk had to carry them out into the world, and as time wore on more and more of them would take it and never look back.

Like its near neighbours the Gavin croft turned the grey stone
of its barn gable to the passing traffic and sandwiched its dwelling
house between that and the byre. The cowshed took the low end
of the long-house *bigging* and that too was traditional, looking
back to a past when it had been necessary to ensure that the cow-
strang ran the way of the *midden* at its gable rather than into the
circle of its folk as they sat round their fire. Across from the house,
beyond the croft close that led down from the road, the kitchen
garden was guarded by a stone wall that baffled both bairn and
wandering beast, its three other sides enclosed by tall beech hedges
and the windowless wall of the milkhouse where the dark was
undisturbed between one milking and the next. Behind that again
was the old crofter's turnip shed and toolshed; it was here that
Willie Gavin housed his trestles and planks, all the tools of his
masoning trade as well as his barrow, his croft implements and
the bicycle that would carry him from home whenever he had
need of it. At the bottom of the croft close, forming the base of
the "U" layout and shutting the steading off from a view of its
fields, was the old stable *bigging* that now housed the calves and,
abutting it, the hens' *cruive*.

The cornyard, with room for a half-dozen small crofter's ricks,
lay behind the barn and its engine-house, where the crofter man's
Ruston oil engine lurked in the gloom, a monster of unpredictable
behaviour that frightened all but the brave. In autumn, when his
hairst was in, his stackyard was the pride of the old crofter's heart;
it was here that he would be found whiles leaning into a stack as
he took a late-evening smoke, with a look on his face that was the
nearest he ever came to contentment. It was here, too, that a bairn
or croft man would come to make the short calls of nature in that
old landscape—so naturally that a man might walk away from
you as you talked, round the corner of a cornrick, and reappear
a moment later buttoning his flies without ever having interrupted
the flow of the conversation. (In any case, it would have been
unmanly to go anywhere else to *pish*; the nearest dykeside or
gable or roadside would also do duty by day, the chamber pot—
only in extremis—by night.)

Screening the cornyard and much of the croft steading from
the road was a scraggy line of elderberry trees (the *bourtrees* of
that old countryside) and a single red rowan. Good godly folk
though the Gavins had always been, they had kept the mountain

ash there to ward off evil and even if Willie Gavin no longer
believed in the witches nor the power of the glamourie they could
cast on his beasts, he would tweak its branches in the bygoing
and, bending down to the bairn with him, whisper urgently:

> Rowan tree and reid threid
> Keep the witches frae their speed.

Maybe it had been planted in Old John Gavin's day or even in his
grandmother's, for once there had been a time when the rowan
tree was a talisman that grew at every croft gable; when, to protect
the beasts, a cross of *rodden* twigs was placed above the byre door.
Long ago that had been, when superstition had gripped the poor
crofter folk and a still-born calf or a cow going unexpectedly dry
was a disaster; glad enough the old folk had been of their enchant-
ments, the things that had made them at times bow less to God
and more to the Devil.

The *bourtrees* and the rowan brought back the past, so that
you would wonder whiles what kind of folk had they been; and
what kind of dwelling had they *biggit* there, those folk who had
first tilled that land? A squalid hovel, like as not, created from
what the countryside yielded. Made of turf perhaps, one-roomed
certainly, with the cow brought in to one end of it when the
days of the year drew in. For folk whom life or the laird might
suddenly move on there would be little incentive to build for
permanence and it is likely their poor dwellings differed little
from those of the century before and so witheringly described, in
The Social Life of Scotland in the Eighteenth Century, by Henry
Grey Graham:

> The hovels of one room were built of stones and turf without mortar,
> the holes in the wall stuffed with straw or heather or moss to keep
> out the blasts; the fire, usually in the middle of the house floor, in
> despair of finding an exit by the smoke-clotted roof, filled the room
> with malodorous clouds. The cattle at night were tethered at one end
> of the room while the family lay at the other on heather on the floor.
> The light came from an opening at either gable which whenever the
> wind blew in was stuffed with brackens or an old bonnet to keep
> out the sleet and the blast. The roofs were so low in northern districts
> that the inmates could not stand upright but sat on stones or three-
> legged stools that served for chairs, and the huts were entered by

doors so low and narrow that to gain an entrance one required almost to creep. Their thatching was of ferns or heather, for the straw was all needed for the cattle.

But in time the Gavins, with the laird's help or maybe without it, had raised a better dwelling on that spot by the side of the track, a house that took the basic shape that would carry down to the 1900s, and in the case of some of the old crofts, up to World War II. It was a layout as familiar in the West, where it would endure even longer, sitting easily on the land and drawing all the materials for its construction from it: the single-storey but-and-ben with a between-ends *closet* formed by the box-beds the folk shut themselves into at night; the walls built of rubble stone and mortared with clay and faced inside and out perhaps with lime mortar. They were but little different, if at all, from the crude dwellings of the farmtoun tenantry a short time before and much the same kind of humble abode in which Burns himself had once, humorously, admitted:

> There lonely by the ingle cheek
> I sat and ey'd the spewing reek
> That filled with hoast-provoking smeek
>   The auld clay biggin'.
> An' heard the restless rattons squeak
>   Abune the riggin'.

The shell of such a *bigging* about the mid-1800s would have been no more than £30 and maybe as little as £20, and the innovation by that time of the *hinging lum* (the hanging chimney) did much to ameliorate the smoky conditions that had so demonstrably irritated a poet's lungs. The *hinging lum* was a wooden canopy over the fireplace, tapering upwards, and extending into the room. Besides that, the fireplace would have an ash-well that needed clearing out only once every three weeks and if the swee had not as yet become a familiar and convenient fitment to swing pots and kettles on and off the fire, there was at least the *rantle-tree*, a crossbar of iron set into either side of the chimney to take the links and pot crook. Floors were earthen—as they would be in some cases right up to the 1930s—the roofs, in the North-east, straw-and-clay thatched, as were those of the abutting barn and byre. *Strae an' clay* thatching would also last long in the North-east Lowlands, a muddy, mucky process that involved running the clay between the oat or barley straw to bind it. Even after the Whinfield croft had been roofed with red tiles underneath, its tenant John Gavin yearly brought the thatching that covered them up to scratch. His grandson, his labourer in the early years of this century, remembers the work: "I used to help my grandfather in re-thatching the croft house. He would have all his thatch ready beforehand as well as the mortar. It was mostly mud, and it was used to keep the thatch in place."

If their folk and their dogs sometimes gave the old crofts a bad name, their poor tumble-down *biggings* did as little to enhance it. In constant need of repair, there were times when they were kept together as much by clever improvisation—a patch here, a prop there—as by the agency of good mortar or the concern of the estate whose interest, in any case, would have to be solicited and which (understandably) would often have preferred to raze the old *biggings* and consolidate their acres with those of a neighbouring holding where the tenant was having better luck in keeping his steading together. It is possible that John Gavin was an exasperating tenant. More than likely, since his lackadaisical negligence even upset his own son. Or, born forty years before the Education Act took the youngsters of that spare countryside into the schoolroom on a regular basis, it may have been that he was incapable of putting his complaints on to paper. It is possible, even, that he could write nothing more than his name. But he had borne long and patiently the steady seep of rain into his byre (and perhaps come to the belief that such neglect was a crofter man's lot) when he stepped into the cowshed with his nine-year-old grandson one morning early this century. Nearly eighty years after, the small boy who had stood that day with his grandfather in the cowshed would recall the incident—and with it, perhaps, the moment when the power of literacy began to change the old crofter-laird relationship and the balance, for once, swung the crofter's way:

In my early years some of the outbuildings of my grandfather's croft were getting into quite a dilapidated condition—in fact the cow byre was not even leak-proof. So I said to my grandfather one day "Why don't you make an appeal to the estate factor for a new byre? This building isn't fit to keep stock in! The beasts are getting soaked . . . Maybe it isn't harming them much, but it's a situation that shouldn't exist."

Old John that day had swithered, uncertain of his ground, unsure what to say to a youngster who did not know how it was between a man and his laird: What could he do? he asked finally with resignation. "Let me write to the factor, Granda, and tell him. It might make him sit up!" Reluctantly the old croft man had agreed. And his grandson remembers:

So I sat down and wrote a letter. I was regarded at school as having a pretty good command of the English vocabulary. So I wrote the factor a nice letter. I cited the grim shape the cow byre was in, and made an appeal. I don't know now whether I signed the letter in my grandfather's name or not—they would certainly know he had never written it. He couldn't. At least, I never recall him writing at all.

Anyway, I wrote this letter and not many days after we had a visit from the factor, who came to see the byre for himself and inspect its condition. And he thought it was in quite a pitiful state and sanctioned approval of a brand new byre, which was then erected and made my grandfather very happy.

I did the same thing with the barn and that was replaced. It was the factor who made the decision, granting a request for a new outbuilding or home. The estate architect then drew up the design—the specifications and dimensions and so on—which was to be adhered to.

But if Old John Gavin had been pleased with his new croft *biggings*, the son who was to follow him was less so. When he came home from burying his father in the kirktoun's cemetery, cold though the November day was, he had taken a walk round the old croft house and its steading. Neither by then spoke well of the old tenant, and as his mason's eye picked out the points long overdue for attention, the plans were already milling in his mind. Yet even Willie Gavin, with all his fluency in calculations, his skill in reading plans and his considerable standing (by then) in the community, felt a countryman's hesitation in writing to the laird. His son, Old John's companion and confidant, remembers:

I recollect, some years after that, after my grandfather had passed on, that my father, who was a master mason, realised that during the winter months particularly the building trade was adversely affected —you know, by extreme frost or the severity of the weather. Or the road conditions would be such that they would find it hard to get to work, to a job they might be on ten miles away and the only means of getting there by bicycle.

So my father thought he would like to take over the old croft himself, on his own. He went to see the factor and of course was granted permission to do this—to get the croft. But the dwelling house by this time, like the rest of the buildings, had got to the stage where it had seen better days. So my father asked me would I write a letter to the factor *again*, this time making an appeal for a new dwelling house!

This I did and it was subsequently granted. My father, being a mason, erected the building himself. . . . Did all the stone work, that is.

The traditional but-and-ben *bigging* that Willie Gavin walked round when he came home from his father's funeral—and in whose equally traditional box-bed he had raised his first cry in the world—he would transform into a two-storey stone-and-lime house the equal of any of its kind on that stark landscape. He would do it single-handed. Within weeks, as soon as he had the estate architect's plans in his hands, he shifted his family into the croft barn and set their box-beds in there after them. Then he started to tear down the old croft house in which he had been born, stone by stone.

The house he built was a bit dour and forbidding (like the man himself, folk would say) but it was a fine croft house for all that with its blue-slated roof and its garrets, dormer-windowed, looking out over the garden to the countryside beyond. Inside, the *closet* was extended and walled off to the ceiling; a wooden porch was built on at the door where his mother had once grown scarlet runner beans, a glassy vestibule that was neither inside nor out but which thwarted the wind that blew constantly at the old woman's back as she sat by the fire. If he had not been a mason man, folk would have said he was getting above himself. In time he would re-build barn and byre to the same standard, discarding the old *clay thacking* for the maintenance-free convenience of corrugated sheet-iron, though he would refrain from painting it the violent red that so many of the croft men favoured (maybe to give their *biggings* the "warmth" that the old red tiles once had bestowed). His two-stalled byre in which his milk cows and his fattening *stirks* stood two to a stall (and chained to the *traviss*) was given new built-in troughs (*trochs*) for the turnips, hayracks (*hakes*) for the beasts' straw and was new-laid with the causey stones that would bring its modernity into line with that of the grand farmtouns. Both *biggings* were lit by skylights let into the slant of the

roof, the barn additionally by a small window in its gable, where
an outside stone stair led up to the small corn loft he had created
in its rafters—a novelty, like the little barn-mill he would install,
about any holding of its size. For all that though, he stuck by the
old tradition in setting its two doors facing each other from opposite walls, something unchanged from the days of the flail; their
through-draught had helped to winnow the grain. And when his
father's old *shelt* had no longer need of it, he would rebuild the old
thatched stable as his calf-house.

The croft though had two further structures that dominated the
lives of its hard-working folk: the water-pump and the privvy.
The first stood by the hens' *ree*, the latter (with irreproachable
logic) across from the *midden* by the old stable's gable. The pump,
the trunk of a majestic larch bored and sunk into the ground above
the old well, endlessly justified the wisdom of the other croft folk
who had stuck loyally by their bucket and windlass, for it went
consistently dry all summer long, leaving Grannie Gavin to carry
her water, pailed and yoked on her shoulders, from the old well a
quarter of a mile away.

The privvy though, like all Willie Gavin's *biggings*, was always
in splendid order and that at least was something to be thankful for
in a landscape where many such offices (where they existed at all)
had fine slap-in-the-wind doors and were so full of draughts you
could catch your death in them. Some had poor fastenings so that
young bairns and shy lasses would have to sit hanging on to a
string on a nail driven into the door. Even so, they might, thought-
lessly, be hoisted off the seat in a hurry before they had made themselves comfortable. Some privvies faced the hill and some stared
on to the road, with a peephole even at the right height in the door
so that a man at his ease could take stock of the countryside (or
what he could see of it). Most, like Willie Gavin's, sheltered behind their croft *biggings* and got busy about the dinner-hour and in
the earlier part of the evening. Willie Gavin, however, offered his
folk and his guests the security of an inner bolt, which could also
be inconvenient: bairns went in and could not be got out (without
prising off the side-boarding) and other folk took to it selfishly as a
retreat from the world for it was a comfortable, solitary place when
things went wrong or for a lass suddenly forsaken—spotless always
and the seat so well-scrubbed that its only danger was splinters
not infection. The floor was as clean, and rich with a fine arboreal

scab where the wood-knots stood through against Grannie Gavin's obsessive scrubbings. Young Gavin boys in particular lingered there, entranced as they grew older by the spencered ladies from the mail-order catalogues already quartered-down for convenience; there was an education, a world of wisdom there on the nail that they were unlikely to learn any other way.

All the same, the John Gunn, with its nail, its swatch of absorbing interest, and its pail (removed and emptied once a week from below the seat) could be claustrophobic on a fine summer's day— so near to the *midden*.

The croft's *biggings* though were the best of it; there was little Willie Gavin could do about its eight and a half sour acres, where all friability was bedevilled by bad drainage and the sedge growing in the marshy part of the ley would be a reminder to him, if he needed one, that he could not call nature his friend for all his love of it. Like his mother, Old John had kept his beasts on the tether, an earlier, easier form of controlled grazing that was less tiresome than cordoning the corn. Willie Gavin, however, had not been able to rest until he had fence-posts into the ground and the paling wire strung three-stranded between them. Raw and damp from the sawmill, they marched in rows down to the burn, demarcating the fields of his small holding, each a little under an acre and a half. Poor though their soil was—"strongish land but somewhat cold and damp", the laird's land surveyor had called it, circumspectly, when he had recommended raising the rent in 1885—the old crofter man never grudged the price of them. Moderate in all his enthusiasms and never easily parted from his *siller*, he went willingly to his bank (the tin box he kept in the top shelf of the *closet* cupboard) as rent-day came round. The croft cost him, in the 1930s, just £7 a year, less than £1 an acre, the same as it had cost his father fifty years earlier. For that recommendation of a rent rise from the start of John Gavin's new lease in 1886 was never implemented. By then that wide countryside of the great farm-touns had gone over the peak of its prosperity and begun its slide into the years of farming Depression.

And the Gavins, whatever else they had been, had been lucky in their lairds. Today the list of entries in the estate's old improvements-and-repairs ledger is a litany of ceaseless wants that tell the story of a fight to better poor ground (500 2½ in. tile pipes in 1904) and, with cryptic "wood and iron" entries, keep poor *biggings* standing. If the Gavins could not get fat on such a holding, neither could the laird, and there must have been years when his crofts were an accountant's nightmare.

As he got older and more respected in the community, Willie Gavin would more easily get the factor's ear to complain about a rotting door or a leaking roof. Likely the laird's man-of-business had always known that the excuse about a winter lull in the mason-ing trade was no more than the crofter man's poorly-reasoned rationale for taking over the holding. After all, the same conditions precluded all but the most routine of crofting chores. The mason man had fooled nobody; what he and the other men like him felt, has been aptly summed up by yet another of the numerous royal commissions on crofting:

> Above all they have the feeling that the croft, its land, its houses are their own. They have gathered its stones and reared its buildings and occupied it as their own all their days. They have received it from their ancestors who won it from the wilderness and they cherish the hope they will transmit it to the generations to come . . .

It is a statement worthy of a better home than a bureaucrat's report. Its sentiments were frequently as true of the North-east Lowlands landscape as that of the Western Highlands. Written long after Willie Gavin's day, it captures his creed entirely.

VI

The "Shifts" and the Seasons

THE SEASONS TURNED and Willie Gavin, like all the North-east
crofter men, turned with them: from seedtime to harvest and
through the dreich days of winter. The cycle of the croft year, the
pattern of its crops, followed that of the farmtoun to whose skirts
it clung, dependent always upon its goodwill. Though the old
crofter man would never willingly let a Clydesdale set foot on his
land, he was beholden like his neighbours to Laverockhill for the
heavier working of his fields and for the spring cultivation of his
soil in particular. That obligation, the contract work by the farmtouns for the crofter men, came out of the past though Old John
Gavin had circumvented it by borrowing his neighbour's *shelt* to
yoke with his own in the plough. But then, he himself had been a
ploughman, as capable of setting up a *feering* and handling a
Clydesdale pair as any man the big farm could send down to him.
Many of the croft men, however, were tradesmen like his son and
not able to speak to a horse without upsetting it, far less set up a
respectable furrow—though that never made them any the less
critical of the ploughman's work. Far from it. Many aired their
views as though they had been match champions in their time.

In Willie Gavin's landscape the seasons of ploughing and sowing
and harvesting held an ancient and comforting immutability, a
rhythm that knitted the pattern of country lives to the needs of the
fields, the old croft men's, whatever their calling, as surely as those
of farmtoun folk. It was a pattern that linked a man with the past
and there was hardly a year when the winter ploughs did not turn
up an old hunter of that wind-scoured plain crouched still in his
cold stone-kist; or a spring when the seed harrows did not draw
their circle round the venerable ruin or pass through the long
shadows of its history and that time when the sword, not the
plough, held the land.

Though he might demur whiles, late-on though it was, that the
ground was not right for sowing or that the *hairst* parks were not

yet ready for the scythe, Willie Gavin fell in with that old country order of things, bowing to the need to work when the weather would let him, mindful that a late-sowing brought a late *hairst* with all the hazards and loss that entailed. Like the rest of the Lowlands croft men he followed the ley-farming principles of the Scottish farmtouns, a system that had been a feature (and the sheet-anchor) of that northern landscape since the mid-1700s. He had no permanent grass for his beasts. His rotation of crops in his humble *shifts* (the crofter's name for his small fields) adhered to the old order (written into many an early farmtoun lease) of the improving lairds a century before: a six-year cycle that gave him temporary leys instead of fixed grazing and that had long made rotation grasses a part of east-coast arable farming. It was a pattern of cropping with many merits, and ideally suited, had the old lairds but known it, to what lay ahead, for it was a rotation with an enviable in-built elasticity: the lying-in ley could be lengthened or shortened according to what was paying best at the time, horn or corn. It was the system that enabled the fine Scottish farmtouns to weather the lean Depression years sometimes a little better than their English counterparts. Its use had taken them through to about 1880 before the importation of wheat from under a more bountiful sun started to affect them. Only then, and only gradually, in the leaner times that followed had the permanent leys been laid down.

It was a cycle that suited the east-coast crofter man, with his concern for stock as well as crops, though unlike the farmtouns, which in the 1920s and '30s were letting their leys lie for four years (and maybe longer), Willie Gavin had little chance of extending the pattern. The old crofter men in that now-distant landscape preferred a six-*shift* system, giving themselves three years' grass, and Willie Gavin held to it. That pattern had been set by his ploughman father at the height of the boom farming days. He ploughed his ley after its third year—back into the *tattie corn* that helped to keep the crofter folk poor all their days for they clung to it, most of them, when they should have known better and when the farmtouns round them had long sown the improved varieties that would have better filled their barns and their meal girnals. The crofter man's limiting "sixth-course *shift*" gave his fields their yearly-changing cycle: ley oats; turnips; clean-land oats; hay; first-year grass; second-year grass. The ley oats got the rich humus of the ploughed-in grass that in an extended rotation might well have supported stock for another year. Their ploughed stubble in turn would lie winter-long and, with the weeds (the *growth*) gathered off, become next year's turnip ground. In the third year the *shift* would take the clean-land corn, undersown almost simultaneously with the grass seed for the fourth year's hay and the temporary pasture that followed it. It was a system as intricately linked and balanced as any Chinese puzzle.

Willie Gavin, like his father, meticulously followed its cycle of renewal and fertility but it never made him rich. The old man's sons-in-law, cottars at the big farmtouns with their mounds of fine dung and sacks of rich lime, claimed always that he was over-thrifty in manuring his *shifts*. Maybe he was. Yet it was not the spirit that was unwilling for he gave his oats as much bagged fertiliser as his pocket could stand and needed all the contents of his byre *midden* for his root crop, the yellow *neeps*, the only kind of turnips he grew (though many of the old croft men also liked a drill or two of swedes). With his oat-straw, they would be the bulk of his beasts' winter diet. It was a sound enough judgement and his inability to do otherwise was no more than a bitter indictment of the straits of the life and the poverty that whiles gripped him, and others like him. And there was no certainty, anyway, that his poor-quality corn would have done any better supposing he had dowsed it in dung.

He made a little hay, as did all the croft men, to add to his milk cows' diet. The *shift* gave him some summer grazing as well as winter keep for with his hay crop off and ricked in the cornyard, he could run his beasts on it till they were housed in the autumn.

His crofting year—like that of the farmtouns—began late in the fall of the year in that ritual that was as old as farming time. With autumn well through and his own cornfields ploughed, Laverock-hill would send down one of his horsemen with his plough and his Clydesdale pair to turn over the old crofter's stubble—though for all the long years of their acquaintance he dared do nothing till he was asked. The old man, he knew, was tetchy about being placed under anything that seemed like obligation, and the arrangement itself had a ritual that hardly varied from one year to the next. It was a sly observation of protocol that left the old crofter with his dignity.

If the mason-man did not catch Laverockhill at the kirk-gate on the Sabbath, he would step over to one or other of his ploughmen at work in a neighbouring field—or carting home turnips to the fine *stirks* the farmer always had fattening in his byre.

"Tell yer maister, laddie, that I would be obliged to him gin he could gie me a turn o' the ploo when he has man and beasts tae spare."

"Fairly, I'll do that, Mister Gavin," the young horseman would promise. "As soon as ever I see him."

So it would be fixed, and with the coast clear, in a week or so the same young ploughman might be setting up a *feering* in the old man's field one morning almost before it was daylight. The task of ploughing the croft *shift* would not take him that long: just a day and a half for an acre and a half, and he could have done better but for the shortness of the crofter's field for he had no sooner got the plough point into the ground than he was out and turning at the other endrig. He would have been a damned sight quicker still, Laverockhill always said, if Jess MacKendrick had not been forever stopping the laddie with jugs of tea and a *piece*, and certainly Grannie Gavin, minding her own farmtoun days and the bareness of the bothy lads' table, would be guilty of that. She was fastidious about visiting ploughmen.

The stubble ground would lie getting the good of the winter frosts and the ploughman would be back before the New Year was long past to get his dram (if it wasn't too late) and turn over the old ley land for half that year's oats, and later still, about mid-April when Willie Gavin had had time to pull and clamp the last of his turnips (for his beasts were still in the byre), to plough the ground for the clean-land crop, the other one and half acres or so of *tattie corn* that the old man would sow. Before April was out, and when Laverockhill's own fields were sown, the horseman would be back with the harrows to make ready the seed-ground.

If he was a bit late it hardly mattered for the low-lying croft *shifts* were always behind the brae-set fields of the big farmtoun in their readiness to receive the seed. And even then, it was never in the state the old crofter man would have wanted it for he was as hard to please about that as ever he had been about masoning. The horseman could as easily have brought the broadcast-sower with him and finished the job. It would not have taken him long. But Willie Gavin would not have countenanced that and Laverockhill knew better than to anger him by suggesting it. For Willie Gavin had always sown his own seed corn (as had his father) from the hopper strapped round his shoulders. It was a ritual the years had hallowed and that took him into the world of the Scriptures and maybe closer to God. He did not speak of it but it was important to him.

The evening before, the bags of seed oats would be set ready in the croft barn and if the weather held, almost before light and as Grannie Gavin readied his breakfast, he would load his barrow to set the bags at intervals down the length of the *shifts*, assessing where the hopper would fall empty. From the nearest, when he stopped in the bout, the hopper would be refilled by Grannie Gavin with a small pail. It was a scene that looked back to an old landscape, to another time and an earlier folk. Feet and scattering fist absorbed the past of the run-rig and the centuries in a heavy symbolism, and set their rhythm on the day. For Willie Gavin it was a moment of commitment and dour though he looked, an aged patriarch striding his parks, that day his heart sang. Behind him would come the harrows, three times over the field, their burying teeth drawing the patterns of their own shallow ridges. In a week or so, ten days at the most, the crofter man would sow the grass seed that would be his next year's hay in his clean-land field, this time pinching the seed between the thumb and forefinger of each hand (not broadcast as before) and the farmtoun man would come down in the evening light with the harrows and stone roller. From the corner of the byre that night as he *muckit* his beasts, the old man would watch this final movement in the orchestration of the spring sowing, grudging the lone Clydesdale's hoofmarks on his land but thankful, all the same, that his corn was in.

The old stubble would lie till May, its furrows baked grey, before it came time to prepare Willie Gavin's turnip *shift*; to set up its drills and cart out the dung to them from the croft *midden*. That was not a horseman's favourite job and he would be glad to see the end of it. He would give the crofter man and his wife a day or two to spread the dung along the bottom of the rows before returning to "split the drills" and cover it, and run the turnip seed-barrow over it. That, too, did not take him long and he would have time for a *news* with Grannie Gavin when she brought out his afternoon tea. He would leave a drill or two in the *shift* for the Gavins' potatoes: in the 1930s, the Duke of York earlies the old man liked would take half a drill; his maincrop, Kerr's Pink, equally well favoured in that old countryside of stark farmtouns and hardy men, or the great Golden Wonder. Willie Gavin had always had a good word on them, small in size though they usually were. He could hardly let you eat your Sabbath dinner without praising their quality so highly that the occasional guest might well go away believing he had invented them.

Like most of the farm and croft men, Willie Gavin liked his turnips sown by the May Term (28 May) and he was late, and a laughing-stock, if they weren't. But that done, he was a happy man. He had seen the last of a Clydesdale on his land till the back-end of the year. For his turnip-singling and their second-hoeing (to keep the weeds down between the rows), the haymaking and the harvest were his own. Apart from his wife, his children and anybody who had been unwise enough to marry into the family and could filially be inveigled, he needed nobody's labour.

Likely he could little afford it. His bill from Laverockhill over the years between the wars for the contract work of the spring cultivations and the turnip-seed sowing had risen steeply, from £4 in 1914 to £20 in 1939. The increase may have reflected the hard times then hitting the farmtouns and even Laverockhill's need to turn a penny wherever he could, even if it was at the expense of the crofter men; it certainly did not reflect in the wage his horseman got: in the 1930s that was being cut with almost every six-monthly feeing market. And the crofter folk were no better off. The time now might be long past when after a bad *hairst* or on their entry into the tenancy of a croft they had to go *thigging* for the seed corn or begging from the kirk's girnal to sow their parks. But there were good reasons still why the croft *shifts* never got all the manure they needed.

VII

The "Bloo Coo" Economy

A CROFTER'S COW was squeezed for every drop of milk it would give, morning, noon and night, and that even into the 1930s, long after the thrice-daily milking had been abandoned by all but the smallest and most impoverished of the neighbouring farmtouns. But the reason was not hard to find, for his beasts, and his milk cows especially, were at the very centre of the crofter's lifestyle, and the basis of his economy. It had always been so, in the Eastern Lowlands no less than in the Highlands: they gave him milk and butter and cheese for his household (and maybe to sell to the grocer when times were good) and, more important still, a calf apiece, every year. It was his *stirks*—his young steers—that paid the crofter's rent. That, at least, was the commonly-held belief and Willie Gavin held hard to those old-proven principles. He kept two *bloo coos*, the North-eastern crofter's traditional animal, slatey-grey beasts whose antecedents were as obscure as those of the crofter folk themselves but whose ability to give a calf each spring could never be despised.

Willie Gavin was mindful of that, as his father had been. When he had the longest day of the year behind him he would take his milk beasts up through the fields to Laverockhill on a rope halter. It was an undertaking hedged round with indecision and for a week or two beforehand he would be asking his visitors, as they took their stroll through the Sunday fields, whether they considered this or that beast sufficiently in heat. It was a delicate question for the middle of a Sabbath afternoon—and for a farmtoun lad who had come to see one of the old man's daughters and might be shy about airing a knowledge that in another context could be held against him.

In fact, it mattered little, for Laverockhill's bull was an accommodating beast at any time and always very willing. A docile animal, who would never have been allowed between the covers of any pedigree stock book, he had offspring in nearly every field in the parish. Laverockhill, maybe aware of the poor brute's lack of breeding, even in the 1930s was charging only a fee of five shillings or so for each service. Indeed, he said affably whiles, the beast was a damned disgrace and a constant embarrassment to him, charging good money for the likes of that when most folk did it for nothing. Sometimes he would waive all payment if Willie Gavin had been *"verra* reasonable" in his account for some small job about the farmtoun.

Old Hector rarely disappointed, and come the end of March or thereabouts Willie Gavin, if he had a young cow that year, might be as often in the byre at nights as in his own bed as he waited for the beast to calve. He was kind to his beasts; a lot kinder than he was to his family, folk said. If he was, he reflected only the hard calculating life of the crofter man and the wealth (no different from that of the African tribesman) that lay in his livestock. He might rise twice through the night, sleepily pulling on his *breeks*, pushing his bare feet into the chill of his heavy boots and throwing his jacket over his shoulders—and lighting the byre lantern, set ready on the kitchen table, on the way out. Going down the close, the cold night mist on his face would wake him, or worse still, the steady drizzle of a grey morning. But the byre would be warm with the breath of beasts when he stepped into it, shutting the door behind him. Edging up the side of his young beast in the stall he would swing the lantern over its head, rubbing its neck, his voice soothing.

"Foo are ye, lass, eh?"

In a moment the young cow would have swivelled her head, turning a large and docile eye up at him to reassure him: *Not yet.* And thus satisfied, Willie Gavin would pull the lapels of his jacket across the front of his flannel *sark* and head back for the house and his bed. Not always though. If the eye that looked up at him betrayed the slightest trace of alarm he would settle down on some straw in a dry corner of the byre, his back against the white limewash of its wall, and take his pipe and tobacco mull from his pocket, to wait. His vigil, even so, might be long and to no avail; in the morning Grannie Gavin would find him, fast asleep, his head pillowed in his bonnet against the wall.

Once, in his old grandmother's time, if not his father's, it had been a woman's job to calve the cow, whether her man was at home or not. But that had been in the time long past when the event had been veiled in superstition and as fraught with portent as the first furrow of autumn. Round the crofts and the small farmtouns then, they too had sat in the byre so that their *bloo coos* would not feel lonely. Up-country, where the past was dark and not always to be inquired into, the beast had been prepared for calving with the titbit of a *quarter* of oatcake dowsed in whisky (which was more than any croft wife got in a similar predicament) and rewarded afterwards with a helping of "pottage". And the tribute to the old gods did not end there: for the first milking a shilling would be set into the bottom of the milk pail and to compound the magic and keep the witches from the byre door the croft wife would remove her wedding ring to milk the first few "strains" from each teat through it. If Willie Gavin had heard of such things and could smile at them now, he would have known their reason and their origin: they too were rooted deep in the crofter's dependence on stock.

The *bloo coos*, their care and their keep, dominated the crofting day and kept every croft wife in thraldom: Grannie Gavin's first out-job after lighting the fire would be the morning milking—and the milking was almost her last task at night. When she shut the milk-house door in an evening, she said whiles, it was like putting the lid on another day of her life. Rain or shine, his beasts extended Willie Gavin's working day, the first and last concern almost of his waking hours. As a working mason, in the winter months he would give his byre beasts their breakfast before he took his own, leaving his wife to fill their troughs at midday. Home at night, he might feed them before ever going in for his own supper. And even the Sabbath brought no respite, as it did with the other croft work. Willie Gavin's father had compromised, whether from fear of the Free Kirk's wrath or due to his own natural indolence, it is hard to say: he milked his beasts but they got leave to lie in the filth they themselves had created until Monday. His son was less fastidious about the one, more concerned about the other: he *muckit* his *bloo coos* and their byre Sabbath or no.

For all but a short time in the spring, while one cow was ready to calve and the other had gone dry (when the Gavins would have to beg from a neighbour) there was always milk on a crofter's table, though there might be neither eggs nor fowl nor any of the other things his holding produced. There was milk in abundance just after the calves were born, a fine surplus that brought a spurt of butter- and cheese-making. The calves themselves would take about a half-gallon each in a day but that still left plenty and Willie Gavin, like most of the crofter men, would look round for an extra calf to get the good of it—one a day or two old from a nearby dairytoun perhaps, where they were hardly concerned about stock-rearing. In the 1930s, the calf would cost about £2 10s. (£2.50) and so long as the milk yield kept up for three months or so, the gamble became a bonus, for at that age the calves would be *coggit* (weaned) and put on to a little hay and turnips chipped small with the *hasher* Willie Gavin had made (from an old scythe blade) or sliced, when he was in a hurry, with his knife. There might still be a little milk for them, too, for the crofter's system allowed a slower transition than the rougher world of the farm-touns.

The crofter man fed his beasts well, giving them some oilcake in with their feed when he could afford it. He was a great believer, too, in the properties of rock salt, and kept a slab always beside the beasts' trough. His belief in the salts was proverbial. They did harm, he claimed (forever seeking converts), to neither man nor beast, and though some folk would have violently disagreed with him, he set an example by dosing himself regularly—with salts for human consumption. They fairly cleaned out the system, he said.

He turned his cows out to grass about the middle of May, certainly not later than the Term Day at the end of the month, depending on the condition of his pasture, and took them back into the byre for the winter before the end of October. Now and then, in open defiance of both the law and the county council he would tether a beast at the roadside to take the lush abundance of the verge in advance of the roadman's scythe (it was a criminal waste otherwise), as most of the crofter men did. Housed, his beasts' feed was *neeps and strae* (turnips and straw)—the diet that fattened many a fine beast for the London dinner table—with a handful or two of hay pulled from the stack at the end of the day, to sweeten the milk and maybe boost the yield.

Not all the crofters' cows were *bloo coos*. Some were as black as Auld Nick and about as reliable and there were brown cows as well, all equally undistinguished by any sign of good breeding. It was getting into the 1920s before the pure-breds of the dairytouns began to make their impact on the crofting scene and the crofter men considered what they could do with the yield of an Ayrshire or a Friesian, sometimes double the old *bloo coo*'s daily one-and-a-half to two gallons.

There was something sad about putting the *bloo coos* away after so many decades of faithful service, but even the most loyal crofter man, with all his conservatism, could no longer ignore the benefits of the pure-bred beasts. About any croft their extra milk was a god-send and for a time the neighbouring dairytouns faced a brisk de-mand for their heifer calves. Willie Gavin though was in no hurry to put his *bloo coos* away, and it was into the 1930s before he did so. Then, traditionalist though he was, he could no longer afford the allegiance. With stern patriotism he switched to Ayrshires.

Not all of them were as docile as his old *bloo coos* had been. Now and then a young beast, annoyed by Grannie Gavin's attentions, would flick a *sharny* tail round her ears, content with that as a pro-test. But some were less easily pleased, and at times milker, pail and stool would be sent flying by a kicker and Grannie Gavin's re-turn to the house would be delayed while she searched for her glasses among the beast's bedding straw.

"Gin ye bring home another beastie like that, Willie Gavin," she would threaten him whiles, "ye will get tae milk it yersel'." Mostly, she would have little to say about it, or about the black bruise on her hip for a week or two after. It was a part of her life and always had been.

The croft men sold their *stirks* at a year old—certainly at no more than eighteen months—to any farmer who came seeking them and showed a willingness to pay something approaching their worth. Though the croft men might be in sore need of the *siller* and not always in a position to haggle, the dealing would be hard. Yet the farmer seldom got the worst of the bargain; he knew that always there came the time, a point finely-judged, when the tide turned for the old crofter man and the beast would begin to eat him out of any profit he might have expected to show on it. It was not feasible to keep the *stirk* longer: he had neither the feed nor the *siller* for such a long-term investment. But again, if he preferred to, the crofter could sell to the cattle-dealers who also came round to his door regularly with reasoned and quiet inducement; men skilled in the salesman's glib art who would give him no more in the end of the day than the farmer. For they, too, were looking for easy pickings in a hard-up society and if the time and the price

Crofter folk: *above*, the way they wished to be remembered. The itinerant photographer of the late 1800s brought them to their doors in their Sabbath clothes. And it was not only the people who turned out. Sometimes the result, *below*, was the kind of remarkable picture that encapsulated all the elements of a life of grim compromise. Hitched here in the plough, in 1888, are a horse and a cow, a pairing typical in the old crofting landscape.

Right: A hardy breed: the years and the work might take their toll, greying hair and beard, but they could not dim that shrewd steady gaze. This Turriff, Aberdeenshire, couple are dressed in the traditional heavy tweeds and the close-buttoned bodice of their time.

Far right: Mutched and aproned, a croft wife of the old North-east Lowlands countryside pauses on her way to the byre in the 1920s. The milking of cows—central to the old croft's economy—morning, noon and night, was the great unrelenting tyranny of her life.

Right: How the crofter man won his crop: usually the scythe was the implement of his haytime and his harvest long after the sound of the machine-harvester was heard from the adjoining farmtoun fields.

Far right: Stopping to sweeten the scythe-blade with the carborundum stone. Note the scyther's leather apron: was this the smith winning his croft's own small harvest after a day at the forge mending other men's machine-harvesters?

Proud toun: *above*, a North-east Lowlands farmtoun of the early 1900s, Barnton of Skene, typical of the farms the crofter men turned to for the contract ploughing of their few acres. Though the binder—*below*, at Denmill of Culter in 1912—was by then becoming common in the countryside, few of the croft men came seeking it. Few, indeed, could afford to pay for its work and some diehards would not have let it on to their land at any price.

Croft *bigging*: *above*, a house of the later crofting landscape, two-storeyed and dormer-windowed and dourly overlooking its small fields. It was a vast improvement on the earlier dwellings, where the smell of the byre percolated through the end wall into the croft's parlour, and that time, *below*, when the plough and the drill-plough had brought together in the traces such an ill-yoked pair as the croft shelt and a bullock.

In the steep uplands fie
of many of the old
crofting colonies the
ploughing—as *above*, mu
later, at Greystones of
Lumphanan—was all o1
way, with the implemen
tilted on to the mould-
board for its return to
the top headland. It was
with the plough that the
crofter's year began, its
ritual culminating in the
spring sowing of his oat
and, *left*, the compactio1
of the soil by the horse-
drawn steel roller.

The kirk and the mill, perhaps the two most enduring pillars of the old countryside. The steam threshing-mill, *above*, was constantly on the winter roads, moving between one farmtoun and the next. The threshing, *below*, brought a feverish activity to a croft's small stackyard but when it was over the crofter had oats to take to the miller for grinding—and, subsequently, the oatmeal to refill his girnal or meal-chest.

Lost art of a lost landscape: *above*, rick decoration, the kind of embellishment that once proclaimed the triumph of another harvest gathered safely into the cornyard. *Below*, modest neat stacks that show the criss-cross roping of thatch common in the North-east Lowlands before the dawn of the combine age robbed harvest of its ancient architecture.

were about right the crofter man could do nothing but strike a
bargain. With the sale agreed, the croft men would let their beasts
go when the drover men came round to collect them. Local droving
continued for some years after the motor-float was a common
sight on the country road flitting the stock of the farmtouns, for
the protracted gathering of the crofters' beasts would have made
its hire for that purpose an expensive business. The float, for all
that, was a fine innovation: it saved the leather of the servant
lass's boots as she dragged an unwilling beast to market at the end
of a rope halter and kept her where she was doing good, in her
mistress's kitchen. In time it would put an end, too, to the drover
men; though their droving was far different from those earlier
times when the beef of that countryside had gone South on the
hoof to the old trysts, they were the last of their kind and would
become as redundant as the wandering packman.

But there was another reason why the crofter men had to accept
the dealers' prices, and it was an important consideration: few
could afford to take a day off from their regular work to take their
stock to the market. And even there the crofter's *stirk* rarely made
the price of a farmtoun beast.

With the hens that squawked in the croft *ree*—impatient to be
let out to scavenge in the stubble or screich in the cornyard—his
milk cows and his *stirks* were Willie Gavin's only stock. It had not
always been so about the Gavin croft. Indeed, folk said, looking
back to Old John's days, there had been a time when it had seemed
more like a menagerie. Then the poultry was to be seen at any time
of the day picking the titbits out of the roof-thatch of the old
dwelling and perched on its low chimneys getting their glossy
feathers sooted with fire-reek. One of his grand-daughters who
came to marry a banking man remembers the croft as it was in the
early days of the century, with humour if not with affection:

> The stock consisted of a horse that did as it liked, two cows and a
> calf, the usual hens, and turkeys that laid away. They [her grand-
> parents] also kept a pig or two . . . and my mother would walk to
> market with a pig in a poke slung across her back, presumably to be
> sold. To reach the byre from the field the cows had to pass in front of
> the house and they seemed to save up their excreta so as to liberate it
> as they passed the house door.

Well, there were many things about the crofting life that never changed, and even in Willie Gavin's time it was always advisable to take a lantern to light your feet through the dark.

The grandson who was Old John's constant companion through the summer months during that same time also remembers the old croft life, and Old John's livestock in particular:

> They had a couple of milk cows and they had a few *stirks* (steers we would call them today), half-grown beasts. When they got close to maturity they would sell them, of course, for beef stock. And they had two or three calves . . . They had a horse there, and a pig-pen, too, where they kept a couple of hogs and maybe a few pigs from time to time. They also kept a lot of poultry, my grandfather and grandmother. They usually had a bunch of turkeys. They were all for sale. And they had a whole bunch of chickens and they kept guinea-fowl for quite a while—for their eggs.

And it hadn't ended there, for besides his collection of hoof and claw, some of the old croft's stock was on the wing. Old John's grandson again:

> My grandmother was a great bee-woman, really adept as a bee-keeper, and produced quite a lot of honey. She would prowl around amidst all her hives—she had quite a few, maybe fifteen to twenty, I cannot recollect exactly—and she would never wear a bee-veil or a glove on her hand. They would never sting her—her hands, her arms, would be covered with them—she would never pay any attention to them. My grandfather though, he wouldn't go near them; he was terror-stricken if he was asked to step inside where they were located.

Willie Gavin would inherit from his mother, along with much else of her character, her fearlessness of bees and when she grew frail he took over her skeps, keeping four or five right up to the end of his days. When the hardy old woman died it was he who went out to the bees to tell them.

VIII

The Heartbreak Life

A CROFTER'S DAY was never-ending. If he were also the smith, the tailor, a mason man or a dyker it stretched regularly to sixteen hours or more through the summer months and was only fractionally shorter during winter. Even then, many of the old North-east Lowlands crofter men pulled their beasts' turnips from the frozen drill when they came home from work, if not by the light of the moon by the fitful gleam of an oil or candle lantern. On any hillside crofting colony on a dark night their lights could be seen, bobbing like will o' the wisps about the brae-face, a sight that raised pity in the heart and poignantly underlined the wretchedness of their lifestyle. For the poor croft man had little choice, especially as he grew older and his children moved away and his wife became frail with the fullness of years and unable to help him with any but the lightest of the work.

Always he was a man on a treadmill; he didn't dare stop. So inter-related were all the strands of his simple agriculture—his cropping and stock-rearing—that if he broke the momentum even for a season, his fragile economy shattered. For his system had, acutely, all the inherent disadvantages of subsistence farming; he was a man without margins, in land or capital, without room to manoeuvre. His was a delicate structure, one part so diabolically dependent on another: his crops fed his beasts which re-fertilised his *shifts* which grew their feed. . . . When his rotation slipped or a crop failed his whole lifestyle faltered or was thrown wildly into an imbalance whose outcome was unpredictable; for that, in turn, put him at the mercy of outside forces which were never favourable to him, that even, at times, viewed his self-sufficiency with antagonism, or outright enmity. There were in the North-east Lowlands no short cuts the crofter men could take in following the cultivation pattern of the proud farmtouns (incongruous though that parallel seems); there was no streamlining possible that would successfully guarantee an on-going crofting viability, far less the maintenance of a modest stability—beyond the kind of speculation that took a holding right out of the crofting pattern and into a world entirely under the sway of those other, alien factors.

It was the stark understanding of this, perhaps unformulated and unreasoned but congenitally understood, that would take a croft man out of his warm bed and into the fields when society folk were hardly home from the ball, and drove him indoors on a summer night only as darkness fell.

There were times when Willie Gavin must have thought himself luckier than most for during the dark of winter when the fierce frosts settled in that pre-chemical age and made the lime-mortar unworkable, there would be few masoning jobs he could do. If he was working away the onset of deep-winter days brought him home to stay for weeks at a time—as it did all the other masoning men of that countryside, even those who had gone to America. They came home with all the *siller* they had made from their skills with stone. There are songs still in that bare countryside's ballad books that celebrate the return of those masoning men to their small village communities and the arms of their hopeful (and determined) sweethearts, lasses who spurned the ploughman and even the smith and knew the fine life they could have as the mason's wife—if he were not also a crofter man:

> I winna hae the sailor
>   That sails on the sea;
> Nor yet will I the ploughman
>   That ploughs on the lea;
> But I will hae the mason,
>   For he's a bonnie lad,
> And I'll wash the mason's apron,
>   And think it nae degrade.

> I winna hae the blacksmith
>   That burns a' the airn;
> Nor yet will I the weaver
>   That works the creeshy yarn;
> But I will hae the mason
>   And the mason he'll hae me,
> And the bonnie mason laddie
>   I'll mount the scaffold wi'.

On the dreichest days there would be little that Willie Gavin could do about his *shifts* or around his small steading, and there was little he would *have* to do unless winter came early and caught him unprepared. Then he might be out in the snow-covered parks, digging to find the *neeps* for his byre beasts, stopping from time to time to blow some warmth back into his mittened hands and stamp feeling again into his feet where the ground struck cold through even the thick soles of his tacketed ploughman's boots and their lining of straw, and the heavy woollen socks Grannie Gavin was constantly knitting for her menfolk. (For an outdoor man in a cold countryside they were a godsend and almost better than a bottle of whisky in your hip pocket.)

But Willie Gavin was a cautious man and it was seldom that winter caught him unawares. Usually, like the best-run farmtouns around him, he would have a *fordel*, a cache, of turnips barrowed home and clamped against the back of the house (under the old thatch from a rick) before the days of storm came on him. There were days, certainly, when he might look out from the kitchen window to watch McCaskill foraging to find a bite for his *stirks* in a steady *on-ding* of snow and be pleased at his own careful nature. When the beige ribbon road to the kirktoun had filled with snow wreaths quite beyond the conquest of short legs, he would yoke Meggie, his father's old *shelt*, into the shafts of the sleigh to take the bairns to the school and out of their mother's way—and maybe, too, because he had a wonderful belief in the "learning" and all the doors it could open. (He had been a willing scholar, encouraged by his mother; a clever boy among country lads who had cared little for their sums and already saw their futures clearly before them: the rough life of a farmtoun bothy until such time as a lass might make a home for them somewhere.) In the right humour the crofter man might order a bag of bran or a roll of wire-netting from the merchant's in the kirktoun for a harder-pressed neighbour, picking it up when he returned in the late afternoon to fetch the children. But he was not known as an obliging man and people thought twice about approaching him, so savage was he about anything that foresight might have avoided.

Yet gradually even a hard winter passed, its unaccustomed ease marred for the mason man only by the worry that there was *siller* going out and none coming in. He would be pleased enough to see the spring when it came and to get back to his chisels and trowels—

cycling away by four in the chill dark of a Monday morning to start his week's work at six, fifteen miles away. It was the last his wife would see or hear of him until the Saturday afternoon. Then with luck he might be home an hour or two before dusk and in time to put the top of a rick through the threshing-mill to get straw for the Sabbath and the following week. Like most of the crofter-tradesmen, however, Willie Gavin preferred to work in his own parish, or failing that, in the ones that adjoined it. That let him home each night to keep up with his croft work, though doubtless there were croft men who were pleased to be in their own beds for other reasons. It would be a slack season of the year, or a night of driving rain, if the croft man was seated by his fireside before eight in the evening.

If spring brought the Clydesdales on to his ground, summer brought its own kind of frenzy for the croft folk themselves. There might be a pause in the year when the *neep* seed had been sown and before the hoeing began, but not for Willie Gavin and the other crofter men. There was never an evening when they could not find a necessary chore in their *shifts* (repairing the fencing) or round their *biggings* (maybe tidying the cornyard).

It was with the singling of turnips, the *hyowing* (to use the word from that now-distant landscape) that the rush began, towards the start of July. By then, the turnip seed of mid-May would be well-brairded, running (in those days of uncertain germination) like thickening threads down the length of the broad drills, burgeoning almost as you watched.

There were crofter men who rose at four in the morning to hoe a drill or two before they cycled off to their regular work, and there was hardly a creature about the Gavin croft—man, woman or child—who could not handle a hoe, and who did not have to. Sons who had gone to be *orra-loon* at some farmtoun, or were apprenticed away and learning trades where the future looked brighter, would be summoned home for an evening or two and given a hoe into their hands to *hyow* a drill or two; cottared sons-in-law who had been *hyowing* all day would cycle down with their hoes for an evening stint at the same job, remembering that earlier time when they had come to see the old man's daughters and been given a *hyow* into their hands instead. For there had never been any doubt but that a lad's skill with the hoe had recommended him to the crofter's notice when it came to considering his lasses' future. Even

the non-farming visitor could find himself enlisted (there was
always time to *news*, the crofter man promised him, quite truth-
fully), and just as willingly a hoe-shaft would be shortened for any
grandchild who showed the slightest aptitude or the inclination to
learn. Its sex was immaterial, as was its age. But that was no grandfather's indulgence; Willie Gavin wanted good work even if all he
was paying for it was a pandrop from his pocket when they came to
the endrig. Keen though he was to have fine *neeps*, however, Willie
Gavin was never in a hurry to lift them; if his circumstances had
permitted it he would have let them lie in the drill (fattening, as he
believed) into the New Year. But they were ready by the end of
October and unlike the farmtoun men, who could feed tares to
their stock in the meantime, Willie Gavin needed his turnips from
the moment his beasts were housed for winter.

Croft folk were hardly out of the *hyowing* before they were into
the hay-making, which was almost as frantic. The crofter man
made his hay in a hurry and while the weather held. By the time
he was spotted on the road on his way home from his day's work,
his supper porridge would be cooling on the window-sill so as to be
about the right temperature by the time he reached home and set
his bicycle against the wall beside it. There were nights indeed
when Willie Gavin did no more than cry in at the window for the
spoon to sup it with and for some *quarters* of oatcake and a hunk of
cheese to follow it. He ate the porridge where he stood and took to
the hay park with the oatcake and cheese in his hand, never setting
foot in the house until the dusk drove him in. His hay-making, in
that time before the machine-baler let alone the nutrient-sealing
grass-drier, followed the traditional pattern: cut with the scythe, it
lay for a day or two in the bout before being raked into wider
windrows and dragged into small *coles* (haycocks) and finally into
big *coles* before being ricked in the old man's cornyard. Though
help was less urgent than for the hoeing, the old man could always
find a visitor a spare hayfork—and there was always a bairn more
than willing to *trump* a *cole* or a rick for him. If not, there was
always Grannie Gavin, called from the house just as she settled
with her knitting or with her behind-hand sewing.

But then the croft life had always been hard on the woman. If
Willie Gavin's day was long, his wife's was even longer; lengthier
even than the working day of the servant lasses *fee*'d home to the
farmtouns—and that was scandalous enough. Grannie Gavin was

up and lighting the fire before the kitchen clock struck five and had
her crofter man's brose kettle on to boil before he had swung his
legs over the side of the *closet* bed. It was a high bed, and when she
left it, over its bottom board, it was as a fugitive or an escaping
prisoner. So as not to disturb him too soon, she stepped down first
to a conveniently-placed chair and then to the *closet* floor. For long
enough her rôle, like that of all the other croft wives, took her back
into the dark of history and the slavery of the old cot-touns of that
earlier landscape where the women had sheared and *stooked*, carried the muck and the peat, and done a whole host of other duties
through a day without end. The croft wives, too, did all those
tasks, long after the censure of society and a new social awareness
had outlawed their continuance even in the rough world of the
farmtouns. If some of them became hard cases, as rough diamonds
as any of their menfolk, that is little to be wondered at, for it was
a life that turned the bonniest lass prematurely into the aged crone.
In their lace mutches, most of them went grim-faced to the kirk,
but in a life that robbed them so often of their womanly grace it
would be surprising if some of them at least had not, long since,
lost all faith in it.

With her man away all day—and often all week—Grannie
Gavin did much of the everyday, outdoor croft work: hoeing, turning the hay in the swath, mucking the byre beasts, pulling the
turnips from the drill and even bringing them home in the barrow,
small woman though she was. Through the rush of her man's
small *hairst* and while the weather held she came in from the fields
only to prepare their simple meals. Her daughters, when they came
of age, learned to do the same and never questioned it.

There was a job for everybody in that old crofting landscape
with its ceaseless pattern of work, even for Daft Sandy. When the
threshing-mill came its croft rounds shortly before the New Year,
his help was constantly sought. The night before, the croft men
would walk along to his folk's place in the evening gloam to ask
could he be sent in the morning, for Daft Sandy had that uncanny
compensating gift of the weak-minded: a strength that could hurl
heavy sacks of corn about as though they were feather pillows.
They were damned glad to have him for they were all of them
older men than they had been and not a few of them already
broken with work.

Daft Sandy would work as though seeking pardon for his life, speaking continuously to himself—raging it seemed—in some high tongue of another time that nobody could understand. He carried the corn and sometimes cleared the chaff as well from the mill's dusty under-belly. And folk were careful to nod to him whiles (whenever he looked their way) to humour him, and would get the beam of his soft smile in return: they knew if he broke loose there was no one could hold him.

That need never arose though and at the end of a mill-day Daft Sandy would go home like a king with a shilling or two in his pocket that the croft man had given him. That night, like many a night, when you passed his folk's place, he might be at the top of the close or hanging over the garden gate—singing to the moon.

Grannie Gavin had never liked the croft life; most of all, as a young wife with her children at school and her husband away maybe for the week, she had found its isolation and the silence of the countryside unbearable and terrifying. Long after, she would confess to the fear and loneliness of dark winter afternoons, a fear that had driven her repeatedly to stand at the head of the Whinfield croft-close in the hope that she might spot—somewhere on that grey landscape—another human soul (a tink on the road, some shepherd walking the hill fields) or, listening, hear the carry of a human voice or a dog's bark on the wind.

That had been in their earlier crofting days, when her man was not long into his father's croft. A grim poverty had stalked their days and want was the constant grey ghost of their lives. With the legacy the old man had left them—leaking *biggings* and the lack of fences, and a *shelt* that did as little as it could to earn its keep—it could hardly have been otherwise. From the moment of his occupation Willie Gavin's family had known what it was to be grindingly poor. There were times when they almost lost hope. "It was nothing but hunger, misery and want," Grannie Gavin would say, long years later and in widowhood, when she had left the life behind her. Good Christian though she was, even then she would be unable to keep the bitterness out of her voice. It was a life that had robbed her of all leisure, completely.

There were nights when, too tired to sleep, her mind had gone back to the days of her young girlhood and the times in the 1870s when she had visited her grandfather's place in the old crofting colony of Lumphanan's Perk Hill. Lying in the *closet* dark at Willie Gavin's side, she would remember her grandmother's advice as she had straightened her back for a moment in shearing her man's meagre corn with the old *heuk*:

"Never marry a crofter, lassie, for it's nae life at all. What comes in fae this year's *hairst*, will gang oot for next year's seed."

And so it had proved; croft solvency was often that delicately balanced.

Willie Gavin's first harvests, threshed out, brought little more than the seed to re-sow and the price of just a little of the manure the sour ground so urgently needed. It seemed for a time that they might all be into the poorhouse, and to keep them out of it young Jess MacKendrick had fallen back on something she could do superbly: her sewing. With her croft chores done, inside and out, she picked up her needle, sewing till midnight by the feeble light of a candle—till she could no longer see the material and was ready to fall off the stool with exhaustion. It was a time still when men's shirts were hand-made in the countryside. Many a farm-toun wife augmented the family's income with such sewing and the young croft wife's skill soon brought her more work than she had time for. Yet she dared not turn it away. Glad of the money it would bring in, she would think nothing of the ten-mile walk that meant an afternoon's mending at the grieve's house on a big farm-toun. And when war came she would continue—making shirts for the soldiers. They were much like the shirts she had always made, except for their colour; maybe they went on to the backs of the same men, the *fee*'d lads of the farmtouns who had left their brown cords lying on some bothy floor to put on the king's khaki. But that was something she would never know. During the four years of war she made over 400 shirts in her spare time on the old German-made sewing-machine she had earlier bought to help her keep up with the work that came her way. When it was over, the army gave her a medal and the Gavins were still in the croft.

IX

The Weaver's Lass

MARRIAGE TO A crofter man was an indenture into slavery. It had always been so, and Jess MacKendrick had known it. Though she was come of weaver folk there had never been a time when, like Willie Gavin himself, she had not had a foothold in the crofting past of that North-east countryside and known what the croft life was like. She had come down into Willie Gavin's bare landscape from the Donside uplands where the air was fine and the Highlands began; there, even now, boarded and silent and high above the stream that once gave it life, stands the wool mill that her folk once worked.

The old mill ran in its heyday and for long after that on the skill of the MacKendricks and closed, some years since, almost as the last of them left it. It weathered the years better than most of its kind because the quality of its goods was exceptional, the best for many miles round, and they found a quick sale over the best London store counters, where the mark-up reflected the standard of the work rather than the standard of living of the folk who made them. Always the *siller* it made had gone into somebody else's pocket, but if its business from time to time took the MacKendricks away (maybe to London for a week to speak with store-buyers) they were as pleased to be home again.

With its sluice unworked, its sightless windows and rusting belt pulleys, the blue wooden mill has become the sad derelict of a newer industrial age, a reminder only of the former self-containment of that uplands countryside. Farther on up the hill is the old MacKendrick croft, Scrapehard, a pleasant cottage now, flower-garlanded on its knoll, with a view of the Highland hills. It carries no memory of bitterness, for Jess MacKendrick's father showed all the sound sense of an intelligent man—and a reconciliation with things as they were—by giving up his croft land to a neighbouring farmtoun, a renunciation of the old style of crofting existence that avoided the spiritual rupture of running two lives, and an action

that brings him down to our time as a reasonable man and a realist
to boot. He had not even kept his own cow, unusual in that time,
and had been happy to carry his milk from the byre of the man who
worked his land. The arrangement had suited the weaver man well:
not for him the trial and the despair of that old dichotomy of cultivation and commerce which so blighted the lives of his cronies.

But not all the MacKendricks were weavers. Early sons, like
Jess herself, had been forced out into the world and soon like their
father showed some singularity or oddity of character: one was a
sawmiller who flattened woodlands as other men sheared corn;
one, a carpenter-turned-coffin-maker in London; and yet another,
also in the metropolis, stood constantly tailed and frock-coated in
the women's fashion department of a top Oxford Street store
though later, for reasons that were never discussed in the family,
he left hurriedly for the backwoods of Canada, to settle down
finally as a market-gardener in Manitoba. There, he lost everything (including his false teeth) in a prairie fire. It was a blow that
might have felled a lesser man, but not that bold MacKendrick.
Out of the chaos (and the insurance), he returned to his original
store-minding trade; he raised first one shop and then another, and
then, in partnership, a whole chain. The good-looking weaver's
lad had come a long way from his early beginnings in the old
bigging above the mill and whatever had happened in that London
store those long years ago (and likely the society woman had encouraged him, folk said), it had done him nothing but good. Only
the later MacKendrick daughters and a delicate son whom the
weaver had fathered as an afterthought had been needed to staff
the mill. Their nephew would remember not only their skills but
the old mill, its operation, and its reputation:

They used to buy up all the wool from folk who brought it in from
the country all round there. They would card it and tease it and do all
the usual procedures needed to convert it into a good high-grade
woollen worsted used in knitting and in the manufacture of all kind of
woven materials. They were experts on the machines, these aunts of
mine, they could do all kinds of weaving, any intricate pattern you
could dream of. They made all kinds of Scots tartans—all the popular
tartans. They were really adept in that particular field. They used to
produce very good quality blankets, too, in this woollen mill and my
crofting mother and father used to buy these from the mill periodic-

ally—though not that frequently, since they invariably lasted a life-time. But the climate of that old countryside was such that a warm blanket was an asset and appreciated in any home.

Jess MacKendrick, as the eldest, had been less fortunate than her sisters, her childhood typically that of a country bairn of her time. Her humble academy was the *fummlers' skweel*, the girls' school, nestling its red-tiled roof among encircling trees where the broad farming strath began to draw in its flanks to become a landscape of smaller brae-set fields and the road took to the high Cabrach moorland. Miss Myers' school took twenty pupils at a time; like most of its kind it was unashamedly fee-paying and without hint of government envy or interference—which was as well, for the way Miss Myers ran it, it might as well have been a military academy. Fortnightly or monthly (depending on the social credibility of the pupil's family) she took from them the 6*d*. (2½p) or 1*s*. (5p) to pay for their learning and daily from each the peat from her father's peatstack or the lump of coal that would keep the schoolroom fire burning and on a wet day dry out their clothes before it came time for them all to go home again.

Weaver man though he was, there seems to have been some doubt about Jess MacKendrick's father's standing: his daughter carried her sixpence fortnightly in the pocket of her inmost petti-coat, wrapped (in case she should lose it) in a page from *The People's Journal*, the weekly newspaper that served that uplands countryside and whose lum-hatted reporters tore round it regularly in their pursuit of every titbit of scandal it would yield (and that could be reliably attributed). It was the only news-sheet that MacKendrick allowed to darken his door and besides the obvious, its uses were endless, for every day of the week in another of its pages Jess carried her lunchtime *piece*: dry oatcakes.

If Miss Myers' régime was rigid and ultra-strict there was no doubt that it got the kind of results that would have gladdened any latter-day dominie's heart. It was what her customers were paying for. She hammered home the tenets of basic arithmetic with the thumping insistence of a big bass drum; hardened the outlines of history in the mind with the dates that only death itself would erase; and managed at times to lift the long recitation of a multi-plication table in the dark of a winter's afternoon to the sonorous chant of high mass.

A little farther along the road, in the separate boys' school, Mr Pithy reigned like an emperor, ready to thrash any pupil within an inch of his life for a misguided subtraction, and it was here that the MacKendrick brothers were similarly prepared for the hard business of life in the same unrelenting routine. In the circumstances the weaver's family, aware of where their best interests lay, turned into excellent scholars and emerged more than willing to take on the world as they found it.

So, it had been neither lack of scholastic ambition nor ability that had ended the young Jess MacKendrick's education at the age of ten. Far from it. It had been that ancient necessity of a hard countryside: the need for the eldest of the family to earn its own crust (and maybe contribute to the economy of the home) at the earliest age. And the *siller* that paid for her schooling had been hard to find from her father's income with brothers and sisters rising behind her, all of them with an equal claim. Yet even then, it had seemed for a moment that the weaver's lass, though she might not realise her heart's wish of becoming a nurse, would at least escape the endless drudgery of the old farmtoun and crofting life.

Her first job had taken her as maid into the home of a woman who was herself a retired lady's maid. Miss Barclay was out of the same mould as Miss Myers; she stood as straight as a stick in her stays, severe and unbending, withering reprimand forever on her lips. Home safely at last from being a "companion" to a lady of quality in Italy (where the hot blood had seemed constantly a threat to her spinsterhood), she paid the weaver's girl only 15s. (75p) each half-year but, in guilt for such parsimony, gave her instruction—a fine finishing to her education, almost—in all the graces of the tea-table and the drawing-room as well as a fine pronunciation of the Auld Queen's English and a liking for the higher caste of religion that was preached in the parish's little Episcopal kirk. This the servant lass attended with her mistress on Sunday evenings, imbibing the grace of its litanies and the gentler modulations of its minister, who saw sin in simpler terms than the Free Kirk did and plainly, in that direction, expected less of his flock.

But Miss Barclay's wisdom, after all, would do the Free Kirk weaver's lass little good. At the age of twelve she was needed elsewhere: to help on her grandfather's croft. Just when it seemed that her future lay in refined service and in the lifestyle of a different kind of society, destiny had turned Jess MacKendrick back to the crofting background from which her family had emerged. After the faded gentility of Miss Barclay's way of life, it was a harsh awakening.

On her grandfather's croft on the bare Perk Hill of Lumphanan, her grandmother, worn by the life and soured by its bitterness, had no wish to hear the Queen's fine English spoken in her kitchen, still less in her byre, and as for the Episcopal kirk, that was damned nearly halfway to Rome anyway. And lady of small deceits though she was, she thought a traycloth an extravagance far beyond the needs of common crofter folk, and maybe even, in its way, a kind of betrayal.

There had, after all, been no escape for the young Jess Mac-Kendrick and even today it is easy to summon into the mind that grey landscape of her youth. The brae-face of the Perk Hill still betrays a little of its crofting past. Its fields, still, are somewhat small and awkwardly set, a reminder in a modern farming age of the days of the crofter men; beneath the trim and harled exterior of the low, single-storey dwellings—even those with the dormer windows of their cramped garrets poked through the roofs—it is not difficult to discern the shape of the old but-and-ben house that once occupied the site. But roof-thatch or red tiles has long been replaced by the cold conformity of grey slates and the seemlier sanitation of a more sophisticated age has added its agglomeration of bathrooms abutting and adjoining. And the years of attrition and farming progress have long driven the old-style smallholder men from the hill and dispersed what was once a colony typical of the North-east's crofting communities.

It was a countryside always where the past lay uneasily in wait for the future, its settlement long a staging post in the affairs of men, its inn as important as its old kirk. The kirk had long been there, bringing men in from the country far round on the Sabbath for the good of their souls, but it was at its inn that the travelling folk of that old countryside sought their first sustenance and their succour after coming over some high pass of the Grampians or fording the dangerous Dee; they sought its shelter before night fell on them, before they pressed north on the old highway. To and fro down the years they had come and gone on their endless errands, the preacher, the packman (the one as vital as the other), the soldier and the wastrel, the thief on his way to grace the gallows tree. Whatever their station they had been glad of the old inn and the kirk that stood by it, a beacon lit in the dark days of the seventh century by Saint Finan as he passed that way, a seeker for the souls of men. His association with the lonely hamlet would descend the centuries in the tortured Gaelic that first gave the kirktoun its name. Among the many who came through on the old road, north and south as their destinies drove them, was another who was more sinner than saint and whose name would adorn the darker cloak of history. They called him Maelbetha; he was Mormaer of Moray. He was going north in a hurry, and with vengeance at his heels; though he did not know it then, he was nearing his journey's end. The man fleeing that fine summer day of 1057 was the chief that an English bard would pass down to our time as Macbeth. His crime was old but it had lain long in his mind: an old man's death, seventeen years since. It had gained him a crown but never the peace to enjoy it. Now the man they called the Red King, old Duncan's murderer, had pursuit behind him; in the words of old Wyntoun, the chronicler now of such far-off things:

> Owre the Mounth thai chast hym than
> Til the wode of Lumfanan.

It was 15 August and the warrior who engaged the fifty-two-year-old usurper of a kingdom in single combat was Macduff. The district has, still, its memorials to that day and its encounter: though Shakespeare took the scene of that action to the woods of Dunsinane (captivated perhaps by their more mellifluous sound but cynically contorting history) he would hardly be able to transpose the wells or the burial cairn that carried the rebel king's name and where tradition had buried him long after he was at peace in another saint's kingdom. After that, the old kirktoun and its countryside had slept through the centuries—as serene as the old warriors in their stone kists below the run-rigs—till the railway came in the mid-1800s. It had carried with it a new kind of religion and a new kind of men who lived it; they called it commerce and there were folk who said it corrupted the soul far faster than the Devil ever did. Its temple was the station they built half a mile to the east of the old kirk; it had its own excitement and in no time at all it had all the appurtenances of trade clustered sycophantically round it.

The railway had reached Lumphanan a few years after James Geerie but there is no doubt it got the better ground, richer by far than the croft man's soil on the skirts of the hill little more than the length of a barley rig from where the Red King died. The battle that James Geerie fought there, too, was mostly single-handed, and like Macbeth's, it was one for survival. Years later, Jess MacKendrick would speak of her grandfather, the pioneer crofter man of the Perk Hill, from whom she would imbibe her fear of God's wrath and an abiding faith in the Word, with a warm affection:

> He was a hard-working, clean honest man. He kept rigidly to the laws of the Book, as he called the Bible, and woe betide any of us younger ones who did not do the same. Some time about 1850 he married my grandmother and bought a piece of land on the edge of the hill, built a house of sorts, trenched the bit of land, had it culti- vated and grew corn and turnips and kept two cows.

Devout though he was, James Geerie had bedded his bride some time before their betrothal only to find her more fertile than his poor ground would ever be, for Jess's mother, their first bairn, had been born, as her daughter would wryly admit "not too long after the marriage". But then, in that lost countryside, there was noth- ing unusual in that.

Herself a grandmother, Jess MacKendrick would vividly recall the life of the croft hill of Lumphanan in the early days of her childhood, and in doing so provide a valuable record of the hard times the crofter men and their families of the 1860s and 1870s faced as they still broke in fresh ground:

> The whole hillside as I remember it was dotted with small crofts; every year they trenched some more ground and generally planted their potatoes in the little hollows they had dug and put the sod back on top—and they had just lovely potatoes! The Perk Hill did not grow turnips well, hence the whins that they cut on the hills. Every- one had their whin patch as well as their whin stone. But the whins were not like the ones you see at the roadside: they were stout, green, single strands and they were cut with a steel *heuk*, with a forked stick to keep them off your hands. They were taken home and chopped fine on the whin stone at the byre door. This was a built, stone erection with a flat top.

The whins that James Geerie's grand-daughter brought home from the hill on her back were needed to augment the meagre diet of his beasts; they were "threshed" on the whin stone with a wooden mallet the crofter man had made for himself from the stout log of a tree simply by fitting a shaft to it. Implement and procedure are at one in demonstrating the oddities and improvisations of the old croft men's agriculture.

On the Perk Hill croft, though still only twelve, Jess Mac-Kendrick had been her grandfather's help more than her grandmother—carrying *neeps* home to his byre in a bag on her back (for James Geerie could afford no barrow); gathering *growth* from his clean land; stones for his laying-down of drains in that time before the tile pipe took the poor man's agriculture by storm and drainage, such as it was, was achieved by arranging flattish stones in an inverted "U" in the bottom of a trench, opened and then re-filled. Such jobs the crofter man could do himself; the heavier cultivation —ploughing, for instance—was done under the old contract system and in that uplands countryside by a team that yet again demonstrated all the awkwardness and elements of compromise that marked its agriculture: a *shelt* yoked in the traces with a cow.

James Geerie's crofting life, running in parallel with old John Gavin's in the lower landscape, was as bedevilled by that insoluble problem: the need for another occupation to keep want from the door. Geerie was a road foreman in that early time when the highway's custodians were the men who sat busily by the wayside beside their *birns* of stones, ceaselessly manufacturing the metalling that kept the countryside's beige ribbon roads passable. He rose at four each day to give himself an hour or two of the flail—threshing his sheaves on the barn floor—before setting out for work. All of her days Jess MacKendrick would remember the thump-thump heard all round the hill as day broke, and in the winter long before that as men worked by the glimmer of a cruisie lamp hung in a safe corner of the barn. Only the Sabbath stilled that insistent morning sound.

The flails of the crofter men were of the traditional type, their design as common to the North-east Lowlands as to the Highland kingdom that lay beyond the bare moors of the Cabrach and began in Strathspey, though their size and weight might differ from one region to the next and depend, also, on whether the man or woman of the croft would be using it. In the Highlands the woods used for the flail were usually ash (for the longer shaft) and hazel (for the shorter striker or swipple that threshed the corn). In practice though, it is likely that a hard-pressed crofter man was glad of any two suitable sticks that could be strapped together and other woods were almost certainly used. Its method of use was more an art than a glance today at the crudely-constructed implement might suggest, though the threshing principle was primitively simple, as Jess MacKendrick would so succinctly recall: "The flail was just two sticks joined by a leather thong. You held by one, the other you twisted round . . . and it came down on the sheaves on the threshing floor—a square of wooden splits to let the corn through on to the floor below and keep the straw for use." To get enough straw to put him over the Sabbath, James Geerie would have to be up betimes on a Saturday and maybe return to the barn when he came home at night if he thought his *fordel* was not sufficient to feed his beasts over the weekend. The straw he needed for his cows; his corn he took to the Mill of Kintocher, beside Craigievar's old castle, when the level of meal in his girnal began to get low.

The sweat would be dripping off the crofter man as he came in from the barn after his morning's threshing to the oatmeal brose Grandma Geerie made for him. She filled his short clay pipe as he supped them, lighting it with the dross from the peat fire and putting the tin lid on it that enabled an outdoor man to have his smoke supposing it came a downpour of rain. She would take half a dozen good "pulls" herself, just to make sure that the pipe was "drawing" properly and that the stem was unchoked, before pushing it straight into his mouth out of her own.

For a godly man, James Geerie was none too keen on cleanliness and went out to meet the world each morning (they say) with a kind of cat's-lick wash that would have made the laziest animal blush with shame. The crofter man's ablution was, to say the least, idiosyncratic. Without ever taking the well-lit clay pipe from his mouth, he filled the drinking jug from the water pail as he went out at the door and cupping a little of the water in one hand swilled one side of his face, repeating the operation, on the other side, with the other palm. He hardly paused even, and his back would no sooner be out of sight round the bend of the hill than Grandma Geerie would order Jess to let the hens into the barn for some rich pickings among the new-threshed corn, a deception that made the young girl think less of her grandmother and which she had later to cover up by gathering the hen droppings left in the barn after she had shoo-ed them out of it. Though it doubtless improved the quality of the eggs, it was a cruel trick, for James Geerie's crops were always poor, their return a promise bitterly unfulfilled. But the roadman's lifestyle allowed him little time for such reflection, or for the smaller pleasures of life, and maybe that was as well for his position, like that of the other hill men, would not bear thinking about.

It was a life, in spite of the croft man's faith—in himself and his ground and in his God—that never redeemed the hope it held out to those early croft men. For his young grand-daughter, her days on his croft at an age when children today are barely embarked on their years of serious education, it was a bitter rehearsal, had she but known it, for her own future as a kitchen maid in the equally hard world of the farmtouns that shared the same landscape and sometimes the same disillusionment. Reluctantly, some days before her thirteenth birthday, and with regret even at leaving her sly grandmother, Jess MacKendrick said goodbye to the Perk Hill and her grandfather's crofting neighbours to *fee* home at the November Term to a farmtoun in her own up-country parish.

Rob Gibbon's was not a grand toun, nor, given Rob's own lack of drive, would it ever be; it was just a middling place that kept Rob and his folk this side of penury and out of the poorhouse, with maybe a bit put away from the fine *hairst* or two that had come his way in a farming lifetime. Mostly, by the time he had paid his *fee*'d bothy lads, his margins were fine. Not that it showed, for all that, for both Rob and his *gudewife* faced the threat of poverty, as the farmtouns began to go downhill from their production peak of the 1880s, with a pretension, in their circumstances, singularly unwarranted.

It was in the last light of a grey afternoon that Jess MacKendrick went home to her *fee* at the Gibbon place. Its track led up from the road through the sad November parks to the steading on its bare rise of ground, its bleak greystone *biggings* unsoftened even in the failing light. Its gaunt dwelling formed the fourth side of the farmtoun's quadrangular layout, a house so dour and chill that you knew at once that charity was mostly a stranger there. The weaver's lass fought down her desire to turn and flee its foreboding. Her knock was answered by the farmer himself, and not for the first time (nor the last) would her small stature tell against her.

"Is Mistress Gibbon aboot?" she asked the tall man who stood stooped and unsmiling under the door lintel, looking down on her.

"She'll be i' the byre," Gibbon said finally, and after a further moment, as the thought occurred to him: "And what would a littlin like yersel' be wanting with her?"

Hidden by the gloaming light the colour flew into young Jess MacKendrick's cheeks as she stood on the door-flag. "I'm nae a littlin," she retorted hotly, bristling with quiet rage, "I'm the new servant lass."

Gibbon's silence had discomfited her, leaving her trembling and biting her lip, but his reply had not been the rebuke she expected. He had shaken his head slowly, wonderingly. "Well, well, gin that be the case, may God preserve us," he had said, shutting the door in her face and leaving her to find her own way to the byre.

All the same, Rob Gibbon had turned out a kindlier man than his sour countenance suggested and the weaver's lass had stayed with him for three years, doing all the kitchen chores for a mistress in insatiable quest of the unattainable—making butter and cheese, washing and scrubbing till her hands were blue with the cold and sometimes horribly chilblained, boiling hens' feed and making calfies' *stoorum*, or gruel, an oatmeal-and-water mixture little different from the brose that went into the bellies of the farmtoun's folk; it brought up the calves' strength after they had been *coggit*. As often, she might be summoned into the fields to break dung down the drills or help with the *hairst*, or maybe to drove one of Rob's beasts to the weekly market at Alford—something she did with an ill-grace (it was damnably wounding to the pride in your own parish) and in which she took her revenge by thumping the *stirk*'s rump with her stick whenever it showed inclination to loiter. On the road back, likely she would not be unburdened and often enough her load would be a young sow in a bag, squealing on her back all the way home. For Rob Gibbon was a *tattie*-man, and like all potato-growers kept pigs to fatten on the *brock*, the damaged tubers; the one was unthinkable without the other and never more so than in that time of farming advance when men became fevered in their minds in their quest for new, fine-tasting potato varieties for the Southern dinner-tables. In that, despite all his endeavours, Rob Gibbon was unsuccessful; he never evolved the potato that would carry his name into the future. What he could do was grow other men's discoveries to perfection: Grampians (inevitably, to show loyalty with his landscape), round and red; Lang Blues and Irish Cup and fine Glenbervies, another rounded variety; and Champions, floury and pure white and as strong then in the uplands fields and the crofters' *shifts* as in the Highlands, where they helped down the winter herring in that ancient marriage that has so long escaped the gourmet's good word but which sustained the Highlands through the vagaries of a troubled history.

The life, though, was a sad down-come for the young girl who had absorbed the graces of the genteel lady's maid; her days were long and their leisure moments few. On the Sabbath she went to the kirk with the Gibbons and sat in her master's pew; it was the day that brought all the parish's folk into the landscape, folk from places far round. Some of them had barely time to take their breakfast brose before they were on to the kirk road, and it might be nearly dark before they won home again after the sermon. It was a diverse society, one, unlike our own, with its fine sprinkling of worthies and dignitaries. It was rich in its lairds, men who ruled their own roosts and gave not a tuppeny damn, some of them, for anybody; their flying carriage *shelts* scattered the Sabbath folk to the roadsides giving you hardly the time to doff your bonnet before you had to step back into the ditch. Some were big men in the world of affairs, as much at home in the fashionable squares of London as on their own hillsides (some of them more so, maybe, for few of them had any great liking for mud on their boots). There was old Knockespock and Lord Forbes of Castle Forbes and Farquharson of Haughton, an affable man who had but lately risen dramatically in local esteem on the strength of a chance encounter in the English capital.

The interest now of such a meeting is not that it was remarkable or that it so eminently demonstrates the old laird's skills but that it fixes his paternal place in that old society. Chancing into Marshall and Snelgrove's one day, Haughton had found a familiar face staring at him from the other side of the counter: none other than a laddie from his own estate and the brother of one of his own, big-house maids. From a parish (or so it sometimes seemed) that supplied the world with shrewd merchants, the young salesman had known his place. Polite and courteous, he had shown no recognition and lesser lairds might have avoided the situation by clutching the cue that was offered them. But not Haughton: he seized the laddie's hand as though he were Stanley come suddenly on Livingstone; his purchases momentarily forgotten, one question followed on the other. What was the laddie's position? What were his prospects? How found he the capital and were his lodgings satisfactory and was he given enough to eat? and—oh! what a strange thing life was, wasn't it, and the world always smaller than you thought. Overwhelmed by the laird's goodwill and concern, the laddie had hardly been able to contain himself till the omnibus took him home to his Clapham lodging house and he could sit down and write home to his mother. Triumphantly, before going down to his supper egg and toast the lad had concluded: "When Scot meets Scot in foreign land, it's equality for a'!" It was a catchphrase that might well have delighted his old dominie's heart and certainly it did Haughton no harm, though Rob Gibbon was less sure about it.

"Maybe so. And then again," he said sourly, "it is maybe damned little he kens aboot it." But then Rob had to pay rent to him.

It was seldom that Rob swore or showed such disrespect for his betters before his young kitchen maid. The child who had come to his door on that grey November night three years before was now fifteen and beginning to grow into young womanhood, pert rather than pretty, a puritan with an impish sense of fun. It seemed, after all that time, that she might stay there until some farmtoun bothy lad took her fancy—or she his. That was the way of it about a North-east Lowlands farmtoun. But as that winter set in Jess MacKendrick became ill, too weak even to lift her head in the kitchen's box-bed let alone climb out of it. The doctor was sent for and came as soon as he could and as fast as his *shelt* and gig could carry him. He was an old man now and had long seen a side of that countryside far different from its bright fields and its acres of bonnie waving corn. When he had examined Gibbon's kitchen maid he took Rob out to the farmtoun close with him.

"It's nae the scarlet fivver, Mister Gibbon," he said slowly. "It's the diphtheeria."

Their conversation was low, brief and punctuated by the nods and understandings of men. In the morning, a horse would be yoked into its farm cart and the cart-well filled with straw. The box-bed would be riven from its moorings on the kitchen floor and lifted bodily aboard, its doors shut and the small patient behind them muffled under a weight of blankets.

It took all the strength of Rob's four horsemen to load the

box-bed on to its cushion of straw and to rope it securely for the four-mile journey. And when they had done so, Rob watched till the cart and its strange cargo turned out at the farmtoun road-end on to the turnpike.

"I doubt," he said, the heavy folds of his face lugubrious, "that the next time four lads have a hold of you, Jess, you will be more lightly handled."

So, sadly, they had taken Jess MacKendrick home to die.

X

A Bride for the Mason Man

MISTRESS SHERIFF, the merchant's wife, watched through her kitchen window as the men in white moleskin *breeks* unloaded their barrows and trestles and planks, their trowels and hammers and chisels—all their masoning equipment—from the long horse-drawn wagon that had brought them up from the station. They had come to build her man the new house he had long wanted and to modernise his emporium, the only substantial centre for trade in that broad and fertile countryside. Mistress Sheriff felt a vague unease she could not put a name to, as she always did at the sight of any sizeable gang of burly working men. For all that, their foreman looked a decent, civil man (little more than in his mid-twenties, she thought), fair-haired, the heavy Kitchener moustache maybe a bit elderly on his square young face. He seemed austere even, avoiding the jokes of his seven companions as he supervised them in the unloading; a man (she thought) not to be tampered with, for he gave his orders easily, expecting no contradiction. His reputation had arrived ahead of him, though now that she saw him he seemed young to justify it.

Even so, Mistress Sheriff remained fretful.

"Whenever the stonemasons come aboot the place, there's aye a wedding," she said.

"Well, ma'am, ye need be nane feared it will be mine," said her maid, most emphatically, pausing only for a moment at her wash-tub to glance out of the window. Jess MacKendrick had survived the scourge of diphtheria by some dispensation of destiny—and when her life seemed forfeit—to put her farmtoun days behind her and enter domestic service, at sixteen, in the merchant's genteel household. She was cook as well as maid.

Their years of confinement between the same walls since then —for the weaver's lass was now in her twenties—had given the two women a bond, an empathy that did not alter for one instant their social standing, one to the other. And in her way, Mistress

Sheriff was as hard a mistress as Mistress Gibbon had been. The merchant's wife's washday was Monday and she had her maid out of bed by four, and standing to the tub on the kitchen floor, in case the day wore past before she had taken the good of it. The rest of the week though, Jess MacKendrick's day stretched only from six in the morning until eleven at night: seventeen hours. And certainly it wasn't her *fee* that kept her there for at 5s. (25p) a week she would not have been worse off at any farmtoun in the district. But there was this consolation: there was never any out-door work she could be sent to.

And the Sheriffs were considerate in other ways. Mindful of the position her man had to keep up in the community (and before the local gentry), Mistress Sheriff kept her maids presentable in black frocks that would be replaced before they got anywhere near to threadbare. These were worn with all the insignia of service, a white cap and white apron and (to lift the gloom round the face) a starched white collar.

There was no doubt about Sheriff's gentility, nor about his standing. A small man with thinning red hair and a rust-coloured tuft of a beard, he gathered pennies from every single transaction that took place over his counters with a skill and assurance that had long been proverbial (and regarded as inevitable) in the parish. It might have been unfair to say that the merchant worshipped *siller* but he certainly made every penny pay its way and the friend-ship was a close one.

He had the speculator's knack: if there was a single want in the community, in the farming countryside, he filled it; he had bran and maize and feed for all kinds of stock; oilcake that could put a bloom on a fattening calf as well as the grass-seed you had to sow to graze it. He had scythes (hanging by day on the wall outside) for your hay or your corn, hay-rakes and forks and byre *graips* in profusion. Inside, the wooden *caups* from which the farmtoun men supped their brose paraded in rows on his shelves along with *spurtles* and *tattie-chappers* whose simple design-lines drew your eye to the quiet taste of some country wood turner. He had galvanised paling wire, plain and *pikit*, and still something of a farming novelty in the northern landscape, the latter coiled on its awkward rough-hewn reels that would soon fill your fingers with splinters. He had wire-netting to keep your hens out of mischief and trap mice round the rick-*foons* for slaughter; *drogs* for man and beast (be sure to specify, he said always; and not to be given to a bairn) and all the provisioning that any farmtoun kitchen had need of—and a lot that some of them never had heard of. He would sell you meal if you could not get to the miller, eggs when your hens went off the lay. And out at the back, in a corrugated-iron shed and with the kind of industry that would today incite mutiny, men sat cross-legged, tailoring on their tables, putting sleeve to armhole with the kind of assured abandon that could put a suit out of shape even before you had worn it and suggested that at times they worked more from memory than the measurements. But there was this you could say for such suits: if they didn't fit the man they were made for it would not be long before another lad came along who could be sized into them perfectly.

It was, in that upland strath, the last outpost of commerce before you entered the wastes of the Highlands, and the little merchant man presided over it in a spotless white apron drawn tightly round the lower depths of his watch-chained waistcoat and the considerable expanse of his own corporation.

Mistress Sheriff kept an orderly house, fearful of the havoc an amiable maid might cause among the menfolk, and the merchant himself, with a fine knowledge of his sex, met all attempts at courting his maid with a venomous "No". His permission, in the manner of that time, was needed to take her to the Oddfellows' Ball, a concert, or the tawdry, tarry-flared excitement of the circus tent, and his refusal was given at such times with such dour finality that the lad who had asked for her company knew better than do the like again. The choice, though, was not always Jess MacKendrick's.

Only on the Sabbath, and then briefly in the evening when they had washed the tea dishes, were the Sheriffs' maids allowed to see their lads in a moment or two of country dalliance and even then, only in the hope that the day would prevent the kind of deed that could bring shame on them.

All the same, and unknown to him, Sheriff's maid joined the lads of the shop (when her master and mistress were in their beds) on many of their midnight pranks—lending her shepherd's tartan bonnet to one of the shop boys so that he could look in, his face pressed to the window pane, on the travelling vanman down to his drawers as he prepared, uncurtained, for bed. The frolic had con-vulsed the pair of them for weeks after whenever they encountered the man who traded the merchant's wares round the lonely farm-touns; and the man himself was plainly embarrassed for ever more in the young maid's company. The same shop lad (and maybe he was a favourite before the mason men came) was her partner in another, older kind of ploy traditionally played at Yule or the turn of the year and against folk one little cared for. One dark night when the house was silent, they had sneaked out, the pair of them, to paint the front door of the Sheriffs' genteel residence with *sowens*, stifling their giggles as they slapped the mealy gruel on to the fine varnish of the wood till it ran in rivulets down the doorstep Jess herself had polished that morning, and which she knew, come daylight, she would be sent to wash yet again. It was perhaps, had she but known it, a necessary act of rebellion for the young puritan lass, caught between the merchant's careful gentility and the earthier world of the crofts. Again, it may have been the outcome of her irritation at her mistress's insistence on having the *sowens* barrel spotless, its girds or hoops clean and shining. It sat in a dark corner of the Sheriffs' kitchen, steeping the last grains of nourishment from the husks of the milled oats so that they would make a gruel supper for the merchant's shopmen, the bane of the young maid's life.

Jess MacKendrick would not have considered herself beautiful; not even pretty. But she was vivacious, her eyes lively and twinkling with fun. It is likely that she attracted the wrong men at times and for the wrong reasons. But Willie Gavin was an honourable man. The young mason, who had finally found lodgings in the married vanman's house, was well pleased with the trim figure of the merchant's maid, small and neat in its dark dress. If she had other offers from time to time, maybe she liked the mason's stolid, steady nature best, even enjoyed the prestige his job gave him as his skill became increasingly praised in their small community. Stone upon stone, the merchant's new home grew under his guidance at the side of the old shop and, with it, the early friendship of the mason man and the weaver's lass deepened into courtship. It grew, for once, with the merchant's goodwill for doubtless he saw in Willie Gavin a man as serious in his affairs as himself; a man who would not take life lightly. It was a judgement based on the two pillars of profound regard: trust and respect.

So, when the mason man's work drew to an end, they had been married with all the dignity that the Sheriffs' new drawing-room could give to the occasion and within the walls the mason man himself had largely built, little knowing they would provide the setting for so personal a destiny. Out of his customary white mason's moleskins, Willie Gavin that day cut a fine figure in his black swallow-tailed jacket and bell-mouthed trousers that narrowed dramatically at the knee. His vest was bound with black braid and his wedding shirt, a lavender shade, with his tie—in the custom of that long-ago time—had been chosen and bought by the bride.

For the journey up-country from his father's croft, he and the guests he had brought with him had hired a brake with seating for two dozen or so folk on seats ranged down its sides. The early July day was with them, colder perhaps than might have been expected for that time of the year but dry, Godbethankit. Horses were changed at an inn in Inverurie, the halfway stage of their twenty-five-mile journey, and refreshments taken that markedly revived the company, kept the chill of the day something at bay and enlivened the rest of the way. The humour had been keen but not outrageous; there were well-aimed shafts about the staggering step that marriage betokened as well as quiet allusion to its comforts (and their consequences). Most of the party, excluding his own family, were mason men like himself, his friends—or as close as he ever came to making any. Willie Gavin bore the brunt of their broad humour that day and their barbs most amiably, a restrained smile shadowed under his black tile hat.

His bride was no less resplendent. Her dress was black, full-length and ruched round the hem, the height of fashion, bought through the merchant's influence and brought out all the way from Esslemont and Macintosh's in Aberdeen. The bridal hat, from the same temple of elegance, was trimmed with flowers and veiled to hide the blush of that small oval face. And though Willie Gavin might not yet know it, she wore blue silk hose and no drawers. There was, though, nothing scandalous about that, for neither did many other women assembled that day in that company; as yet the fashion for under-drawers had percolated north only to the most fashionable circles.

So they had stood together in the merchant's front room so that their bodies might be given one to the other in the embraces of matrimony. Inside, in the solemnity and silence, Mr Brander the Free Kirk minister's high and fluting voice, rising with sonorous

grace, gave them God's blessing, and on the heels of each supplication came another, from outside the new sandstone walls, raucous
and shrill:

"Herrr-in!"

"Fresh herr-in!"

"Herring tae sell."

Between the prayers and the plain hymns, between the words
that would unite Jess MacKendrick and Willie Gavin in wedlock
for all their long years, the fishman's voice rose and fell in its
own liturgical chant oblivious of the consternation it was causing.
Nobody moved to silence him and it seemed to many that day that
the omens were not as they should be. Others, however, determined
to make light of it, for the young folk's sake, saw the comical com-
bination of the high-minded Brander with lowly herring and would
long remind them of it. Most were happy to sit down to the feast
that followed and fell to drinking to dispel the memory of it. They
danced late in the old storeroom the merchant had cleared for the
celebration to a keen fiddle and an even higher-strung fiddler. And
by then, they had all of them all but forgotten it.

If the drive up-country had been restrained, the humour of
their return to Willie Gavin's low-lying countryside was less so.
Now they had the bride with them, changed for the journey to her
new home into another of her purchases from the fine Aberdeen
store: a blue, tight-bodiced dress with a decorous high neck and a
long wide skirt, and over it, a short velvet bolero. Against the nip
of the night air she had a black cape with a Queen Mary ruched
collar. The blue bonnet with velvet ribbons that tied under her
chin had two brilliant yellow feathers anchored in front, like some
proud cockade, by a massive buckle. The merchant's maid that
day, folk said, was out of her box and dancing on the lid.

If the night air was cold, there were those who did not feel it;
they sat, swinging easily with the sway of the vehicle, so well-
warmed with drams that even the dour presence of the bridegroom's mother could not dishearten them. The whisky, as always,
had broadened the carnal horizons and as bottle after bottle
emerged from under what had at first appeared to be singularly
ill-fitting suits, the banter, too, became broader. As well as the
bride, they also had the cradle with them, rocking gently with the
motion of the brake between the two rows of folk, a temptation
for every wag with a quick wit and, at that moment, with more

whisky in him than was good for him. It was painted a pale blue on the inside, dark brown on the outside; its presence, one merry character suggested, showed more faith in Willie Gavin than he had.

The sallies brought shrieks of well-modulated shock from the womenfolk.

"Ye'll need tae ca-canny, Willie. That crib has only room for ane."

"Yer sure it's gaun tae be a laddie then, Willie—painting it blue inside, like that," one voice mused.

"Mair likely it'll be a lass," said another, with the kind of quiet authority that brought silence to the buzz of talk.

"Why dae ye think that?" the first voice asked finally, its trailed wonder broken by the steady sound of the horses' hooves on the road. It trailed into further silence before the reply came, reasoned and clear.

"Why nae? He will hae the pattern in front of him at the time."

Night hid the bride's blushes, but broad though it was, direct even in its allusion, the humour seldom added the offence of prurience. There was mock comfort for the weaver's lass from a woman's voice, matronly in the dark and wise in the ways of men.

"Never ye heed them, lassie," it hinted, "we'll see tae it that Willie disnae cause ye any concern this nicht."

By that time they had taken Willie Gavin's folk home to the croft (where Old John, nothing loth, had broached his own bottle) and set off again on the final few miles to the little quarry-toun where the mason man had rented two downstairs apartments in a house with more tenants than it had room for. With the groom's formidable mother set down the mood was ever-merrier and it was a raucous crew that entered the little village in the early hours of the morning, waking everybody in their beds.

The bridegroom was seized almost as the brake stopped and long before its unsteadier passengers could summon the courage to dismount (or fall off) and bundled bodily inside by his mason colleagues, followed by their wives and lasses, all of them now intoxicated if not with drams with the heady excitement that had suddenly taken hold of them. Bodies jostled each other in the constricted dark of the lobby where the bridegroom resisted peevishly, thrown against each other by the young mason's struggles. Lasses became pinioned for long moments against walls by dominant male forms, impromptu embraces that registered every contour and suspender. Things got worse as the struggle got keener; men who had descended finally from the brake to dry land (unaccountably unable to shake off its motion) followed on, colliding with door-jambs and with each other and eventually with the mob in the lobby. Grappling hands in the anarchic dark gripped velvet thighs and buttocks as men shaken loose from the mêlée slid down them to the floor. Finally though, they managed to drag Willie Gavin into his bedroom and the more high-spirited—lasses as well as their menfolk—fell in through its door after him. Bedding the bridegroom was still a common enough custom in that old coun-tryside and it was an occasion, for all the Free Kirk's thraldom, that generated its own sweaty carnality.

"Aff wi' his breeks, noo," a voice said, its breathlessness a tribute to the mason's ceaseless resistance.

"Haud him, then! Haud him!" cried another, querulous and impatient. Willie Gavin was instantly and ungently spread-eagled on the floor, two of his companions perching on his shoulders with a further two pinning his feet. A candle was brought to let them better see their work for the group encircling the bridegroom had cut off the glimmer of the oil-lamp.

"Lowse his galluses, can't ye," the first voice instructed.

"His boots first, ye fool," protested another. "How in the hell are we gaun tae get his breeks aff wi' his boots on?"

Men, one at each foot, unlaced Willie Gavin's patent boots, their drunken fingers prolonging the excitement for the bolder lasses peering over their shoulders at the prostrated form, who squealed their delight as the groom's boots were flung under the bed.

"Now ——" The first voice again.

"Wait!" It was as quickly countermanded by one of quiet authority. "Have ye gotten the bolster case?"

"The bolster ——?"

The men holding down the mason man looked up surprised —almost sobered—by their own stupidity. "God, no . . ." They looked from one to another; in their drunken excitement the whole point of the custom had almost been forgotten.

But in a moment, women's hands had slipped the case off the bolster on the bed and dropped it over the ring of heads.

"And tow?" that authoritative voice demanded. "Ye'll need

string—strong string—for God's sake!" Exasperation laced the quiet tone. "Ye'd think nane of ye had ever bedded a bridegroom afore."

As suddenly, string was produced.

"Richt then ——" The man who had unbuttoned Willie Gavin nodded to the men at his feet. "Pull!" Simultaneous yanks slid the bridegroom's fine bell-bottomed wedding *breeks* from under him.

"Again!"

With the chorus of approval, the men took fresh purchase on Willie Gavin's trouser legs and heaved—and only then was it noticed that the loops that kept the bridegroom's drawers hanging, like his *breeks*, from his braces had somehow got caught round the buttons of his trousers. Lasses jostling to peer over their men's shoulders suddenly shrieked and turned to hide their faces in convulsions of excitement; and the best man, fevered though he was by the drams and his exertions, did what he could, seizing hold of the tail of Willie Gavin's shirt, dragging it down and holding on like grim death to it while the mason man flailed on the floor apparently unaware of his predicament—or his own excitement. Finally his drawers were again dragged over him and though he fought strongly against them, they got both his legs into the bolster case and pulled it up to his waist. A short further battle and both his arms, too, were inside it and the case brought up to his chest.

"Wha's guid at knots?" The quiet voice that had taken command registered a small note of triumph. A volunteer bored forward and soon the strong string was stranded round and round the top of the bolster case and the man it contained bound tightly and incapable of all movement to free himself. Thus, incongruously imprisoned and still in the wedding splendour of his swallowtailed jacket, Willie Gavin was put into the bridal bed and the blankets drawn up to his waist. Satisfied, the members of the party gathered round to crow their delight and gape at the mason man's plight. They showed a deep mock concern for the bride, the weaver's lass come newly among them:

"There ye are, Jess—he will nae be a handful till ye this nicht. See till it that ye get a guid nicht's sleep noo."

"I'd nae let him oot of there the nicht gin I was you."

"Gin ye do, lass, it's nae good kenning what could happen."

Jess MacKendrick bore their sallies good-humouredly; finally, there was a drift towards the door, a last sly warning:

"Mind ye noo, Jess—prevention's aye better than cure."

The remark lit a fresh wave of hilarity, and their laughter spilled out to the night and the quiet of the little quarrytoun, leaving Jess MacKendrick alone with her mason man. Though she might, reluctantly, tell the story of that night and the "vulgar affair" of the bolster bedding when pressed to do so, she never told of the rest of that bridal night. But one thing we know: Jess MacKendrick at twenty-four had been little accustomed to the ways of men or indeed to the rough intimacy of their caresses. She was not a prude; far from it. But she was well-versed in the precepts of the Good Book and had held to them as staunchly as her old crofting grandfather did. And then there had been Sheriff, overly-protective of his servant maids at times and anxious for their reputation, so easily lost in that northern landscape (where, alas, it was seldom that no one was the wiser). Mistress Sheriff, too, had been strict: from the start of her service with the merchant's household— within a matter of days—the weaver's lass had been enrolled (at 6*d.* a year) as a member of the Scotch Girls' Friendly Society, which did its best, in the long and sometimes uphill fight, to stave off ruin among the countryside's kitchen maids. When she went to Willie Gavin's bed eight years later it was with her virtue intact, innocent of lovers and with a certificate from the Society to prove it. It gave her bridegroom a written guarantee of her virginity though it is unlikely he would have asked for it and anyway, could not have been in doubt of it. Long years after, in her nineties and in a society long grown used to the indiscretions of young lovers and untroubled by them, she would speak of the Rules that had kept her pure until her marriage: "I did not find the Rules hard, as I was just brought up to them from infancy. I won't say I've kept them all—reading the Scriptures every day—but even now I never begin my day, whatever I'm going to do, without first asking the grace and guidance of God for myself and some others . . ."

Her observances and her creed, all the same, came very close to truly reflecting the Scotch Girls' main injunction, set out at the top of its "Rules for Daily Life" on the back of its member's card: "*Seek ye first the kingdom of God.*" The Rules themselves were six in number and in the religious climate of that earlier time by no means extravagant:

1. To pray morning and evening and especially to remember the Associates and Members of the Society every Thursday evening.
2. To read a portion of the Bible at least once a day.
3. To attend Divine Service, if possible, at least once every Sunday.
4. To avoid reading bad books and magazines.
5. To endeavour to spread no scandal and to repeat no idle tale to the disadvantage of others.
6. To dress simply, according to your station, avoiding all exaggerated fashions.

The Society's slim, white-lidded guide began with a prayer and ended with the words of the society's hymn and the chorus that encapsulated its simple message:

> True friends help each other,
> Gladly give and take;
> Bear with one another,
> For sweet friendship's sake.

And it explained, among other things, fearful of all the temptations the fashionable faced, how inadvisable was the stretching of a dress budget too far, instilling in the bygoing its Presbyterian precept of thrift:

We determine to dress simply, according to our station. This does not mean that we are not to dress prettily and well; on the contrary, we are anxious that all belonging to our society should look well but we must not spend on our dress more money than we can rightly afford. Sometimes, for example, we may have to buy an article less attractive to look at than we would wish, because it will "last well".

It was good advice, just a little superfluous for any kitchen maid whose pay was only 25p a week and for one who would become a crofter's wife in a lifestyle where the lessons of thrift were brutally instilled.

According to the Society's guide the Rules were "no more than any well-brought-up, high-principled girl is already trying to carry out in her daily life". All the same, there was one thing, at least, in the Scotch Girls' Friendly Society's Rules that the young Jess MacKendrick would disagree with, which she felt appallingly lacking in Christian charity. The guide made clear its unbending unacceptance of those of blemished reputation:

Those girls *only* are admitted as Members who have borne respectable characters; and should any Member unhappily lose her character, and therefore her right to be ranked with the others, she would
forfeit her card, and cease to belong to the Society. It is earnestly
hoped that all will remember that they have a character to keep up,
and will resist by God's grace, those small beginnings of evil, which,
if yielded to, so often end in terrible sin.

For the back-slider then there would be no forgiveness, no sympathetic hearing or understanding, only expulsion. And for Grannie
Gavin, as well as the lass she had once been, that had never seemed
right: "There was just one thing I never liked about the Society.
They expelled the sinner when she was most in need of kindness
and help back to the right road." Besides her purity and the
cradle, there were other things aboard the brake that summer
night that the bride was bringing to her new home: the things
bought in her employer's shop a short time beforehand. When the
shop had closed for the night (and after she had given the merchant his supper and washed the dishes) she had been invited into
the little man's emporium to purchase the simple plenishings she
would need for her new home down the country. Sheriff himself,
impressively aproned as though for the Lady of Haughton herself,
had stood behind its counter, noting the items and their prices as
she brought them to him, choosing from the cluttered shelves. He
could hardly have thought that his account, preserved in an old
woman's *kist* and proclaiming him James Sheriff "draper, clothier,
grocer, seedsman, wine, spirit and general merchant" and under-
lining the twice-yearly custom of that farming countryside with
the reminder "all accounts payable at Whitsunday and Martinmas
terms" would one day constitute a document of humble history.
Its fine Gothic heading gives the merchant himself some standing;
it is from another age when commerce, still, had a touch of dignity.
Its list reflects the wants of a kitchen maid when she came to move
into her own domain for the first time, and in 1893, the young Jess
MacKendrick's wants were few:

		£	s.	d.
1 bed cover 5/- 9/-		—	14	—
1 pr cotton sheets		—	4	—
½ doz dessert spoons		—	1	—
1 doz dinner spoons		—	1	9
½ doz egg spoons		—	—	6

	£	s.	d.
2 pr blankets 15/6	1	11	—
1 watering pan	—	2	6
1 girdle	—	1	6
1 chamber	—	—	8
1 frying pan	—	1	2
1 pail	—	—	9
basin 6d bath 1/3	—	1	9
ladle 6d jug 1/6	—	2	—
scoop 1/6 spitoon 6d	—	2	—
9 tumblers 1/6 6 glasses 1/–	—	2	6
teapot 6d stew pan 1/8	—	2	2
boiler 2/6 basin 3½d	—	2	9½
pan 6d pie dish 4 by 8 1/–	—	1	6
lamp 2/3 6 bowls 6d	—	2	9
¼ doz teaspoons and cream jug	—	3	—
2 jelly dishes 1/–	—	2	—
1 ashet 8d doormat 1/10	—	2	6
9 plates 2½d	—	1	10½
1 zinc pail	—	1	—
4 brushes 8d	—	2	8
10 yds bed tick 1/–	—	10	—
1 tin kettle	—	1	2

Besides demonstrating all that money could buy in that bygone age, the account reflects something else: the eclectic wandering of young Jess MacKendrick that summer night as she took the pick of her master's shelves. Some of the items now have their own piquancy, their reminder of another time: the spitoon, for instance, that great monument to the strength of thick ploughman's twist, and the chamber pot, a necessary convenience when the alternative was a cold walk in the night to the chill of the outside privvy. Mr Sheriff gave them all his blessing with his "Paid" on the old queen's head, to which he added his signature and his thanks, as well he might for the maid who had served him so loyally and for so long. Assuredly there *was* a fine dignity to trade!

In that first year of her marriage (with her man away at his mason work all week) Willie Gavin's bride had taken a *hairst fee* to help towards the rest of her "providing". It was at the small farmtoun, not far from the little quarrytoun, of her man's uncle and aunt: there she gathered and bound the harvest sheaves behind the bothy lad (who was hardly old enough to be in control of a scythe and would be lucky to finish the *hairst* with both legs). Kinship though was not strained, for she got leave to eat with him too at the noon mealtime on a side table in the kitchen, while the master and mistress had the main board to themselves. "But now you're *related*," folk said, incredulous when she told them.

"Aye," she would say, impishly, "distantly related."

By the time the next year's *hairst* came round, Jess MacKendrick was heavily pregnant and not able to take a harvest *fee*. Even so, some folk said, Willie Gavin had taken his time about it.

XI

A Life without Luxury

A CROFT HOUSE was seldom comfortable and the human frame
was never cosseted. In a hard world the chairs too were hard,
though that bothered nobody for there was little enough time to
sit on them anyway. It is likely that such mortification of the flesh
explained why the crofts threw up more than their fair share of
Free Kirk ministers, contentious and uncompromising and so
strong on denial. It was an environment calculated to make its inmates cussed and that, undoubtedly, many of them were.

Grannie Gavin's kitchen was as much a part of the croft *biggings* as the byre or the barn, an extension of the croft life and never
a "home" except in the late hours of the evening or when the door
was *snibbit* against the winter's night. At all other times it was a
place where folk sat briefly (and usually only to food) before shrug-
ging on their jackets again and going out to the fields. Its privacy
was such that to be alone its occupants would take a walk ben the
road or lock themselves in the John Gunn. Its stone floor, when it
was not dominated by the wooden washday tub on its three-legged
trestle, or the plump churn, was a thoroughfare through which
much of the commerce of the crofting day passed: Willie Gavin
himself to the girnal (the meal chest) to make the calves' *stoorum*;
Grannie Gavin making passage to and fro with the hens' pot that
dangled through most of the afternoon from the *swey* hook, hotter-
ing its hideous pottage of potato peelings, bad turnips, all manner
of morsels the humans had not had the stomach for and heaven
knows what else. By the end of a wet day, the floor would be swim-
ming with water—the rain that ran off boots and oilskins unheeded
as its folk came and went on their outdoor errands. And if the fire
blazed, only the cooking pots got the good of it for folk were dis-
couraged from sitting down not only by the lack of luxury but by
the biting wind that whistled in through the ever-open door.

The croft kitchen's furnishings were minimal, mainly functional
and ranged, usually, against the walls so as not to get in the way of

the day's business. It had a dresser tiered with plates and cups recumbent in stacked saucers; a tall chest of drawers, recessed at one side of the chimney breast, a small table at the other; the main table, covered by the saving grace of frayed oilcloth, a token, in that day long before our own wipe-clean age, of crofting poverty, for tablecloths were so rare a sight you could hardly enjoy your food off them. They were reserved for grand occasions and the visits of richer relations, some of whom looked down from the walls. Heavily framed and silent in their faded sepia, their serious faces unblemished by life, they were the old and representative young of far sprigs of the Gavin family. Few of them looked like themselves for there was not a pimple or a blackhead between them and their appearance in the flesh was always an anti-climax and a sad disappointment. Among them was a stranger, as dour as the rest and so seemingly unyielding that he might have been one of the family. He was not; his name was Charles Spurgeon. It is impossible now to say where the Baptist pastor touched the lives of the folk of that bare domain but clearly his stern countenance had some dominion over them. From beside Willie Gavin's old shaving mirror near the window, he stared down, his gaze as austere as the old crofter man's own. It may have been that once there was a time, in the days of revival, when the Baptist man's sermons were read round the croft *biggings* for there would have been much in his creed that would have been relevant to the crofting existence.

The grey stone floor's only adornment was the *clickit* rug that lay before the fire, though that was mainly for the comfort of the evenings: during the day it would be rolled up and thrown against the wall for the fire was the focal point. A croft wife's day revolved round it. Washed—as it was daily—the floor gave off the aroma of soured dust, a smell, like the scent of the clover fields or the stench of the muck *midden*, that became one of the touchstones of a croft bairn's later life.

Though there was variety in its seating, the kitchen had only one substantial armchair, wooden and red-varnished, its armrests worn and smoothed by years of rubbing hands but its stature instantly recognisable. Even so, it was not a comfortable chair; its seat, painted black (the better not to show the dirt from a working man's *breeks*), was also wooden and as unyielding as the others in the room. It was called the Throne; it was Willie Gavin's chair and even in later life while its hard seat chastened the old man's work-weary frame, its straight back gave him a ramrod stiffness, as though he were on parade by the fire. Its design, its square-built lines, had affinities with the traditional wooden chairs of the Gaelic kingdom though the Lowlands crofter himself had none. The Throne was sacrosanct: it emptied as if by magic at the mere sight of Willie Gavin coming home over his *shifts* or as he passed the kitchen window on his way in to his supper. Indeed, there were folk who dared not sit in it by invitation even when he was known to be miles away in case he should come suddenly home and surprise them—far preferring the guiltless ease of one of the kitchen's table chairs, which were shaped to cup the buttocks. For all that, they were a "hard sit" and folk did not overstay their welcome. Mostly, Willie Gavin's household made do with what they could get—stool or table chair—to drag in to the fireside in the evening.

The crofter man, like all the Gavin men in their own homes, and as James Geerie of the Perk Hill had done sixty years earlier, took the left side of the fire, though there may have been nothing traditional in that any more than seems to have been the case in the Highland landscape. But there was a parallel in other ways. As Dr I. F. Grant, in her delightful and authoritative record of that lifestyle, *Highland Folk Ways*, says: "Whatever the seating accommodation might be, the man of the house always had his special seat by the fire while his wife occupied a lower one or a stool on the opposite side. I have never heard that the right or the left side was specially appropriated to either partner." In Grannie Gavin's case, the millwright son who had made the Throne had, in the 1920s, made a lesser, female chair for his mother, a companion piece to the croft man's own seat, though the old stool she had so long occupied for her sewing and nursing remained also at her side of the fire and it was that, mostly, that she drew in to the fire between the byre and bedtime.

Reviewing Highland seating, Dr Grant continues: "A charming feature is the number of very small children's chairs that one finds, some of them, elaborate, craftsman-made chairs with arms, others replicas of the local type." In the Lowlands crofting and farmtoun landscape, too, there was a similar custom and many of the croft houses contained miniature versions of the traditional seating for the bairns. The Gavin household was no different: it included a child's seat that was an absolute model of Willie Gavin's own, a mini-Throne that a young Gavin male (on a night spent in his grandparents' care) could draw in to the edge of the kitchen's *clickit* rug between the old folk's chairs and, glancing from one to the other as he puffed solemnly at a "pipe" fashioned from an old fir cone and a twig from the elderberry, assimilate the traits of the dour Gavin character and come to know the things that would be expected of him.

But it was the meal girnal (as also in every cottar house and farmtoun kitchen of that countryside) that was the most crucial piece of furnishing, as it had been for centuries. Inherited, like the old croft itself, it stood under the kitchen's small back window not too far from the fire, maybe as much for Grannie Gavin's convenience as for the conditioning of the oatmeal in it. The youthful companion of Old John Gavin's later years remembers still the tramping of the meal, the girnal's importance and its place in the crofting economy:

> Oats were the main crop in that particular area—I don't think there was any wheat grown at all—and they used to be taken to the mill to get them milled or ground for the folk's own use. My grandfather used to take his crop to this miller named Watson—he was an old friend of my grandfather—and they would get enough oatmeal to last them for a whole year. And they had a special container, called the girnal. They used to pack the meal in and the kids would all have a bath the night before and they would tramp the oatmeal with their feet.

He recalls, too, the look of the old Gavin girnal. It is unlikely that its constructional details were unique.

> It was about five feet high and a pretty fair width too. It was hinged at the centre front and you could lift the front down fairly low so that you could dump the oatmeal into it. But there was access, too, from the side to the meal for the croft wife just taking some, a moderate amount, to bake oatcakes or make porridge or brose and such-like.

It was in the kitchen, too, that many of the old crofter folk kept their *sowens* barrel, its shiny hoops scoured clear by the sea-sand brought round, by pony and cart, by a man from the little seatoun where Willie Gavin sent his oats when he had any to sell—the seatoun, they said, that his missing grandfather had come from. The sea-sand was sold by the half-stone or the pound. The *sowens* barrel shared some of the girnal's symbolism; both were ever-present monuments to the importance of oatmeal (and a reminder of its dreadful monotony). But it was the girnal that was vital, the repository of the kitchen's largesse; where the space was tight, the *sowens bowie* would be relegated to the milkhouse.

The fire that Willie Gavin had installed in his new-built house had been determined by functional considerations more than any question of comfort for its occupants. It was a range, that rage of the farmtoun kitchens that put many a servant lass on to her knees before it—with the emery-cloth and the black-leading brushes—before the sleep was out of her eyes. All the same, it was a fine fireside by crofters' standards and many would have liked it. It had an oven built in under one of its two hobs, or *binks*, and the fire itself —set so high that you could get frostbitten toes while its heat took the skin off your face—was set behind three bars and closed on the three other sides by the fire bricks that helped to hold in its heat. From its glowing heart at the ragged end of washdays, Grannie Gavin plucked the red-hot "bolts" for the box-iron that smoothed the creases of her man's Sabbath shirt. The dainty flat-iron might do well enough about the Big House for the governess's petticoats or for the frills of the laird's fine shirts but in a croft house it would have been an irrelevance and at Whinfield, as else-where, it was the heavy dreadnought box-iron that reigned un-challenged down the years, giving its users the kind of wrists that could thraw a chicken's neck without noticing it.

Willie Gavin had not stinted, thrifty man though he was. His high fireplace had a *swey*, swivelling out from one corner and into the room to allow the hens' pot and the black iron kettle to be lifted on and off without also consigning yourself to the flames. It was an impressive piece of ironmongery in its polished state; from it dangled not only the *crook* on which the pots were hung but also the *links of the crook*, the chain links into which the crook fitted. These were the unsophisticated Regulo of the croft and farmtoun kitchen: you could not immediately turn down the blaze, but what you could do was adjust the height of the pot above it by hitching the *crook* into a higher *link*.

There was hardly a moment of the day when the *crook* did not carry its burden: the *girdle*, the griddle, hung by the ring of its semi-circular handle, and the hens' pot in turn usurped the big

kettle which "sang" above the flames in instant readiness to make
the kind of tea that shook strong men right down to their boot-
tackets. On the *bink* alongside sat the teapot, warming its chipped
enamel and waiting.

Above that, on the mantelshelf, sat the tea caddy, its kimonoed
Chinese lady headless now where Grannie Gavin's thumb and her
persistent hospitality down the years had worn the paint off—for
she would have the tea into the pot before she knew for sure whose
footfall it was on the step. Beside it, enflanked by the ornaments
that had come from kindly folk and a day here and there at the sea-
coast, ticked the kitchen timepiece, one of the many clocks the
punctual mason man seemingly could not live without and which
whispered through the silent house with conspiratorial urgency,
Make haste . . . *Make haste* . . . They were uncanny, the clocks of
Willie Gavin's house; you could swear that at times they held con-
versations among themselves.

On one side of the fire's wooden surround hung its most important piece of furnishing: the small bellows that blew fresh life
into it whenever it faltered.

For anything that came near to comfort you had to walk
through to the ben-end of Willie Gavin's croft house, the *spence*
or *horn-eyn*, as Grannie Gavin called it, using the words that came
out of the past of that far countryside and that were, even then, all
but forgotten. There the floor was wooden and black-varnished
round the edges where its dull pink linoleum square reached un-
successfully for the wainscotting. There, too, the furnishings were
of better quality, sometimes even with a small hint of luxury.
There was the black-rexined sofa where the semi-invalid could
pine comfortably and lie out a day or two with the fire lit, or where
anyone with a sprained ankle might seek sanctuary while it mended;
the crofter man's own winged armchair, its armrests patched with
bicycle solution, where the horsehair had been on the point of
escape. Beside it, so that he had only to swing his head over it,
was the spitoon bought all those long years ago in the up-country
merchant's shop, its white enamel now badly chipped.

Around the room stood chests, deep-drawered and mysterious
and seldom opened to the world; a glass-fronted tall cabinet with
a selection of china figures, each a memory from a moment in
Grannie Gavin's life; and, on a small table by the fire, the fine
oil lamp with globe and elegant chimney that lit only the dark

Sabbaths of winter, when its brass pillar gleamed in the firelight. Before the hearth, enclosing its long-handled poker, shovel and fire-tongs, stood the brass fender and the footstool you were not to put your boots on.

Here, in the ben-end of the house the silence and the dust might be undisturbed between one Sunday and the next, maybe for months on end if the summer was fine. It was a silence presided over still by the woman whose iron will had long dominated that crofting household: Willie Gavin's mother. Turbanned with tulle, she looked down from her brown frame above the mantel with the same dour gaze on all who entered there, factor and *fee*'d laddie alike, a tribute to the terrible realism of the photo-portraiture of her time. Her eyes (you would swear) followed you all round the room and gave you good riddance as you left it.

It was a room, above all, that had its social nuances, for it was here—in the croft parlour—that folk got married for better and often for worse and where the minister came ill-willing, knowing the day could no longer be decently postponed and that he would be back too soon to the christening that followed it. It was, always, the place where serious business was done; where a man with important proposals (or serious grievance) would be shown to have out his speak. Not least of them was the factor, the laird's man of affairs. When he came he would be conducted into it, with Grannie Gavin scurrying before him to give the best chair a wipe with her apron in case his fine tweed *breeks* should get dust on them. And it was here, finally, that folk lay quiet in their coffins for a day or two to say goodbye to their friends and put their long croft days behind them.

The remaining ground-floor room was the *closet*—the *culaisd* of the Gaelic landscape. It led directly off the kitchen and housed the brass bedstead that was the matrimonial bed and the bed, brought with them from the little quarrytoun and their young married days, in which Jess MacKendrick had given her mason man five bairns and, between times, some moments of pleasure, hurriedly taken. Its satellites, pushed under the eaves in the attics, were black iron on whose ends there blossomed the black roses that held together the tracery of their intertwining bars. Their mattresses, like that of the *closet*'s bed, were chaff-filled, the chaff being renewed once a year when the steam-mill came into the district on its threshing round.

Throughout, Willie Gavin's fine house was panelled with strips of narrow boarding varnished light brown to give the patina of a seemlier grandeur; lace curtains graced the sashed windows, but and ben, and on their broad interior sills geraniums and begonias flourished as the croft folk themselves never did, taking most of the daylight. At night, illumination down the crofting years had been first the bog-fir taper, the cruisie lamp with its rush-light and its lurching shadows, the tallow candle (which took Willie Gavin's folk up to their garret beds still in the 1930s) and the type of small paraffin oil lamp that today commands a fortune in the antique shop. In the circumstances, a croft bairn's greatest gift was to be born with good eyesight.

Even the porch, that architectural afterthought of a cold climate, did little by day to improve the warmth of the house for the steady foot traffic through it kept it as open to the weather almost as the close itself. But by night, with its outer door rammed shut, it almost succeeded. Built entirely of wood, the porch was the half-way compromise of stoically hopeful men who refused to believe that the weather was as bad as it seemed and who had resisted for years the need to incorporate some such functional structure at the doors of their dwellings.

Given its makeshift character, the porch could be said to be neither indoors nor out. It contained the thick mat that stopped some at least of the croft's mud passing in to Grannie Gavin's kitchen floor. In it, too, stood the water pails filled from the pump, and near them the washbasin on its marble-topped table, its cold location a discouragement to protracted ablutions and beyond doubt typical of the kind of arrangement that threw up a race of hardy men who washed always with their shirt on and could run the razor round their chins without ever wetting its neckband.

If there was a semblance of cosiness at all in Willie Gavin's house it came from the welter of *clickit* rugs that littered its floors. They were everywhere and the collection grew yearly. Thick and strongly-backed by further layers of the tough seed-corn sacks on which they were hooked, they absorbed all the old pairs of *breeks* and black stockings the house's occupants had no longer use for. They kept an agreeable distance between you and the stone cold of the floor.

Cutting the material into strips, Grannie Gavin hooked her rugs by the winter fireside, improvising the patterns as she went along.

Given the preponderance of stockings in the rag-bag, they would invariably be bordered by black, but within that sombre outline would be an in-filling of fine swirling patterns of colour that soothed the eye. There was little doubt ever about where the pale pink *clippit cloots* had come from—or that the dash of equally pale apricot was the remnants of another kind of garment that was rarely joked about in Willie Gavin's house and never mentioned in front of the bairns. All the same, there would be the occasional wet Sabbath when a newly-made rug would cause its moment of mirth where the menfolk sat, in the best room.

"You've surely been gettin' yersel some new pairs o' drawers, Wullie?" someone would say, all serious on it.

"Maybe then. Maybe . . ." The crofter man, surprised for the moment, would be dourly non-committal, as in all things. "But what is it mak's ye think so, man?"

The joker would look down solemnly at his feet and the pattern below them. "Faith, man," he would hoot, unable to hold in his merriment longer, "I can see yer auld pair in the rug here."

Yet, if the comfort of Willie Gavin's croft house at times seemed minimal, there were others much worse; his neighbour, Lang Andra, would take an earth-floored kitchen almost into the television age. And its panelled rooms were a far cry from the old walls Willie Gavin had been born into and the dark interior of the single-storey dwelling he had so remorselessly ripped down. The old crofter man's daughter, nearing eighty, remembers that earlier *bigging* still: "It had three rooms—a kitchen, a closet and a room end. In that you got the smell of the beasts coming through from the byre, so it wasn't very healthy for folk . . ." In the days of her girlhood the old croft house's living end had ". . . two *binks* at the fireside and a *swey* to hang the big iron kettle on, and a dresser and a *deece*—something like a settee—and a home-*clickit* rug, with a footstool, fender and fire-irons".

There must have been days when Jess MacKendrick thought, in her new croft *bigging*, of all the improvements the years had brought with them and remembered that old dwelling on the Perk Hill that had been her grandfather's croft house. Yet, amid all the changes some things had remained, ingrained and traditional, among them the importance of the meal girnal and the impregnability of the *gudeman*'s chair. They gave continuity to her crofting life.

The walls of my grandfather's house were built of stone and clay;
very low they were. The house had a thatched roof and it was very
dark inside. The roof had couples but no wooden roof, just boards—
"wattles", they were called—with strong stalks of heather intertwined
with them, like the darning on a sock, and over that a thick thatching
of broom. The house itself had just two apartments, a but and a ben,
divided by two box beds placed back to back to divide the rooms,
with a press at both ends. There was a big meal girnal in the corner
of the living end, filled with meal that came from the Mill of Kintocher, and a bench between that and the bed: it was a wooden seat,
and it had a back. There was a *plat rack*, as we used to call it, with the
plates all set in rows and spoons in front of them. There was, of
course, the usual tables and chairs, with Grandfather's large one; a
big blue-painted box at one side of the fire—the *saut backet*—a bellows at the other, and of course the floors were earth. Grandfather's
seat was called the Throne and nobody else sat in it when he was
there.

There was a big wide fireplace; it was always well-filled with peat
and turf. It had a wooden canopy—a *hinging lum*, they called it—
that came over it. The grate had three smiddy bars and the *aise*, the
ash, was pushed through a trap-door out at the gable. The windows
were twelve inches by twelve inches and they did not open. The
stones round them were white-washed to make more light inside.

Even the thrifty placing of peat with divot on the fire had its traditional pattern in the hard crofting world of the Perk Hill: just a
single peat was set at the centre and the turf divots arranged
around it.

It might seem now, these long years after, that the finer nuances
of life would surely be absent from such poor and simple dwellings
or that their folk might be lost to those small and gentle graces
that have their enhancing effect on the quality of life. That was not
always the case; far from it. Old John Gavin's daughter had played
the harmonium that sat on the earth floor of his *spence*, his parlour
room. If she played the psalm tunes on the Sabbath when the Free
Kirk folk met in her father's barn, it is likely that through the week
she played the tender songs of Burns as well as the rumbustious
songs of that countryside. She would not have been alone in that.
Throughout the crofting communities there were others who dis-
tilled the elements of a hard life into song and poetry, whose gifts
indeed might in time lead them elsewhere. And comfortless though

their lives were, for as long as the peat fires burned on the crofting hillsides there were hardy wives who never forgot to end their day on a note of grace, repeating the words of the *smooring* prayer as they "rested" the fire to keep it burning through the still hours of the night:

> In the name of the Father,
>   the Son and the Holy Spirit,
> Thanks be for our life,
> For peace in our home,
> And for matchless grace
> This nicht and ilka nicht.
>   Amen.

The words are beautiful still in the sanctity they seek, the most moving perhaps of all the incantations that come down to our sophisticated time from the lips of the old crofter folk.

XII

Kebbucks and Kail Brose

WANT WAS SOMETHING the croft bairn grew up with; he expected nothing better and he was seldom disappointed. And if, as was so often said, he was always willing to go to school because it was less arduous than staying at home, the lure of education was certainly, in the later days of the crofts, enhanced by the taste of early school dinners—usually rabbit, a benign laird's gift from his keepers' guns. The dinners were a boon beyond mere gratitude and if the croft child were fortunate too in having a chum with a fastidious middle-class stomach, he could even have two dinners and go home at the end of the afternoon with a full belly. Such charity had only one serious consequence: much as the stew might please the bairn, it could put the adult off rabbit for the rest of his days.

Yet that did not make his gratitude less, for want was as old as that landscape and ingrained in the folk memory of its people. Its dark shadow had haunted the hindmost days of the 1700s with a series of ill-years that had taken a tragic toll and given musty grain the lustre of gold. And later still, other ill-*hairsts* had visited their own calamity upon the countryside, a constant reminder of its fragile ecology.

It was not that the landscape lacked good basic foods. Far from it: it raised the finest beef and oats, prize potatoes, and eggs and poultry as good as any, with partridge and pheasant on the hill and the moor and fish in the burn. But the crofter man, like the cottar folk of the farmtouns, enjoyed none of it; he got no game pie and but rarely a bite of the beef he helped to raise or the chickens he fed. The moor and the hill (and even the burn) were the laird's, and his hens were a part of his crofting economy. To kill one, outside of some important family occasion or reunion or the high festivity of Yule, would have been unthinkable. Though the Gavin croft at the turn of the century had been teeming with guinea-fowl and turkeys that strutted and preened and gabbled their glottal chorus to the point of irritation as they scavenged round the old croft *biggings*, Old John's grandson and companion never tasted turkey until he was a grown man on the other side of the Atlantic. He recalls their importance, indignant now at the suggestion that they might have brought variety to the bare croft diet from time to time:

> The turkeys were all for sale. I never tasted turkey in my life till I was a married man. That was living—eating turkey, in those days. The croft folk would never even have *dreamed* of eating turkey. To do so would have been the most ridiculous thing you could possibly conceive of...

It was no different with the produce of Great-grannie Gavin's considerable number of beehives. Though a little honey might be used to make the *hairst*'s honey ale, most went for sale, Old John *yoking* his *shelt* to take it the seven miles to a merchant's near the railhead, where it got a passing trade.

It was a landscape in which the recipes, some of them as eccentric as the folk, passed down with a careless abandon and usually without the benefit of a recording "receipt book" from mother to daughter (the only dowry she was likely to get) compounding the kind of culinary disaster that gave many a croft house and farm-toun kitchen a bad name (and sent visitors home for their supper). Equally, it perpetuated now and then an inexplicable and exceptional excellence.

It was a landscape in which the Auld Alliance had left its legacy as surely in the home as in other areas of life. Though *velouté de volaille* would not have been everyday fare (since it took a chicken) there is little doubt but that it sometimes graced the croft table in the disguise of *feather fowlie*, a soup remarkably similar that managed to wreck the savour of the Frenchman's fine cooking in the process. *Stovies*, that stomach-filling dish that could take a country-man from his breakfast brose to his brose supper, and which fell so frequently into the croft menu, may have an equally illustrious affinity with that gourmet's cuisine: there are those who see the recipe's method—and the name—as deriving from *étouffée* (meaning to stew in a closed dish).

They may be right, but to be sure it was a terrible come-down. The dish the crofter's wife so adroitly concocted about the middle of the day would have sent any conscientious chef into a decline.

Fat kissed the stewpan and was allowed to melt before a small onion was cut and added and allowed to brown in the fat. When the fat was very hot, sliced potatoes were added, laced with salt and with pepper and dowsed with a tablespoonful or two of water. The left-overs of the previous day's beef or mince (and that would be little enough) were spread on top of the potatoes and the whole permitted to simmer for about three-quarters of an hour. Then, stirred up with a spoon, the *stovies* were ready to eat with accompanying oatcakes and a glass of milk. There were wives, certainly, who abided by that North-east Lowlands recipe; others who *birsled* them so long in the pan that the slivers of onion shrivelled to cinders and usually took some of the burned bottom of the pan with them when they left it. When they didn't have left-overs of meat, the croft wives added a wry humour instead—and called the dish *Barfit Stovies* (Barefoot Stovies).

There was many a day, indeed, when a croft diet was so poor that it needed a bit of humour to help it down and there were other examples of culinary wit. One "making" of broth, for instance, could go on so long you could imagine that you would never see the end of it: the second day it would be called Yavil Broth, the third day (with a frowned-on irreverence) Resurrection Broth.

Away from the sophisticated taste of France, Sheep's Head Broth was a lot closer to home, though undoubtedly it would have gone down better in a foreign language. It took the bit of the animal that nobody else wanted (or had the stomach for) and combined it with the kind of ingredients found in every crofter's kailyard. A vital preliminary, however, was the children's walk to the blacksmith's—to have the sheep's head singed at the forge. That was a necessity, the old folk said, for good broth of its kind.

Salt herrings came to the table without such ceremony and often from the crofter's own barrel if his holding was well off the beaten track. They were eaten with the fingers (as were most kinds of fish) and partnered by potatoes, traditionally boiled in their jackets. The *tatties and herring* had a strong following all through that old countryside, and sometimes even ascended the social ladder to appear in a modest gentleman's house, upgraded for his dining table by having the herrings set out on one *ashet* (from the French *assiette*), the potatoes on another. Then, in the kind of quandary that never troubled the crofter's table, the finger-bowls would have to be brought out to provide some semblance of refinement.

There was no doubt about the dish's wide appeal: *tatties and herring* yoked together like a cart and a Clydesdale, the one unthinkable without the other, the potatoes' blandness taking off some of the strong flavour of the fish.

For long the red herrings (salted and smoked) were a staple in the poor folk's diet. Soaked overnight, to draw some of their sting, their raw saltiness, they were usually boiled on top of their accompanying potatoes. Bought regularly from the fisher lass who came round with her creel, and later off the fishman's cart, they even found a favoured place on Jess MacKendrick's table—in spite of the havoc they had wreaked on her wedding day.

There was little on the croft wife's menu that did not come down from the distant past; that, like the old language of the North-east Lowlands, did not find its last bastion, its final foothold, in the croft house before fading forever from the landscape. The basics did not change, though thankfully they got slightly more plentiful. The food of the rural communities of the mid-1700s had a close rapport with what was still coming to the crofter's table 125 years later. Thus William Alexander, looking back to the earlier time as he sat down in the late-1870s to write his *Notes and Sketches Illustrative of Northern Rural Life in the Eighteenth Century*:

> So with only their porridge, their sowens and their kail . . . supplemented at exigent times by a dish of nettletops or "mugworts", it is not to be supposed that the food of the common people was ever luxurious. Their favourite drink was home-brewed ale, which they manufactured to pretty good purpose. . . .

The home-brewed ale gave way, even at the croft table, to tea, earlier to be found only in the laird's house. But that was the only difference the young Jess MacKendrick would have noted in the 1870s at her grandfather's Perk Hill croft. She would remember the main dishes of the Sabbath dinner, the mid-day meal, the best of the week: cabbage brose or *claith* broth made with barley. In a variant, one of many on the brose theme, the cabbage was *chappit* (mashed) small, mixed with milk, sugar and cream and eaten with oatcakes.

Then, in that bare, wind-scoured countryside, as for many years before and after, the oatcake was king. In its time it had been eaten by bishops (with their morning dram) and it would be found in the *aumery* (from the French *armoire*) of many a kirk manse up to—and maybe beyond—World War II, where the incumbent had grown up with it and formed an addiction. It was like a bad upbringing; a man could never get away from it. Oatcakes came to the croft table with everything; the first dish plumped down on the table oilcloth as the mealtime came round was the wooden oatcake *truncher*, piled high. Oatcakes accompanied saps, *stovies*, soups and broths of all denominations and practically any other dish you could think of. Most of all, they were quite inseparable from the crumbly blue-veined cheese all the croft wives made and whose bacterial content did not bear thinking about—and which had come to maturity (not to say over-ripeness) sitting chessilled and muslined in the stone cheese-press standing a few paces from the dung-*midden*.

The oatcake went to the school with the bairn for his playtime *piece*; with the tradesman as his dinner snack. When a man sat down to eat it, he took part in Scottish history. Its anvil was the *girdle*, the griddle, that followed the hens' pot on to the *crook* of the *swey* in mid-afternoon. Rolled flat and circular in its raw, newly-kneaded mix of oatmeal and water that also mingled fat and a shaking of salt and bicarbonate of soda, one round followed another on to the griddle where it hung above the flames. On the griddle the "round" was quartered into *farls* and these when baked were toasted to a dry crispness on the toaster that hung from the top fire-bar. With cheese, the *farls* followed the breakfast brose or evening *sowens* as a second course, the only one you were likely to get.

In the North-east oatcakes, singularly and collectively, were called *breid*, misleadingly but evocatively, for the word aptly sums up their rôle: the staff at the centre of northern rural life. As such, they were baked in croft kitchens throughout the North-east right up to World War II. Only then, with the end of that holocaust and the readier availability of the factory-made article, so uniform in taste and texture after the individuality of the past as hardly to engender anything like the same loyalty let alone excite an addicted palate, would the griddle be put away—banished, like so much else, to the gawping wonder and speculation of the antique shop. It is a far cry now from that time when the iron stalwart was hardly put away from one day to the next.

Maybe it deserved better, for the *girdle* too had an old and honourable rôle, its history stretching into the Celtic mists of Wales, Ireland and Brittany as well as those of Scotland herself. The word, in the view of some knowledgeable opinion, is from the French of *gredil*, though equally there is room for supposing a descent from the Gaelic *greadeal*, the hot stones on which the old Gaels toasted their oat bannocks. But let none doubt its glorious past. The fourteenth-century chronicler Froissart, who would have known about such things, claimed that the Scottish soldier of that earlier time carried with him a flat metal plate and with it a small wallet of oatmeal. With a fire and a little water he had his sustaining oatcakes in no time. Give him a sword or a halberd as well and you had something unstoppable. If there were croft wives who baked dainty *breid*, thin *farls* that melted mealily on the tip of your tongue, there were more who baked in the substantial traditions of such hardy men. Grannie Gavin was one of them; on her thick oatcakes you could have marched for a day or more.

From the same source—the meal girnal, re-stocked yearly—came vital variations on the oatmeal-based diet: oatmeal brose, and the more occasional porridge that took the same ingredients and more time and with a kind of culinary *savoir-faire* put them on to a plate instead of into a bowl or a *caup*. And there was *sowens*, of course, which repeated the same basic trick with poorer constituents (the milled husks of the grain) but sought to disguise the fact by being sometimes pourable—into a bottle, for instance, to take to the *hairst* field.

The better the oatmeal, the better the porridge or brose, naturally, though there were folk of that far countryside who believed (with many another superstition) that good porridge could only be made by stirring clockwise with the *spurtle*. There was a belief even that porridge must be eaten standing up. For a treat, and usually for the supper, porridge would be made from bere meal, made from good barley instead of that more commonly milled, from oats. It was stronger to the taste, with its own very distinctive flavour.

Sowens, whatever they came in, arrived with a testimonial—Dr Johnson's no less. The jaundiced old man of English letters (with so little good to say of oatmeal), during his famous 1773 tour of Scotland, at Tobermory "took sowans and cream heartily". (He also had a good word on Scotch broth with barley.)

A croft's *sowens bowie* stood usually in the cool of the milkhouse dark. In it, the corn *sids*, the husks brought home from the miller's, steeped for a week or more until the residual grain was soaked out of them. Then the barrel's contents would be emptied, sieved into a pail. There were two kinds of *sowens*: supping and drinking, the latter sweetened with syrup, the supping variety served on a plate like porridge.

It was to the milkhouse dark, too, after the calves had been given their share of it, that the milk from Willie Gavin's *bloo coos* was taken, steaming and *yoaming*, hot from the udder to the chill of the polished stone shelf and the shallow dish in which the cream would rise. When it had done so it would be skimmed like a crust —into the big earthenware jar on the equally-cold floor—to keep for the churn. For the butter for the croft table, like its cheese, was home-made long after both might have been easier bought off the grocer's van. Traditionally it was made in the milkhouse though more often a croft wife, with cooking pots to keep an eye on and a new bairn in the cradle, would take her churn into the kitchen.

Making butter sounds simple; in fact it wasn't. It might prove impossible even. In the days of the old crofts and farmtouns, there was difficulty with the temperature: both extremes, hot or cold, brought problems and in winter especially, to ensure success, many of the old crofter wives would warm the butter cream by the fire-range before emptying it into the churn. There were paddle churns (on which you turned the side handle) and plump churns with their plungers (older and traditional). Jess MacKendrick, all her days, stuck faithfully with the past and the plump churn made for her by her millwright son, but there were as many croft kitchens where its place was finally usurped by the smaller versions of the paddle churns used in the farmtoun dairies.

Near the end of the butter-making, the butter-milk was drained off, and many of the croft folk drank it as an ambrosial draught. Young crofting Cleopatras even saved it to later wash their faces in it, believing that it enhanced the complexion. Finally, cold water was put into the churn to "firm" the contents, and in with it went the dosing of salt that so often made a croft wife's butter as savage as her tongue.

But the abiding staple of the crofting families, as of the folk of the farmtouns, was brose, of one sort or another, relentlessly made to appease ever-hungry stomachs. Besides water brose, the basic concoction from which all other variants stemmed and grew in their bewildering complexity, there was milk brose—though this, because of the value of milk in the crofting economy, was less seldom seen on the croft table than in the farmtoun kitchens.

In its basic form, what brose did have was the merit of over-whelming simplicity: a few handfuls of oatmeal thrown into a *caup* (the wooden bowl from which it was traditionally supped), a little salt after it, all stirred with the spoon as water or milk was poured over it. Such an easily-prepared dish could give a croft wife an extra half-hour in the harvest field—something never to be scoffed at as the weather held and the croft folk battled to bring in their crops.

Kail, as honourable as oatmeal, was for long years as central to the northern existence and kail brose, unappetising as it sounds, was at one time almost universal as the mid-day meal, a sustainer as vital as the psalms of the crofter's Free Kirk and richer in vita-mins certainly, if not in iron. It was always, in fact, more nutri-tious than palatable, which may be why the croft folk supped it one way and every way, trying anything that might mitigate its monotony. Again, in its basic form it was not difficult to cook, and God knows, the Scots had always had plenty of practice. In the popular way of the North-east Lowlands (though certainly it varied), the kail (colewort) was torn into pieces and put into a pan to boil in water for a couple of hours—maybe even longer, for that could only be for the better. Then the kail was "pulped down". Next, that older, stauncher standby, a *bicker* of brose, was made, adding butter and salt and pepper, with the *bree* (the liquid) from the kail pot. When the brose was made a further libation of the *bree* would be poured over it. Meanwhile—the way many of the crofter folk preferred it—the mashed kail was mellowed with a nob of butter and further mashed in the pot to be ready as the second course. This would be eaten off a plate, the brose having been supped from the bowl in which it was made. Just occasionally, the kail, mixed with butter, might be spread on a *farl* of oatcake, as a between-meals titbit. Turnip and cabbage brose, made on the same principle, allowed the same eccentric permutations. But kail was the standby, its hold on Scottish history as immeasurable as the oatcake's practically, and if once there were bishops who took an oat-bannock with their morning drams there were, later, minis-ters of wilder evangelical fire who rejoiced in the name of "kailpot preachers". They got their name not from any dullness in their sermons, as they held the crowd in thrall at some great five-day communion, but from the fact that their impassioned oratory kept the folk of that countryside from their Sabbath dinner.

Though the culinary leap was hardly momentous, oatmeal *could* come to table in other forms: as *skirlie*, for instance. The cookbooks of today that give it countenance at all, lavished as they are with the sumptuous still-life feasts of fancier fare, will tell you with the kind of enthusiasm that is tantamount to recommending avoidance, that *skirlie* can be an accompaniment for meat or game, or even fish. In the old crofting kitchens, with its chipped onions first well *birsled*, mixed with oatmeal and the mixture cooked till it took on the lustre of dull gold, it accompanied nothing grander than boiled potatoes (often mashed) and came to you with the glass of milk you so desperately needed to get it down. Once, for the festive occasions that punctuated the year, even the shortbread was made from fine oatmeal. Indeed, the subsistence factor of the old crofting life would have delighted today's self-sufficiency pundit, even if he might have cared little for most of its dishes. Though beef (after that time when the killing of the mart beast had been a yearly custom) came from the butcher the rest of the household's food was home-grown. Out of Willie Gavin's carefully cultivated garden there came the carrots and the occasional cabbage that would partner field-grown potatoes and turnips. In the *yard*, too —its main provision almost—grew the strawberries, currants (red and black) and the green and russet gooseberries that became Jess MacKendrick's preserves, put away in the *press* to appear on the tea-table only when visitors came.

The croft eggs, though plentiful enough, were not part of that self-sufficiency; they were not eaten recklessly. They were part of the croft's produce, for sale to keep the bailiffs from the door. Often they were preserved for the winter, when the hens went off the lay, in waterglass in a big *pig* or earthenware jar. This method of preserving was practised also when egg prices were low; first, as a means of minimising the market glut; second, so that the family could later use the preserved eggs and offer the newly-laid for sale when prices rose again.

Such was the bareness of the crofter's table that only the man of the house might have a supper egg occasionally. He ate as well as circumstances allowed and that was by no means lavishly. The reason was sound enough: it was on his strength that they all depended. If the breadwinner was not able to work for any length of time in those pre-dole days, they were all of them—the entire family—out of a home and into the poorhouse where the texture of charity was sometimes sadly thin.

The diet at Willie Gavin's table was no better than most, and considering his craft skills it was perhaps more frugal than it need have been. In the early days, as he took over the poor fields and rebuilt the old *biggings* inherited from his father, his *siller* had been sunk single-mindedly into the croft and his family got barely enough. His daughter, in her late-seventies, recalls uncomplainingly the want and the dietary monotony of those days in the early part of this century as Willie Gavin pursued his impossible dream: "There wasn't much to live on at that time. We would have had kail and kail brose for dinner and peasemeal brose for supper—or maybe *neep* brose or *sowens*. My mother used to make cheese and we often had *crowdie*." *Crowdie* was a kind of almost-instant cheese made by squeezing the curds in double muslin and then hanging the "cheese" out to dry on a nail on the wall. For Willie Gavin's children that was a treat, like the top off his supper egg, which each of them received as their turn came round, or the small piece of his supper herring spread on a corner of oatcake (to make it last), which came round in the same rotation. If such want left marks on the soul, none of the Gavins showed it.

By the 1930s, the Sabbath, if no other day, brought beef to the Gavins' table. Boiled to make the broth that went before it, it came on its *ashet* with a cordon of carrots and turnip segments plucked steaming from the pot and with the broth barley still barnacled on them. To follow there would be a simple sago or tapioca pudding made (like the broth) the day before and allowed to settle into *rigor mortis* in its enamel dish. It was a feast after the frugality of Lumphanan's Perk Hill colony.

Sabbath tea, after such largesse, was a simple affair: oatcakes and Grannie Gavin's blue-veined cheese or maybe the luxury of a boiled egg if the hens were laying; bread and butter and (if you were lucky) a smearing of redcurrant jelly; maybe even the special treat of a floury bap. A maverick big Abernethy biscuit might also appear on the plate from time to time, but since there was never one for every guest it gave the young Gavins their first lesson in ethics. Such was their reluctance to disgrace themselves (or their parents) that often, sadly and to their dismay, it went untouched back to the cupboard from which it had come, to become the mason man's dessert the day after.

Though the Sabbath meal might be more leisurely than most, folk did not linger at Willie Gavin's table; the croft's board was no place for social eating and the old crofter man himself had little time for that. As soon as he had finished his pudding he pushed his plate from him and if you were still putting away the last mouthful or two—forcing down the chill sago—his glance of displeasure was indication enough that you had not been in sore need of it. But that haste was the only unseemliness. At the crofter's table, as in his mason squad, he allowed neither bad language nor coarse stories and any man who did not realise it never got the chance to repeat his mistake. Having given the back-slider a moment or two, the old crofter man would reach into his cords for his Stonehaven pipe and the round tobacco mull that polished ceaselessly in his pocket—a signal that the meal had ended.

XIII

Mutches and Moleskins

IF THE WEDDING folk saw the brief exchange between mother and daughter just before the bride boarded the brake that would take her down-country to the quarrytoun and into the midst of her man's folk, maybe they smiled to themselves, assuming the tenor of the conversation: a mother's last word on the ways of men and wifely duty; absolution in advance after all the years of sternly-preached denial.

They would have been utterly wrong.

Jess MacKendrick's mother's advice that day concerned something much closer to her heart, an important matter in that now-distant countryside: family pride. "See to it," she had said, "and mind and always put yer man oot tae his work wi' white breeches and black sheen." A wife's reputation could hang on such things but Jess MacKendrick's was never in doubt for she did both nearly all the years of her married life and Willie Gavin set out each Monday morning as though he were going to an Oddfellows' meeting and never less than a worthy example to the men of his masoning squad.

Every Saturday evening when he came home from his week's work, his mason's white moleskins, the hallmark of his trade, would be spread-eagled on the croft's kitchen floor almost before he had time to step out of them. And down on her hands and knees beside them, his wife would first smooth soft soap over them before beginning with the scrubbing brush. With the cleaning of the family's shoes, and for as long as Willie Gavin made his living from his trowel, it was almost her last task before the lull of the Sabbath. Appearances had to be kept up—all the more so if you had no *siller* in the bank and little meal in your girnal. And that had been true long before Willie Gavin's time.

It was the Sabbath still that drew the folk of the countryside out in their finery, as it had done when Willie Gavin's father was a boy. Then, in the 1840s, were the ploughmen "free from the plough for one day . . . done up according to taste in rough grey tweeds, and with the ends of their brilliant neckerchiefs flying loose". On the same kirk road trudged "one sturdy old dame with close mutch, ancient shawl of faded hue and big umbrella implanted firmly under her arm, fine as the day is . . .". Beside her clanks a servant lass in heavy tackety shoes. The picture, so delightfully evocative of the fashion of the time, is drawn for us by William Alexander in his *Notes and Sketches Illustrative of Northern Rural Life*, written just over a hundred years ago. Fairs and market days too, among the very few holidays of the crofting and farmtoun year, were other occasions that brought the country folk out in their best attire. Few events drew them in greater numbers in the North-east Lowlands than Aikey Fair in Aberdeenshire, where there was practically nothing that was not traded between the drams and among the raucous cries of the chapmen. Again, the same author, writing of that slightly earlier time when the crofter man's grandmother had been a girl, gives some indication of the country fashions the folk of the mid-1800s had left behind.

> The men appeared in the old-fashioned homespun, woven and tailored coat and vest, with big pockets and big buttons, knee breeches and hose all made of wool of sheep reared at home. They wore shoes with large buckles; and some of the rustic dandies came dressed in white trousers and vest. The women also were in their "braws", and those of the fair sex who could afford it appeared in white. They generally wore high-crowned gipsy mutches. Then, as now, in matters of dress, the common folk trode on the heels of the gentry.

Clearly the craze for trousers was something new in the countryside and, quite predictably, the mood of change was not to everyone's liking. Thus a minister, of the same landscape, about the same time, in that most remarkable series of Scottish records, the *Statistical Account*:

> The dress of all the country people in the district was, some years ago both for men and women, of cloth made of their own sheep wool, Kilmarnock or Dundee bonnets and shoes of leather tanned by themselves. Then every servant lad and maid had a quey or steer, sometimes two, and a score or two of sheep, to enable them to marry and begin the world with. Now every servant lad almost must have his Sunday coat of English broadcloth, a vest and breeches

of Manchester cotton, a high-crowned hat and watch in his pocket. The servant maids are dressed in poplins, muslins, lawns and ribbons.

The minister was not well-pleased. But the interest of his quaint lament lies now in its confirmation of the way the fashion wind was blowing. What irony, that it was always the kirk road that brought out the excesses of fashion!

Yet up to 1840 anyway, and into the days of Old John Gavin's childhood, there were folk of the North-east who still wore the linen and cloth spun by a woman of the family. And James Geerie, when he set out from his up-country croft in Lumphanan in the 1870s for Sunday worship (often alone, for his *gudewife* was not the ardent worshipper he would have wished) was still wearing the coat and breeches of the old landscape. But pious man though he was, there was one way in which he kept remarkably up to date with fashion: his heavy road-foreman's boots were thrown aside for the lightsome grace of elastic-sided ready-mades. His grand-daughter would recall the rest: "He wore a high Gladstone collar with a black silk neckerchief hanging down, long hose with garters, with white toes and white tops, made from strong mill worsted." His weekday wear would have been that honoured garment of the northern countryside, the sleeved waistcoat with its back and sleeves of black jean (a cotton twill), worn with moleskin *breeks*. Women's fashion then, around the crofts and farmtouns, was as delicately poised—between the primness of the mid-Victorian age and an earthier past, for as Jess MacKendrick would remember, they wore two petticoats but nothing under them beyond their home-knitted stockings so heavily gartered on the thigh that they almost stopped the circulation. The petticoat worn next to the skin would be made from *sark* (shirt) flannel; that over it, fully-pleated round the skirt, from wincey. Over both went a wincey skirt. The stockings worn through the week were brightly-coloured, those of the Sabbath a sombre black. Topping every-thing was a *vrapper*, a kind of jacket with long sleeves.

Some thirty years later, about the turn of the century, croft fashion was well settled into styles that would pass down the years. By then, for sure, Old John Gavin was favouring tweed for the Sabbath and for all the other important affairs and occasions of life. His likeness about that time shows him as well-suited as any eminent Edwardian, the wide skirt of the jacket falling away from a high button. The photograph shows a small-built man with moustache and full whiskers and (despite his years) a full head of hair elegantly quiffed at the front—a man with some claim to be thought handsome had his lack of height not denied him. There is a dim and now-distant memory of him as a man with a liking for the old plush waistcoats that were once the rage of that northern countryside, and that would have been entirely in keeping with his jovial character. But it was a trait that could hardly have pleased his wife, for the velvet double-breaster with its pearly buttons was never seen on the back of a gentleman; it was the stamp of the rake, at best of the up-start. Blue was the favoured colour though red was more outrageous and just the thing for a man who wanted to leave his mark regardless of good taste. His grand-daughter would remember quite definitely, though, the ill-assorted pair who set out for the kirk each Sunday from the Whinfield croft in the early years of the century and her grandmother's fashion in particular.

> My granny was a great tall lady and Granda was a real small man with a moustache and long beard. Granny wore a long skirt and a blouse and apron and when doing dirty or heavy work she wore a sack-apron. When going out she had a nice black dress, with buttoned boots and a black velvet cloak with bead trimming all over it, and a wee hat the shape of a mutch with lovely mauve flowers on it. She wore black knitted stockings. She only went to church with this on. . . .

The mutch was a persistent fashion in the crofting countryside and among the lonely mud-girt farmtouns and, in a commoner context, lingered long in the language to describe the old scarf a croft wife might throw over her head to go out to the byre or to work in the *shifts* alongside her man, or more likely by herself in his absence. In its original form though it was a baby-shaped bonnet that tied with ribbons under the chin, and in its time its lace frills framed not only the sweet features of many a winsome lass but the face of many a matron where endurance was more strongly written than beauty and looks, where they had been early bestowed, had soon become sallowed (often) with peat reek. Frequently, in sepia'd prints from the past, the flinty gaze from under the frills is a reminder of the steely woman a croft wife had to be.

Crofter fashion changed slowly. Willie Gavin's mother looking black-browed down from her frame in the ben-end, besides being heavily turbanned in tulle, wears a tight, dark bodice. Many years later, her daughter-in-law, similarly framed—her hair dragged back to a bun and her face made austere by the photographer's flash—is similarly bloused. Without decoration, the bodice is puritanical and Prussian-collared for in the close and circumspect fashion of her day Jess MacKendrick showed neither bosom nor barely an ankle to anyone but her husband and her doctor. Though the 1920s would put her daughters into the mass-made frocks of the flapper society, she never lifted her hemlines more than would clear the mud of the old croft's close.

On the Sabbath, like all respectable men, Willie Gavin himself quit weekday moleskin for the dark green tweed he so strongly favoured and wore in defiance of the seasons with a waistcoat of the same weight and colour (where else could he put his watch, or anchor his watch-chain?). It was a suit made of as stern stuff as the man himself, which was just as well, for in the great tradition of Scottish tailoring it gave its occupant plenty of room to move inside it. It seemed whiles that it would long outlast him, and finally, it did—a testimonial to a thrifty countryside where folk did not ask was a fabric fashionable but was it hard-wearing. With it he wore brown boots of supple leather that made the kirk-miles a lightsome walk.

Married in black, Jess MacKendrick, for all sober and Sabbath occasions, never deserted it though after the splendour of her wedding day, her croft life with its ceaseless chores was a decline into drabber greys. It was all a far cry from the neat maid's uniform of her servant days with the up-country merchant. Now the most persistent fashion of her working day, like that of every croft wife, was the sacking apron (made from a washed corn-seed bag), which she flung round her waist when she rose from her bed in the morning and removed, sometimes, only when she went back to it at night. Her workaday bodices she made from her man's flecked wincey shirts when they could no longer bear the scrutiny of the masoning world, cutting their tails to make a new collar-band and piping that with binding so that it might wear even longer the second time round. Her seamstress's skill and ingenuity were endless, a byword (and sometimes an embarrassment) even in a society well used to thrift and making-do. She made all the family's clothes bar the new tweed suit her man might need, or be able to afford, once in a blue moon (and only after a good *hairst*) and the dress that might be needed for some special occasion. In the thread-bare days of their early crofting life she had cut down her own clothes for her daughters as they came to adolescence, causing many a bitter tear, for though she could easily transform the gar-ment, she could never disguise the giveaway of the fabric. Bairns' clothes were adapted to meet the needs of rising Gavins; collars and cuffs were endlessly turned till everyone lost count, for in the crofting community, as in the cottar's house of the farmtoun, the hand-me-down was a way of life, as inevitable as the seasons. In-deed it was said that as brother followed brother into the classroom the woman teacher, though she might not know her new pupil, could instantly recognise the *breeks*. Understanding women that they were, they never gave the pupil less attention because of it. The *breeks*, anyway, would still have been a novelty to the bairn, for until they were four, Willie Gavin's sons in the early-1900s were kept in frocks (coming to no psychological harm because of it), graduating then to the usual small boys' attire for that time and region. Willie Gavin's daughter remembers the crofting child's fashions of that day just as vividly. The boy's outfits were "breeches and long stockings, a sort of jacket with an Eton collar that you wiped clean with a cloth. They had strong boots in winter and went barefoot in summer." The girls of the crofter man's family "had on a frock and pinafore, real long, with black knitted stockings and buttoning boots". It seems certain that they took the school-road better clad than their old grandfather had been in the days just before the mid-1800s. Here is a description of the country school-bairn of that earlier time, from *At The Back o' Benachie*, whose author, Helen Beaton, has left us a remarkable folk record. The desperate saving on materials is evident:

A boy from a cottar house was usually dressed in moleskin trousers, the legs made narrow and short. The coat was the same material, the sleeves being made usually too small, which, altogether gave the child the appearance of having jumped out of his clothes. In winter the boy's hands were often bleeding through the dirt from chil-blains and hacks. His hair was usually very long and always looked tooslet. He wore a red gravat round his neck on which the "water mark" was plainly visible. The boys had no greatcoats in those days; but if the weather was very stormy, an older brother's jacket or an old plaid was donned.

A crofter man's working fashion, like the rotation of his crops, followed that of the farmtouns and the wincey shirt was king. Worn in the fields open-necked or closed with a stud, it had a collar-band so that in an emergency (or for a visit to the doctor) a man could go home from the parks and make himself presentable for better company simply by attaching a white collar with studs front and back, or more elaborately add a dickie front. His wincey shirt would be taken off for bed; it was just about the only thing that was, for the old countrymen spurned pyjamas—if they had heard of them at all—and slept in their flannel *sarks* and their long drawers, glad of the residual warmth as their feet left the *clickit* rug for the cold of the *closet* bed. (In stormy times there were men even who did not scorn the benefit of keeping their socks on under the blankets.)

With the factory-made shirt still the kind of luxury that a man would buy once in a lifetime, Jess MacKendrick made all her men's *sarks*. And like many another croft or cottar wife of that North-east countryside, she made them for payment for the men whose wives were less skilled with a needle (or less in need of the *siller*). Even in a parish where such a skill was by no means uncommon, she could sit in the kirk on the Sabbath and see never fewer than a half-dozen of the *sarks* she had made, not counting Willie Gavin's. One of them would be on the miller, so taut across the great barrel of his chest that there were times when she waited to hear the seams splitting. A big man, like a well-bred bull, the miller's twenty-stone bulk would have made a mockery of the stock of any draper's shop had he been at pains to step into it. But if he got his shirts made at the same price as other men (with maybe only a penny or two more for the extra bit of cloth needed), he milled Willie Gavin's oats at the same price as everyone else's. In the way of millers, north and south of the Border, he prospered well and retired finally to the house he'd built and called Millbank. The sly humour was not lost on his old customers. It had been that right enough, folk said, thinking little of his joke.

The shirting the young croft wife mainly worked with was the favourite of her day—wincey, which mixed wool and cotton and

had ousted linsey-woolsey, combining wool and linen in an in-
ferior fabric. But with equal flair, running her eye over the set of
a man's shoulders and the tape measure round his chest, she made
the half-sleeved flannel *sarks*, the under-garments that the men of
that dour landscape wore next the skin in the days before the
sophisticated *semmit*. (Not a few of them, in fact, continued to
wear flannel *sarks* long after the *semmit* came round the country in
the travelling draper's van: it was a poor thing against the comforting "felting" of flannel, a garment for a man who could put a
coat on his back on a day of storm.) Into old age, Grannie Gavin
knitted all the men of the family's socks, completing a pair in two
or three evenings at the fireside and sometimes in less time if the
need was urgent. She wove the kind of thick woollen socks that
brought comfort to the feet encased the day long in heavy landsman's boots, genteel grace in cashmere for the shopman's ankles
or for those in gentler occupations. Latterly, with her children up
and away and her shirt customers at last seduced by the shop pro-
duct, there was never a night (the Sabbath excepted) when she
did not come in from the milking to pick up her knitting from her
chair. It lay there ready to be resumed at any moment, assumed
and set down almost without thought.

A croft wife's weekday wear was as little in the height of fashion
as her man's. It was based on the kind of tight bodice that Jess
MacKendrick made and the long skirt, in some heavy material.
And if a wife cast her inmost petticoat on a winter's night before
putting on her nightgown it would be only for reasons that need
not detain us here. For the work of the croft *shifts*, and to keep the
wind out of her hair, she might don one of her man's bonnets but,
fearful of the warning of Deuteronomy that "women shall not wear
that which pertaineth unto a man," never his trousers. Mainly,
for her chores round the croft *biggings*, it would be her shawl
she would throw over her head and shoulders. That had long
replaced the plaid, from which it descended, and had even odder
uses. As her bairns came, Jess MacKendrick had worn her shepherd's tartan shawl in a way traditional in that North-east Lowlands landscape: folded lengthwise so that its two ends fell longer
down the front of the body to conceal her pregnancy. The shawl,
like the plaid, was a classless garment. Popularised by no less a
figure than Queen Victoria herself, it endured round the crofts long
after the cardigan came into its own, a practical fashion that would

linger as surely in the Victorian *ambiance* of the genteel sitting-
room till the shawls' old owners no longer had use for them.

If the Sabbath broke the weeks of toil one from another, it also
brought with it another kind of regeneration. It was the day that
the croft folk changed their clothes and in doing so looked back to
obscure Celtic ritual and a lost past as relentlessly rooted in the
folkways of the farming North-east, even in the 1930s, as in the
Highland glens. That day a man set out on the rest of the week not
only spiritually and physically healed but fresh-laundered with a
clean flannel *sark*, clean drawers and clean shirt and socks. Only
in the heat of summer would the drawers or the flannel *sark* be
cast off, and even then, only until he had the hard work of *hairst*
behind him. Summer and winter, Willie Gavin's last job on a
Saturday night, before the Sabbath came on him, was to take off
his working boots in the barn and pack into them a fresh lining of
the straw that would cushion his feet through the week to come.

In all Jess MacKendrick's wedded years, croft fashions changed
little—except perhaps in one notable area. On the day of her marriage, the mason man's bride had not worn knickers. Nor had she
done so for some years after, for they were practically unknown in
that old countryside except among women of quality and fancier
ladies (especially the latter, folk said). It took a winter of storm
and the quiet word of a neighbour to get her into them, and then,
a long way from the stylish shops and working more from rumour
than sample and taking her pattern from her man's, she made her
first pair of cotton drawers. They had long legs feminised with
frills.

Latterly, as the crofting years drew to their close in the 1930s,
there would begin to appear, walloping on the clotheslines of the
crofts and farmtouns, a garment that had percolated north with
the flapper society and the head-long advance of the mail-order
catalogue. Measured against the croft wife's early underwear, it
gave some indication of the way that sophistication had raced
north in the intervening years. It invoked indeed some of that
spirit of romanticism of the Auld Alliance and in our own time
would duly emerge, further abbreviated and lace-trimmed, as
French knickers. In those earlier days, however, they came round
surreptitiously in the battered suitcase of the chapman-sikh and
were known in that countryside of good oats and fine bulls by the
droll name of "free-traders"—a calumny that resulted from their

most conspicuous lack: leg elastic. Their appearance was enough to raise suspicion about many an innocent wife's character, and almost certainly, there were wise men even then—the elders of the parish—who looked at them and foresaw the downfall of a society.

XIV

The Pattern of Harvest

AS THE YEARS came on him Willie Gavin's *hairsts* grew harder,
taxing him more, so that he must have wondered whiles would
each be his hindmost. Glad he would be each year to put the task
behind him. For all that, it pleased him when it came, that high-
point from which the year hung. His crofting economy might be
based largely on his beasts, but it was his harvest *shifts* in all their
glory, bright with corn, that gave his life significance. It is diffi
cult now to know the old man's mind, to understand his delight in
his small harvest: it was something from another time, a thing of
the spirit in a bare landscape.

It was part of the dream of the crofter men that each *hairst* when
it came would bring them abundance, the yield they hoped for. It
never did. Yet, having sheared his corn a man won a victory in his
soul. Whatever the condition of his crop, he had then a month or
two when he almost breathed freely, without responsibility, with
nothing committed to the soil or the seasons except his *neeps*, still
swelling in the drill, and they hardly counted. There was little
hurt even the frosts could do them. And even if his *hairst*, after all,
left him little to sell to the corn merchant, just to have staved off
disaster was enough, itself a reason for rejoicing.

In that the old crofter men joined the mood of the farmtouns,
for the *hairst* brought its onslaught of work all round the countryside in which their small *shifts* sat—a strange festival it was, part-
slavery and part-thanksgiving. It was a time that united men as
did no other season; that more deeply renewed the bond between
folk and the soil, for its treachery as much as its bounty could
strengthen the chains. It was a time whiles when the mind slipped
the years to call up earlier harvests and the haunted folk who
sheared them, when one saw again the old patterns behind the
binder's technology. For the crofter folk, indeed, the pattern
of harvest was practically unchanging. If it immured them in
the past—divorcing them in the 1920s and 1930s from the

machine-modernity of the farmtoun harvests around them and accentuating their loneness in the agricultural landscape—it was a pattern, none the less, that looked back more directly to the ritual harvests of a lost countryside.

Willie Gavin's small hard *hairst* was repeated on every croft in every parish throughout the North-east Lowlands; while the clackity-clack of the mechanical cutter-bar carried to them on the clear air of a fine harvest day the croft men wielded their scythes in their patchwork fields, looking anxiously over their shoulders in case the black clouds were massing behind them and the weather should break before they were done. Maybe they looked, too, at the worn women gathering and binding behind them. They would stop, the weary lot of them, in the middle of the long afternoon to seek the shade of a stook and ease their backs against it as they *sookit* drinking *sowens* from the glass lips of the china-stoppered lemonade bottle they had brought with them; or sat, as thankfully, for the sweet reviving tea and floured baps brought out to them under the folds of a teacloth in a wicker basket. These moments were one of the delights of *hairst* in the days before the lonely combine and the zippered beercan; work paused briefly and there was banter and a high good humour as folk got their breath back.

Yet the old crofter men were hampered in winning their *hairst* in a way that would not be so today: the Sabbath then, the one day of the week that was their own, was inviolable. A silence lay on the still fields and nothing impinged on it; it was broken neither by the swish of the scythe nor the sound of the reaping machine. And even on his Sabbath afternoon stroll round his small parks Willie Gavin would not straighten a slipped sheaf in the *stook* without first glancing in the direction of the croft *biggings* to make sure Grannie Gavin was not watching him. He knew, should she see him, that he would be given his rascally character. But if she knew, or suspected him whiles, nothing was said—though the mason man's caution long caused sly merriment among his companions of the day and especially among the younger men who had come to look over his daughters. Only the fluting of Free Kirk psalms from some barn service, carried across the hush of the land, would disturb the quiet, their dolour at odds with the triumphal fullness of nature.

There were crofter men ill-placed to win their *hairsts*: the road-man (*fee*'d home for a harvest to some farmtoun in an attempt to make ends meet); the blacksmith (too busy by far at that time of

year with the needs for other folk's *hairsts* to think of his own) and
farmtoun horsemen and grieves who could not reap their own
crops till they had gathered somebody else's. Sore was their plight
and their loyalty torn as they toiled, wanting only to be home.
Their hardy croft wives, nothing daunted, would go out with the
heuk by themselves to shear the croft crops while their men were
away; it was fine, after all, to have your own *hairst* in and the *fee*
for the work of another.

Those days now are only a memory in old men's minds. But
their activity was intense. Though the mechanical harvester was a
practical reality in Old John Gavin's day—from the 1870s, anyway—it was always something for the farmtoun fields. Hired, it
had to be paid for; and, of course, it was an impossible investment
for any croft man even if he had the horses to harness into it. So,
down the years, his scythe had been the crofter's best friend: it
captured his hay when the clover was sweet, his oats when they
came to ripeness and began to *reeshle* on the stalk. It had a name in
that spare countryside—Rob Sorby, from the name on its blade.
And if that particular make of blade had as good a following as any
good whisky, there were also men who would hear nothing said
against the Tysack. New blades were bought at the *smiddy*, where
the smith fitted them to the *sned*, the wooden frame of the scythe,
a job not nearly so simple as it seemed. It needed its own skills in
alignment and adjustment if the implement was to be sweet to use,
not cumbrous and unwieldy, a thing without grace.

With his oats coming to ripeness and the promise of a fine harvest hanging in the summer air (as it sometimes did) Willie Gavin
would take down his scythe from its nail on the toolshed wall to
check the truth of its blade and the strength of its stay. He would
sharpen it and oil it and make a mental note (as he did before each
harvest) to buy a new carborundum stone next time he went to the
kirktoun. There had never been a time when Willie Gavin had not
sheared his own crops and brought them in. It was a strange
loyalty, a loyalty to his *grun*, that drove him. Beholden though he
was to Laverockhill for a *yoking* or two of a Clydesdale pair and a
plough and for most of the cultivation of the spring work, he
would not let a reaper or a binder on to his land from fear of the
harm the weight of the machine might do. A cottar son-in-law
fee'd home one year to the big farmtoun on the hill, who had
borrowed his Clydesdale pair and a binder one evening and

brought it down to the old man's *shifts* to save him the long hours
of slavery under the sun had been sent home again with damned
little thanks for his pains, and fell so far out of favour that he knew
never to do the like again. But maybe it was not the weight of the
machine that worried him, only that it came between him and the
hairsts of his ancestors. There is nobody knows now, one way or
the other, for Willie Gavin, even to his friends, could be a close
and secretive man.

The old crofter man began his *hairst* bouts at the top ends of his
shifts, cutting across their width, walking back to begin the next
bout, working slowly, inexorably, down towards the burnside. Old
man though he was in the 1930s, he was still as tidy a man with a
scythe as he was with a trowel. Bout after bout—each about four
and a half feet wide—the rhythmic sweep of his blade, right to
left, took the grain to the side of him, to fall neatly in a narrow
swath. The blade's sound in the summer air fell sweetly on the ear,
harmonising with the scyther's rhythmic movement. You could
almost hear the changing note—feel the drag of the blade, as
Willie Gavin did—as it became blunted and the crofter man
stopped to sweeten its edge, setting the tip of the blade on the toe
of his heavy boot as he *straiked* it.

Willie Gavin took all the straw he could get—he had need of it—
leaving little more than three inches of stubble. Behind him, as relentlessly as Old John's formidable consort had once done, Grannie Gavin bunched the fallen grain into sheaves, her hands seizing
the straws that would make the band, dividing them and twisting
them with that deft assurance she had known almost from the
cradle and certainly from the days of her girlhood in the Perk Hill
croft colony. Quickly she enclosed each sheaf, tying the band and
tucking the ends under, tidily. Row upon row, by the *yoking*'s end,
the sheaves would lie like the lines of battle dead, their eared heads
in the direction Willie Gavin worked. When Grannie Gavin went
in, about noon, to prepare dinner, he would lay his scythe against
the fence and begin *stooking*.

Working again across the *shift* he would seize the sheaves where
they lay, tucking one under each armpit as he strode across the
stubble to settle them into *stooks*. If the old crofter managed to
make it look easy, it was anything but that. It was hard work and it
always had been. The *hairst* field had its pattern, like so much else
in the seasons of that old countryside, and in a good year when the

stooks stood proud it delighted the eye. In a bad *hairst*, it was something else again: a crying in the heart of you as the grain flattened
and tangled under the constant *blatter* of rain till it was almost
beyond handling. Then the bouts of harvest were haggard, their
harmony and pattern lost by the harvester's need to scythe as he
could, undercutting the twisted crop where it lay.

The steady swish of the scythe was a sound that echoed down
the years in a croft bairn's mind; a memory that united the generations, as it did the Gavins. How little the old pattern changed!
Here is Old John Gavin's grandson, the old man's summer companion when the century was new:

> My strongest recollections of my young days were in the time when I
> was aged between nine and thirteen or so . . . I used to spend the
> major part of my holidays with my grandparents, at which time they
> were usually busily engaged in taking off their crops. I recollect those
> days as being very, very happy and pleasant. There was no such thing
> as binders or even reaping machines for the croft folk and the crop
> was all handled by the scythe. My grandfather did all the scything
> and my grandmother and I did all the making of the sheaf and bind-
> ing it. After a fair bit had been accomplished I would abandon the
> gathering to work on the *stooking*. At that time, my grandmother
> used to make a batch of honey ale every season. This was taken in a
> stone earthenware jar to the field, the jar being cast usually into a
> *stook* to keep the sun's heat away from it so that it would remain
> palatable. There was no alcohol in it.

By then, Old John and his spouse were both into their seventies,
and needed a short nap after dinner before going out for the afternoon *yoking*.

Yet if that memory is of hardy folk, it is also of something else,
that strange equation of harvest time: hard work and happiness.
The years had changed nothing at the Gavin croft—except that
with that formidable old woman gone where they brewed no
honey ale, the drink taken to the *hairst* field was now *sowens*.

Blessed with fine weather, it would take Willie Gavin a week,
maybe ten days, to cut and *stook* his three acres. He would cut his
ley oats first, moving, immediately that *shift* was done, into his
clean-land crop. Bad weather could make his *hairst* a fragmented
and protracted affair. But it was never the straightforward operation of a farmtoun harvest, for into it had to be fitted the tending

and milking of beasts as well as the odd funeral or two that might take the best part of an afternoon. It was a fine time though, for a man to go, with the *hairst* golden, or cut and standing tidy in the *stook*, and Willie Gavin had always thought so—though it was a damned inconvenience to his neighbours.

Yet slowly the *stooks* would rise on the cropped stubble of the old croft *shifts*, immaculately ranked, north to south in their ancient alignment so that the sun at noon struck along the length of their bunched heads. A week in the *stook*—ten days at the most —and if the weather was with him, Willie Gavin's oats would be ready to take home to the cornyard. In the early days, when he still had Meggie, his father's old *shelt*, as well as the cart to yoke her into, that had been an easy task; his *hairst* had come home in style in the manner of the farmtouns'. But in time the old beast, like its master, was gone, and Willie Gavin, like most of the crofter men, brought in his crop with his barrow, building a harvest frame on it to take the sheaves.

It was a method that aped the *hairst* carts of the farmtouns, where the Clydesdales bore home the loads. The croft barrow, however, rolled home under the power of human sweat and Willie Gavin was a tired man before he had his crop safe and into his small stackyard. A Clydesdale between the shafts of a Laverock-hill cart could have done the crofter's *leading* in an evening at the end of its day's work, without tiring either its horseman or the beast itself. But Willie Gavin set his face as firmly against that as he did the trespass of the binder; he would not have allowed it. Even so, in the up-country folds of the hills, there were crofter folk worse off, and men so poor that they had to bring their harvest sheaves home (with a big rope sling) on their backs, the same way that they brought a young sow home from the market.

So, like a fulfilment, Willie Gavin's sheaves came home. He tipped them, one barrowload after another, in the cornyard until he had a sizeable *birn*, a heap he judged enough to be the beginnings of a rick. For a start he managed by himself, building from the *foon*, the stack foundation, of springy spread brushwood, throwing the first sheaves into the centre, building up the "heart" of the rick before he began to splay them, heads inwards, round the circumference of the *foon*. The stack grew, tier upon tier, the crofter man still keeping up the "heart" of the rick so that outer sheaves would run the rain *out* not *in*. Layer was kneed upon circled layer, until it was no longer possible for him to continue unaided. Then, magically (because she had been watching from the small back window) Grannie Gavin would appear round the corner of the barn (mutched and aproned even on a day of heat) to fork up the sheaves to him.

Willie Gavin was a careful man; he built slowly, laboriously considering his trade, coming down the ladder she would prop against the stack to walk round and round his work. Taken from her butter- or cheese-making, she would lose patience with him at times:

"Dyod man, what needs ye tak' such pains aboot it? It will stand tae the wind and keep oot the weet, and what else is there that matters?"

But Willie Gavin would not be hurried; he *biggit* to satisfy something deep in himself. Yet the truth of it was that the crofter man for all his skill with stone could never manage to give his cornyard the kind of simple grace he could so easily bestow on a new farmtoun barn or byre. He never *biggit* a house with more care, but his stacks were neither proud nor handsome. Waterproof he could make them, certainly, but that symmetry that marked a master's skill eluded him and in his later years he never *biggit* his stackyard —got all his crop in—without one of his ricks being thankful for some prop to lean on. His small *hairst* would raise three or four ricks in the cornyard behind the croft barn, poor things beside the stacks that filled the farmtoun yards and so modest in stature as barely to lift their heads above the height of the barn roof: ten feet, little more, to the *easings*, the point at which the builder began to draw them in to their conical points.

Their thatch would be ready and waiting, the last of the straw from last year's harvest. On one or two wet mornings the old crofter man would have been in the barn *drawing thack*—straightening the straw—in readiness till it faired enough to let him out again with his scythe. Crofter men in other parishes might use *sprots* (rushes) from the bog or the burn bank as thatch, but whatever the *thack*, it would be lashed down with rope criss-crossed in the traditional tracery of that North-east region.

Grannie Gavin would be glad to see the *hairst* sheaves home and into the cornyard, for then too Willie Gavin was a happier man: he had (in the language of that farming countryside) "gotten winter". His crop was secure and his crofting year had ended. And that was a matter for congratulation among the crofters no less than in the world of the encircling farmtouns. To have your *hairst* home dry and in good order was a small triumph.

"I see you have winter, Willie," folk would call, meeting him on the road as he brought his beasts in for the milking.

"Aye, just so," he would cry back at them, jovial almost, well-pleased to be at one with farming men. And then, for modesty's sake: "An' nae afore time."

It delighted him, all the same, to be among the first of the croft men to have his harvest in, though in that he was handicapped by his cautious nature and was never the leader. He would not cut a corner here and there as some men did or risk a hot rick—and maybe a fire—in the process. But he was never the last, and there was little chance of his being so, so long as Puir Angus was among them.

So the pattern of harvest passed down the years, giving its continuity like the kirk with the crofting past. But if that gave a kind of reassurance, it was also a bitter condemnation. It showed the croft for what it was: an anachronism, a unit out of its farming time. And that, in turn, was never more deeply demonstrated than when it came time to thresh-out the corn stacks. Here, more dramatically than in anything else, the years *had* brought crofting change.

Old John Gavin had been early at the flail, every morning bar the Sabbath, turned out of his bed by his strong-willed wife to give them straw for the day when by all accounts he would sooner have lain there quietly at her side. Like James Geerie of the Perk Hill, Old John had threshed on the barn floor, stripped whiles to his under-*sark* and no doubt cursing, unkirk-like, the necessity that drove him to it. But by his son's day it was different: the steam-mill—the contractor's portable threshing-mill, moving winter-long between one farmtoun and the next—had become a part of the country scene, a thing of wonder and a terror to every Clydesdale in the land, for they would sooner leap over the dyke (cart and horseman and all) than face it. Even so, with their threshings so small, the crofter men would have to approach the mill's owner in a body to have any hope of raising his interest. And even then, Old Henderson would grumble and *girn* at them: there was not one of them with anything more than a *yoking*'s work to his machine. Forbye, it took him longer to manoeuvre the mill into

their small cornyards than ever it did to do the *thrash*, always supposing he did not tip the whole caboodle—engine, mill and bogie—
into the roadside ditch in attempting it! But Henderson was never
a happy man for all the *siller* he made (folk said) and was ill to
please with lesser work so long as the big farmtouns wanted him.
He complained bitterly when he did come: it was as well that his
crofting customers, like all his others, had to buy the "firing" for
his traction engine (he said) or he would have been bankrupt long
since.

If the steam-mill caused a stir about a farmtoun, its half-day at
a croft was pure upheaval. It turned the normal routine upside
down and caused claustrophobic congestion in its kitchen for it
was the practice, as well as common Scots hospitality, to feed the
mill crew—twelve men at the fewest. Lumps of beef would be
brought from the butcher's the day before to make broth in the
washday pot, wiped round for the occasion. Trestle tables were
set up in the kitchen, or sometimes in the barn, and to augment the
worn kitchen spoons the best cutlery was ripped out of the canteen
where it lay bedded in silk between one christening and the next.
In the excitement of it all, in his early crofting years, Willie Gavin
had been able neither to sit nor stand; and Jess MacKendrick's
kitchen would have come to a halt completely had not both Puir
Angus and Lang Andra had the good grace to go home for their
dinners.

Later though, the Gavin croft would avoid the disruption of the
steam-mill's visit. Willie Gavin would have his own barn-mill,
something unique in the crofter community and a blessing that put
him beyond the bargaining and the desperate petitioning and gave
him, perhaps, his only real measure of independence as a crofter
man. His son, Old John's young companion, recalls how the croft
got its mill:

My younger brother took up threshing-mill construction as a livelihood. He was quite good at it: he had a great reputation for building
the threshing-machines that were installed in each farmtoun's barn.

When the croft crop was harvested they would build it all into
stacks in the cornyard and these would be made more or less waterproof against rain, to an extent like the roofs of the buildings, which
were thatched. And as they needed grain or straw they would bring
in one of these stacks at a time, into the barn. Mostly, when they

started to move the stack there would be a considerable number of rats, running in every direction ...

And my brother, he built a threshing-machine ... and it did a good job and it was certainly a step much beyond that of using the old flail. It was powered by a motor and the grain would all be bagged, of course, and subsequently taken to the miller for grinding.

In fact, Willie Gavin's little thresher, an ingeniously sized-down version of the bigger mills that huddled in the dark of the farm-toun barns, was the envy of every crofter man in the district. With its drum, corn riddles and conveyor belt and two straw shakers, it did everything that the larger barn-mills would do. And though a few of the other croft men, by the 1920s, might have the kind of small portable thresher that was pedal-driven furiously by the croft wife as she also fed the sheaves into it, that needed a strong purse as well as a strong spouse! Mainly, the croft folk would continue to wait upon Mr Henderson, hopeful of soliciting his sympathy.

Willie Gavin enjoyed his independence, and maybe not only because it went against his grain to ask favour. There was a feeling (remembered still) among his family and neighbours that just because he had a mill he had also a bee in his bonnet about threshing, as strong in its way as his insistence on winning his own *hairst*. Certainly it was the view of his sons that he sometimes put on the mill when he had no need to. In retirement, it is admitted by all who knew him, the old man's decisions to *thrash* became increasingly eccentric, taken hurriedly and unpredictably between his morning brose and stepping in for his dinner. But, his mind made up, there could be no gainsaying him.

"Wumman," he would say, coming in to the kitchen and hanging his bonnet on the back of his chair as he sat down at the table, "we will need to thrash this afternoon."

It was fair warning that, whatever other arrangements she might have made, Grannie Gavin would be needed in the barn to feed the sheaves into the mill-drum.

The power for the little thresher-mill came from the old Ruston oil engine, housed in the shed behind the barn and transmitting its drive by a shaft through the dividing wall. It had been bought cheaply, secondhand, and it was not long before the old crofter man knew why. Crouched and waiting in the dark, fume-filled engine-house, it was a cantankerous thing. It took Herculean strength—much more than the old man should have exerted—to crank its heavy flywheel into motion. More than that, it took an accomplished sleight of hand, not to say magical adroitness, to slip the cranking handle free of its engaging "dog" as the engine finally "fired" and careered into motion. Such encounters blanched even the features of hardy men. Failure to achieve the dissociation in the critical instant could put the cranker in peril of his life as the handle whipped round and round in an ever-increasing frenzy on the spinning flywheel—ready to be hurled off at any moment. Once it had gone through the roof unhindered by the worn corrugated sheeting while the starter huddled petrified in a dark corner. Understandably, there was a tension about the Gavin croft whenever the mill had to be put on; when a volunteer had been selected (on a Saturday afternoon, say, when extra hands were available) he stepped into the engine house alone while his companions gave what good advice they could from the safety of the shed door.

All the same, there were times when Willie Gavin's famous engine stayed silent and sullenly unresponsive without even the encouragement of an occasional chuff-chuff. Men panted at it in relays, taking off their bonnets to wrap round its handle and so prevent themselves getting hand blisters. Fear heightened the responses so that over the years Willie Gavin's oil engine achieved a notoriety that matched the fame of his little mill, and with it, a number of names, none of them the maker's and few of them that Grannie Gavin would have approved of had she heard them. But she never did. Starting the engine was men's work; the women-folk stayed in the house, waiting for the first steady thump-thump of it—and ready to attend to the injured.

The day, at times, might be well done before the threshing was begun but at the end of it Willie Gavin would have a barn full of fine fresh straw and in his small loft, where the mill's conveyor cups had taken it, there would be a quarter or two of oats ready for bagging to take to the miller's or the seed corn merchant. That night, as he stepped in for his supper and the plate of bere-meal porridge Grannie Gavin would have waiting him, he would be a man well-pleased with the world and all the folk in it. There was no doubt that the threshing heightened his blood. Nobody knew why, for the old man's hard *hairsts* never gave him anything near the yield he had hoped for. But then, there was nothing new about that; the croft folk were long inured to it and took its inevitability stoically, as they did so many other misfortunes.

It was, after all, no more than they expected: the grand *hairsts* grew in other men's fields, in the parks of the fine farmtouns where, in the days before *hairst* a man might bury himself to the armpits in the golden waving grain. All the same, the crofter men often connived at their own failure by sowing *tattie corn* year in, year out. Always it was a poor yielder, giving only seven quarters or so to the acre, a poor return against that of the farmtoun fields. Well into the 1930s most of the crofter men clung with cussed insistence and misguided loyalty to the old strain when there were improved varieties, long-strawed at that, which would have bettered their yields by at least half again. But then, the crofter folk were like that: as unwilling to change their seed as they were to put away their *bloo coos*. Some, shackled by tradition, compounded their plight by keeping back from their own crops their next year's seed, so weakening the sad strain further. Willie Gavin was no different. Only the quarter or two he did not need either for seed or for household oatmeal went to the feed and grain merchant. Maybe they just about paid for the oilcake he needed to fatten his *stirks*.

XV

The Summer Folk

THE LATE END of summer brought another crop home to the old crofts: the visitors who came, drawn by the season or driven after a year's sterility of city streets by the need to re-nourish their roots, gulp lungfuls of good air and a desire to rest the eye on a green and remembered landscape. They were the folk with connection in that old countryside; who could not live in it and could not leave it, their loyalties now so strange and torn. Their yearly pilgrimage emphasised the *raison d'être* of the old croft dwellings: their appeal as a home and the family's hub.

Sometimes a man would return briefly from Canada or the States with a cultivated drawl to buy a bull at the sales and take a wife back with him, sure of the pedigree of both. Sons came home from southern police forces to help with the *hairst*; lasses who were nurses or teachers brought intended husbands from Edinburgh and Glasgow and Dundee and from their respective professions to be looked over: poor lads most of them, hapless in their Argyle socks and Aran pullovers, for they could neither bind a sheaf nor set a *stook* and were of no mortal use to anybody, except maybe the croft daughters who had taken a liking to them. Clever sons, too small of stature for the country life but with the kind of pernickity minds that made them masters of other men's *siller*, brought home womenfolk, socially superior, from far counties and some of them English, sophisticated *jauds*, knowing and teasing; they smoked and they drank and they painted their faces (and God knows what else) and wore short flapper frocks that showed sometimes a portion of knicker-leg. They called everybody "Darling", small boys included (to their eternal embarrassment) and demanded hot kisses at bedtime. For all that, they would be invited to come for their supper some evening and just for once Willie Gavin, when he came home, would wash his face and his hands before sitting down to an unaccustomed fine spread. Later on, the lad (and sometimes the lass, too) would take a dram with the crofter man and not know that it was a hint to go home. They would sit on, with their speak of the southern ways, so that the mason man would have to get out his bottle again to give them encouragement.

"Ye'll hae another nip afore ye go," he would say heavily, hoping this time, surely, the allusion would not be lost on them.

It was a sociable countryside then, at that time of year, while the *rowth* of *hairst* went on. It was fine to have the young folk back for a while, to re-cement for a week or two the close texture of the old society, and the croft kitchens about the end of the day would ring again with their humour—boisterous, abrasive and slyly allusive but never foul-mouthed. Willie Gavin enjoyed their company; liked it, without resentment, for the view of the world it brought to his fireside. In the course of a summer he might discuss the disaster of an English *hairst*, the problems of building with bricks as well as the rubber plantations of Malaya and (with some young missionary who spoke still in his own broad Doric tongue) the cropping rotations under a hot Swaziland sun. Given the right man and the right topic the crofter might talk well into the night, as absorbed as though he were bound there himself come the morning.

The young McCaskills who had done so well at the school were regular yearly guests. Known since the days of their childhood, they came home, the three of them in turn usually, for the hay-time and to help their father put past his harvest—to scythe and bind and *stook*, tasks as natural to them still as breathing. When there was a lull in the work or the weather broke they would be invited to Whinfield for their supper at six. They were allowed to stay late and have out their speak, for with their clever minds they were interesting folk.

One year Angus, the youngest, a Metropolitan police-sergeant, brought a lass from the Shires, all rosy and dimpled and with a shingled bob that showed off her delicate neck to perfection. For a fortnight she was the speak of the parish as she billed and cooed about him, not able to keep her hands off him even in decent folk's company. It was "darling this . . ." and "darling that . . ." and "Isn't that so, darling?" Poor Angus (folk said), to have landed himself with such a *limmer*! For days on end the older croft bairns trailed them surreptitiously through the landscape, hoping they could learn something to their disadvantage. But desperate though the lass looked, if young Angus got a roll in the corn there was none of them saw it.

That was unusual, for it was a countryside without cover, unkindly to lovers. Hardly a year went by without some of the visiting young folk being found in a grassy lie, at the edge of the corn by some old crofter man who had gone out in the gloam (with the gamekeeper gone home) only to set his rabbit-snares.

Fiona McPhee was a nurse and as bright as a button. She came regularly home with the *hairst* to rekindle old passions and flirt with the menfolk and spoke of the body and all its parts (even in front of the bairns) as if it were no better than a binder. She was *verra clivver*, folk said—and strong on high heels and displacement of the uterus.

But there were years when her oldest flame, Geordie McCaskill, never won home. He was a mission helper and it was the Depression years. Down in Liverpool's dockland, his mother said, things were so bad that he could not be spared. The croft folk believed it: from what Geordie had decently been able to tell them it was a *byordinar* place, a bit like Hell, with its women all painted and powdered, ill-creatures all of them, waiting on sailors; they did *that* for a living. Geordie could not get away for they were all of them in sore need of the Word.

The Gavin croft too had its family guests, most of them Grannie Gavin's relations, for the MacKendricks had always been sociable folk. Rob, the second eldest of her brothers, came, a regular refugee from his own grim *hairst* in the Home Counties, and no sooner was he there than her youngest brother came downcountry to meet him. The one was manager of the wool mill the MacKendricks had run for so long, the other sold coffins in Harrow.

They came as fugitives from their respective responsibilities and their social positions—into the freedom of Willie Gavin's landscape. Without loss of dignity (or trade) Rob could enjoy his ale at the inn in the kirktoun; Will could swill the dust of the looms well and truly from his throat without fearing any loss of authority. Together, they came home late to keep the crofter man out of his bed ("Where the devil can they be till this hour, Wumman?") or at least make sure he did not lie easy in it.

Rob had a strange charisma, for an undertaker: he was no sooner known to be in the countryside than folk flocked to see him, filling Willie Gavin's house from all corners of the parish. He was Somebody and enjoyed it: he was worth a penny or two folk said, and he never denied it. The pomp of his arrival, indeed, would hardly have disgraced royalty, for he travelled north not by the rigours of rail but in the cabin'd ease of the steamship *Caledonia*, which he left in Aberdeen harbour not a moment before he had sighted the hired car sent to meet him. From its window, as it sped the turnpike road, his eye drank in the countryside; he would be ready to give his verdict whenever he was set down at the top of the Gavin close, and as soon as the crofter man had shaken hands with him and taken charge of his cases.

"The *hairst* will be late this year, Willie."

Some years maybe: "The oats are looking well, Willie."

Or chancing his townsman's arm, as he looked down the old croft's *shifts*: "You'll have a good crop there, Willie."

A stocky, black-moustachioed man with the unfortunate pallor of the burial parlour, he wore his bonnets as broad as those of any ploughman and set squarely on his head—a habit that at once gave credence to the thought that they were not his normal headwear and but newly out of some London draper's drawer. His soberly-refined suits had the kind of cut you could not find in any fifty-shilling tailors, and his patent shoes were unblemished by even the smallest wrinkle.

His appearance betokened what everyone so strongly suspected: a more than passing acquaintance with *siller*. That, the young Gavins were told (when Rob had gone home), he'd made by burying the English in large numbers when they were taken off by the big 'flu epidemic. He had worked night and day, all the skills of his carpentry stretched, till he was forced into ready-mades to keep up with the demand. Poor Rob: he had taken ill himself after the epidemic was over, out of sheer exhaustion of body and spirit. And when he had some come to himself and squared his accounts, he found himself a rich man, set for life. On the strength of it, he had taken a wife late in life and now had a daughter, neither of whom he exposed to his northern relatives.

There was little doubt but that his brief summer sojourn was an escape, a time from the world and his affairs about the sedate streets of Harrow, where he was known to wear the genteel bowler and maybe even that higher badge of public service, the striped *breeks*. Besides his broad bonnet, there would be croft days when he would come down to the informality of shepherd's tartan trousers, worn with his funeral-black jacket. When he took through the countryside thus attired, he was an impressive—if alien—figure. There was hardly an afternoon that did not find him on the road for he was asked to tea here, there, and everywhere. He took leave to look over many a roadside dyke in the passing and be quite cantingly critical of the work going on beyond it. He would be scathing about the *stooking*, the capability of the man on the binder. Yet his presumption was soon forgiven him, for there was this you could also say for Rob: if he was quick with his opinion, he was not slow with his *siller*, in the inn or elsewhere. Short of that small-talk that beguiles a bairn, it would not be long before he was reaching his hand into his pocket to compensate the child with a silver coin. The children of the countryside soon came to know it and went far out of their way whiles to encounter his good-will.

In other ways, too, he was a man of singular habits, and almost all of them played hell with the croft morning. He would not sit to his (late) breakfast till he had washed and shaved and put on his collar and tie—a ridiculous refinement in any croft kitchen. And when he was ready to sit down, so to speak, he would insist on eating his porridge standing up, his back to the fire, in spite of all the inconvenience it caused.

"Sit ye doon man, an' tak' yer pairritch in comfort," Grannie Gavin would advise him (in the interest of avoiding further delay), trying to get at the pots on the boil behind him.

"No, Jess, thank you," she would be told solemnly. "I'm fine as I am. It's the straight sack that fills the quickest."

It was a truism that any *fee*'d farmtoun laddie could have vouched for but typical of the droll aphorisms the Harrow undertaker would hurl about him during the course of his fortnight's stay. His personal-cleanliness habits especially, drove the old crofter man clean out of humour at times, especially if the *hairst* was bad.

"It's as weel, Wumman, that he did not bring his family wi' him," Willie Gavin would say, when the coast was clear.

"God be thankit for it," his wife would reply, in fervent agreement, her gratitude for that overwhelming for the moment her horror of vain usage. "Gin I had them here as weel, among my feet, I would never get a cow milkit nor a hen meated."

Yet the sovereign or two he would set down on the garret's chest of drawers when Willie Gavin had taken his cases out to the car wonderfully softened the memory of his visit, and when he left it was always with a cordial "Haste ye back" ringing in his ears. Since he was paying for the car and it had to come back to the parish anyway, he was never short of a send-off. All the Gavins who could get away were inclined to pack into it, to make his departure something of an outing.

Aboard the *Caledonia* for his voyage home, they marvelled at the way he spoke to the crew and to the steward who took his cases below. And they marked his sadness.

"Ach, it is a pity that all good things have to come to an end," he might say as they all stood on deck taking a look from the harbour round the fine granite town.

"I'd like fine, Willie, to have an acre or two of ground . . . Some small place, when I retire. It would be fine to be out from among the coffins for the last of my days."

Maybe he truly wished it; we cannot know now, one way or another. He was held by a position, a woman and a bairn; yet he may have hungered for that old countryside he had known as the weaver's laddie. Or maybe it was only a dream that he had; a dream in his head. But Rob MacKendrick never came back to his native landscape to stay and put down roots again. Nor did Fiona. Nor Geordie, who spent his life helping folk who were even poorer than the crofter folk themselves. Not even Angus and his shingled lass from the Shires, for she had gotten Angus in the end. There was word for a time that Angus *might* come back. But he stayed away and bought a fine house and his bairns spoke nothing but school English.

So, yearly, the young croft folk went back to their city beats and their matron's rounds, their lathes and their ledgers; to stronger suns and darker continents. When they had gone the country would be quiet, the *hairst* sheaves home and a stillness on the land as it came into the fall of the year. They were the summer folk; they had broken that old continuity of family and landscape, broken away from the crofting dream. Though they might feel the pull, they would not be coming back to re-people the old crofts. That had saddened Willie Gavin and Lang Andra McCaskill and, for all we know, Puir Angus McPhee. It seemed they might be the last of their folk to work the small patchwork fields.

XVI

A Thread from the Past

THE GAVINS, LIKE the rest of the croft folk, shaped no destinies, not even their own. Their lives were dominated by the prices of meal and corn and what a *stirk* would bring in. Yet their crofting years would bring undreamt-of change. On the land the machine-age would transform the old patterns of agriculture; travel would move from shank's mare to the threshold of the jet age.

Old John Gavin had been a man in his prime in the days of railway mania, yet he never boarded a train in his life. His grandson and favourite companion was with him in the early-1900s when the first motor car was seen approaching along the narrow beige road that ran past the croft and the old crofter had to be persuaded not to run for his life. His turkeys and guinea-fowl, equally terror-stricken, scattered in all directions and did not come home for days. When the first motor-bicycle came to the Gavin croft the old woman who so fearlessly faced the bees brought out a box of matches when it came time for the guest to leave—and then quickly retired from the scene to await the explosion. Grannie Gavin was twenty-two and maid at the up-country merchant's before she saw her first bicycle, a wooden bone-shaker. The shop-boys who later bought iron-made models would be forbidden to take them out on the Sabbath. . . . Train, car—the ubiquitous bike most of all—would bring a rural revolution as far-reaching as the one that had first brought the crofts themselves into being, bringing an end to country life as the Gavins had known it.

Yet there would be continuity of a kind: it came down at Grannie Gavin's fireside on the nights when she kept her grand-children to let her daughters and their men to a harvest supper or the bacchanalia of a Hogmanay ball. These were the nights that knit the generations; when story and legend passed down from the lips of the old to the credulous, receptive minds of the young.

The past came vividly alive at Grannie Gavin's knee; she was a

great tradition-bearer—to use a modish and pompous word that
had no currency in her own time and even now takes away the
warmth of her recollection. Painstakingly she untangled the crofting past, never tired of answering a bairn's foolish questions. It
was a fragile thread but she spun it with fine colours and the kind
of striking detail that would stick in the mind and come back to
you long after she had gone. Though she had worn black for best
for as long as any of her grandchildren could remember, she was
by no means in mourning for her life (though God knows, she had
reason enough). She was a merry story-teller and her grandchildren listened, silent and wide-eyed. On such nights, in the 1920s
and 1930s, in the hushed glow of the oil lamp and the dance of
firelight, it was the spell of a hard landscape that passed down and
with it the lore of the Gavins and the MacKendricks and all their
folk, imprinting identity. Often she would return to the days of her
own childhood and to her grandfather's small place on that wind-
swept hill where the early crofting life had been at its most primi-
tive.

"Where was that, Grannie?"

"On the Perk Hill."

"Far's that?"

"Up the country, lassie. In Lumphanan."

"Is yer grandfather's hoose still there, Grannie?"

"No, lassie. It is gone these many years noo—like nearly all the
folk."

"What were they like, Grannie? Yer grandfather's folk?"

"They were just poor crofter folk, like oorselves." With a
chuckle she would glance at Willie Gavin seated at the other side
of the fire, herself enjoying the joke, her listeners as yet too young
to catch its irony. But they would listen as she told of the Hill and
the old croft life.

Later, scarfed and bonneted against the night air, they went out
to the byre in a body as milking-time came round, the little ones
going down the croft close on Willie Gavin's hand, as yet barely
able to stand and apt to sit suddenly down in its mud if released.
They stood quietly against the byre's lime-washed wall while
Grannie Gavin milked the beasts, their voices stilled for once by
the leap and menace of the shadows brought to life in every corner
by the flicker of the candle lantern. Outside the wind haunted the
old croft *biggings* but inside it was warm with the breath of beasts,

a solitude made mesmeric by the steady slurp-slurp of the *bloo coos'* milk rythmically hitting the side of the enamelled pail.

Coming back up the close, if the night was not chill, there might be time to take a look at the full moon, a yellow disc that hung in the sky over Lang Andra McCaskill's chimney.

"Is that God's lantern, Granda?" It seemed, on the face of it, not an unreasonable supposition.

"Dyod laddie—likely it will be, then." The old crofter man would see no need to refute it.

"They say there's a man in the moon, Grannie."

"An' sae there is, laddie. See ye . . ." The milk pail would be put down for a moment while the young Gavin was lifted to get a better look. "D'ye nae see his een an' his side-whiskers?"

Long he might look, the young Gavin, unwilling to accept defeat. Finally, though, he would be forced to admit that he could see neither eyes, nose nor dundrearies—caught, as he was, between the desire not to disappoint his grandmother and the honesty in all things that was constantly preached at him. Yet even that young, he knew the value of compromise.

"I think, Grannie, that must be the back o' his heid."

Indoors again they were in the private world of Granda and Grannie Gavin. Coats were hung on the passage nails, not to be needed till morning. Now night folded in on the croft *biggings*. Grannie Gavin took off her outdoors apron (finally) and found her knitting and the old folk settled in their chairs at each side of the fire while the bairns played (and as frequently squabbled) on the rug between them. There were minor emergencies in which the smaller children were excused the cold trip with a lantern to the John Gunn. All the same, the proprieties would be observed. Little girls were seated behind their grandmother's chair, shielded from curious glances; small boys took cover behind their grandfather. Both parties would be asked, repeatedly, had they done "their business" and if not, advised and instructed, their grandfather in particular counselling pressure should it be needed.

"*Birss*, laddie. *Birss!*"

Decorum came to disaster only when a young bairn, feeling ignored, so far forgot himself as to rise and bring pot and results on to the rug.

Here was the softer side of the hard mason man, one that the world never saw, as he and his wife, between the wars, again surrounded themselves with children. Willie Gavin liked his grand-children, folk said, better than he had ever liked his own. But maybe it was only that he had more time to give them.

In the young Gavin laddies who might keep him company in his small fields, he inculcated the old ways, maybe judging whiles the man the bairn would become. What he passed down was a landsman's skills. A likely lad would be given a light spade to assist the old man on some crofting task and would be reminded as they came home again and into the croft close:

"See til't that ye clean and oil that spaad, laddie, afore ye put it awa'."

If the boy showed aptitude, he would be allowed to quarter the beasts' *neeps* with the spade; he would be taken to the hoeing with a cut-down hoe and encouraged to walk home from his *yoking's* work like a man, the hoe's shaft across the small of his back and his arms crooked round it. He would be invited to pat cow rumps and hold *stirks* by their halters, and in time to judge crops for their ripeness. He would be given a hay fork to turn the hay in the swath and when he was older and stronger, the *smiler*, the hay-rake, to pull the swathes into windrows. And on a day when the old crofter man took it into his head to *thrash*, he would be given the same fork back again and put into the barn corner to clear the straw as it came off the little mill's shakers.

For such a lad, Willie Gavin, hard man though he was, could make concessions: coming home from the hoeing the lad might have his boots brushed for him with the besom at the croft door before they both stepped in for their supper; a blind eye might even be turned were he to be seen for a moment among the garden strawberries. In time, it might be that the laddie would absorb some of the old man's compassion for dumb beasts and for those folk whom life had maimed.

And there was something else their old grandfather taught the young Gavins: that to survive you had to win. In those long winter evenings with the milking done, he would bring out the *dambrods*, the draughts, that he loved so much, to take on all-comers. In that he made no concessions: he had to be beaten fair and square. It was not that he lacked pity, far from it; only that in a hard world he saw no point in pretending it was otherwise.

With his wide antiquarian interests, it was Willie Gavin who re-peopled the historical past of the countryside for his grand-

children, making them understand how close they stood to the
men who had once walked its old baulks and its burn banks.

"Fa was it bade in the auld castle, Granda?"

"The Forbeses, laddie. Gey cheils all of them."

Excitement would dance in young *een*. "Did they hae fechts,
Granda? Battles, like long ago? Folk fechting wi' swords and such-
like?"

If Willie Gavin was not the man to tell lies, neither would he
willingly have stunted a young imagination; he would get round it
neatly. "Well, I never heard tell o' that, laddie, but maybe . . . They
were sair times lang syne." In truth it was not only its history that
took the mason man still on a walk to the castle on a fine Sabbath
but his admiration for the men who had *biggit* it; he went to marvel
at the way its mortar had weathered the years. He would have
liked fine to have built a castle in his time.

"Did they fecht at Harlaw, Granda?"

"I kenna gin they did or no'."

"Didnae the king himsel' come once to the castle?"

"Long syne, I believe. Jeemes the Saxt, not long after they had
biggit it."

"They say that one laird saved a king's life."

"Aye, and so he did, laddie. The tenth laird. He was a colonel of
horse at the Battle o' Worcester. Doon in England that was, in
1651 or thereaboots. The poor king had his horse shot from under
him. . . . The laird, he swung his whole troop around him ——"

"Was the king kil't, Granda?"

"Na, laddie. . . . The laird does nae mair but pit the king intill
a sodger's coat and pits a bleedy rag roond his heid to make him
look wounded-like—and then sets him on his ain horse an awa' tae
safety, aff the field!"

Strange they thought it that history had brushed so close to
them there by the fire on a winter's night; strange to think now of
that laird, who had lost all his *siller* in the disaster of Darien; or
the one who came after him, bankrupt but defiant, entrenched
behind the old castle's wall till the Redcoats came to evict him.

"Was it a ruin lang syne, Granda?"

"No, when my father was a young man there were folk still bade
in it."

Bedtime came always too soon for the younger ones, for under
Grannie Gavin's roof they had expected indulgence. Again there

was discretion as long cotton nightshirts were donned behind either grandfather's or grandmother's chair. A song was sung to forestall tantrums and dispel a few tears, the old crofter man joining in as he took their hands and *convoyit* them as far as the foot of the stair.

> Wee Willie Winkie rins thro' the toon
> Upstairs and doonstairs in his nichtgoon.
> Chappin' at the windae, crying at the lock
> "Are a' the bairnies in their beds
> —it's past echt o'clock?"

Tiny feet tramped their thumping accompaniment, one step after the other, their disappointment forgotten—and suddenly found themselves at their bedroom door. Prayers were said on *clickit* rugs before they climbed under the blankets—muddled orisons that made appeals in their own behoof and for all known and remembered Gavins and all others believed to be deserving cases, the tones of supplication slipping from the school English into the lurching Doric of their own landscape as vocabulary failed them. It is impossible to say what the Almighty made of these garbled messages but, their penury apart, He never did badly by the Gavins and for all their mishanters they never lost faith in Him.

Under Grannie Gavin's care the young ones slept three to a bed under the panelled eaves of their grandfather's garrets, a small Gavin girl between two Gavin boys whom she would cuddle in turn, all innocence yet in her bedding. High on its shelf above them, sconced in its black-enamel holder, the candle was allowed to burn till sleep had claimed them.

The older Gavin grandchildren sat on with their grandparents. Secrets were shared, confidantes made as the firelight dwindled. The speak now would be "grown-up", almost between equals. Affection kindled laughter and even Grannie Gavin herself might be quietly teased. Willie Gavin, they were led to believe, had not been Jess MacKendrick's first love. There had been another, whose name had never been dropped in their hearing, though the reason for his fall from grace was known: he had attempted liberties with Grannie Gavin's young person. Knowingly unknowing, her older grand-daughters slyly abetted such revelations.

"But did ye nae take him back, Grannie?"

"No."

Quiet pressure would elicit that the poor lad, thus disappointed, had gone on to misbehave elsewhere and had been immediately banished from the young Jess MacKendrick's circle.

As often, it was her adventures that seized them: her escape, once, from a blazing attic, her journey home in the kitchen's box-bed in Rob Gibbon's cart.

"Ye was goin' tae die, Grannie, wasn't ye?" Endlessly, insistently, they would need confirmation of that.

And there were other things too, known darkly of Grannie Gavin's past, that were rarely spoken of and might be gleaned only from the guarded gossip of her daughters as they sat round their own firesides. Among them was her encounter with The Convict. Now and then, as the fire wore down and Willie Gavin filled his stump of a Stonehaven pipe for the last smoke before bedtime, a spirit, emboldened, would say:

"Tell us aboot the convict, Grannie—when he captured you and ye didnae ken what tae dae. And he made ye sew a button on till his troosers."

Grannie Gavin, her head mutched still from the byre, would nod gently, staring into the last of the fire, her voice quiet as she told them.

It had been the gloam of a winter's afternoon and only herself about the croft, busy in the kitchen. Sensing his presence, she had turned from the fire to see him, half-hidden in the lobby's shadows. There had been *news* round the country, word from the kirktoun; she had known. He was a dangerous man, so they said. And maybe he was, for all that. But what the young croft wife saw that day was a man driven to the end of his tether by days on the run and exposure; a man in draggled clothes, stolen like enough in the night from some farmtoun that had unwittingly sheltered him—a need and a necessity that had immediately pin-pointed his flight. They had stared at each other, gauging their fright, one of the other.

"You're by yourself?" he asked finally.

"Aye, man." If he sensed the fearless spark in the little woman facing him, he saw also her pity.

"Have ye food? I've no' eaten for days." His accent was from somewhere in the South.

"Little enough, but ye're welcome. Sit ye doon."

Cautiously, listening for noise in the house or in the gathering night outside, he drew the chair out from the end of the kitchen table, between her and the door. It had not troubled her. From the meal girnal she brought the trencher with its piled *farls* of oat-cakes; from the press she set down kebbuck cheese and watched him wolf into it.

"I hiv second day's broth . . ." she offered. "It will tak' but a moment to heat."

"And tea?" he said. "Wid ye make tea?" It was more plea than command. She picked up the iron kettle from the fireside and went to pass him into the porch when he seized her wrist in a desperate grip.

"Where're ye gaun?" He had half-risen from his chair.

"Tae get watter man, from the pail."

"Oh, aye." He sat slowly back on to his chair.

Close to him she saw the state of the clothes he had stolen: the misshapen heavy jacket that some bailie maybe kept behind the byre door to take him across the farmtoun close on a day of *dinging* rain; the *breeks*, buttonless and held by twine, from God knows where, but likely from some shepherd's bothy and used only for the dipping.

"Yer claes are sodden man. Ye'll catch yer death."

Reassured, he released her wrist and when she returned from the porch and filling the kettle she saw he had hung his jacket to dry on a chairback, close to the fire. He broke oatcakes into the broth she set before him, supping it untidily.

"Warm," he said.

She nodded, watching him. "The tea will be drawn in a meenit."

"Hae ye threid?" His broth finished, he had stood up and was looking down at his buttonless trousers. "And a button? Tae mak' me decent."

"Aye, man. But ye'll need tae come near the fire to let me see." She took a mug down from the dresser and poured his tea.

So, in the firelight of that darkening room, Jess MacKendrick had sewn on the button that would save the convict embarrass-ment, he in that moment, more her prisoner than she his. As she stuck the needle back in its cushion on the mantelshelf and put her thimble away, he had shrugged back into his jacket, still damp but at least a little warmer. Under the growth of beard the face had seemed that of a decent man, without evil in it; it was hard to think of the ill he could have done.

Future ploughmen, farmers and crofter men? Perhaps, and already the boy pupils of this small school, paraded for the yearly visit of the photographer, show a stubborn individuality. Fashion ranges from the Puritan-style collar to bow-tied elegance; from warm, leg-warming breeches to short socks and bare knees. Yet all have the kind of sturdy, thick-soled footwear a country child needed for his long walk to school.

Meeting points: *above*, a typical North-east Lowlands smithy, at Lyne of Skene, Aberdeenshire. The smiddy, with its litter of worn wheel-rungs and forlorn ploughs, was where countrymen met while their Clydesdales were shod or an implement mended. *Below*, a country kirk in the Cabrach, in Banffshire, stands lonely amid the still fields. Folk came from far crofts and farmtouns to worship in its pews—and to lie finally in the quiet of its kirkyard.

Men of trade: *above*, a fine example of the old country emporium, at Bridge of Alford in the 1890s. It sold everything from sugar and soap to scythes and cattle-cake and accounts were settled twice-yearly at May and Martinmas. *Below*, the travelling country dealer of the same period, a trader in discarded trifles. He rendered no accounts; his deals were impromptu and if he bought rags he paid for them in chinaware.

Right: Country smith: an old smiddy with old-style chimney at Dallachy in Banffshire. For safety, the roof is tiled above the forge. The two-pronged hand-tool is a pluck.

Far right: Country wife: a quiet scene from the old lifestyle that seems idyllic yet poignantly emphasises the sometimes solitary life of the croft or cottar woman.

Country kitchen: folk did not linger here, and in this bare interior, probably of the 1880s, everything has been swept aside for the comings and goings of the day. Furnishing points: the deece, left, and the wall plate-rack, right. The fireplace shows the links and the crook on which cooking pots were hung as well as the hobs on which black kettles sat. To the right of the fire, hanging on the wall, is the small hand-bellows, and, in the right-hand corner, a little wooden armchair for the child of the house.

Even where a crofter man or small farmer could afford a mechanical reaper, harvest still took his wife and daughters, *above*, out of the kitchen and into the fields to bind and stook. If the task was quicker than the long days spent with the scythe, *below*, it was just as tiring. In time though, machines would end the old work patterns of harvest.

Caught, by the camera. The poacher, *above*, was a familiar sight in the old landscape, a lone figure in the closing dusk, for a rabbit or hare was always a tasty addition to a diet based mainly on oatmeal. It was a time, the early 1900s, when the men of the farmtouns—like the horseman, *below*, at Meiklepark of Oldmeldrum—would cook one in its skin in the hot ash under their bothy fire.

With both horse and farmtoun cart beribboned and garlanded with greenery, this North-east group, about the turn of the century, were probably on their way to a seaside picnic or the summer games. Wherever they went, they travelled lightsomely, for they have a bearded piper as well as a young melodeon-player on board.

"Ye've a barn?" It was the most tentative inquiry.

"My man will be home directly," she said.

In a moment he had been gone, into the deeper dark of the croft house lobby, a shadow an instant later flitting past the kitchen window.

"God be wi' ye, man," she had said, not knowing if he heard her. It had seemed wrong that any human should be hunted so— like a beast.

When Willie Gavin himself came home she would tell him what had happened to the second day's broth she had been heating for him, and though the poor convict's other crime was never known, he went into the Gavins' folk-lore forever as The Man Who Ate Willie Gavin's Supper.

In the last blink of firelight, from the skeletal account and their knowledge of their grandmother's ways, the young Gavins would fill out the portrait of that encounter in an old countryside. They would be the last generation to gather through those long winter evenings round the old croft's fire—the last to know the old crofting life and the ways of the folk who lived it. For all their grandfather's encouragement and his dour discipline, some of them would not be able to tie a *hairst* band or know the need to clean and oil a spade. But they would remember an old man's steely character and a croft wife's charity. None would choose to work on the land. Their only inheritance would be the memories of the crofting Gavins. It was a past binding on the soul.

XVII

The Bonds of Friendship

CROFTER FRIENDSHIP was a fragile thing; it could be ruptured abruptly by your cow in the other man's corn. Yet deeper down there was an underlying unity in crofting society that drew folk together. That it was so was less than surprising: theirs was a community in which self-help, though constantly preached, was a fallible commodity and mutual aid more frequently the hard necessity of a hardy lifestyle. Differences there might be but, for all that, a man would not willingly stand by and see his neighbour lose his crop or in desperate want. Bad illness would bring help, a willing spade or a scythe from along the road, from somewhere else on the hill; death itself, where a man without sons had gone without gathering his *hairst*, the kindly aid that would tide his widow over until such time as she decided her future. The womenfolk, when family tragedy took them from home, or childbed claimed them, would milk each other's cows and feed each other's men. It was more than mere neighbourliness for sooner or later they knew they would need repaying in kind. For the same reason a man was careful not to too far outrage his fellow-crofters; though he might not himself be a regular kirkgoer (and there were few who did not owe allegiance somewhere), however rough his character or his crofting, rarely would he provoke censure by blatantly working his *shifts* on the Sabbath.

The New Year traditionally was the time—as in the world of the farmtouns—when the crofting community came together to resolder old friendship and bury (for a time) ancient vendettas; when passions cooled and all debts were acknowledged. It was a festival in that harsh landscape—like old Beltane and Lammas and All Hallows—that for all their kirkgoing came perilously close to the pagan. It had to do with the earth and the soul, with nature and portents; its theme was renewal, the rebirth of the year and through that the rebirth of the spirit. Like most of his kind, Willie Gavin held to Aul' Eel (Old Yule). It was the trait of a persistent man, and one widely shared in a region where the elderly, refusing to nod to the calendar's change of a century and half earlier, still counted their days by the old feasts, Handsel Monday, and Fastern's E'en (with its bannocks and brose) and lovely old Candlemas among them. It was a calendar, that old one, whose seasons and days more closely marked their everyday lives (and their backward agriculture); its customs at times had long roots in the past that didn't bear scrutiny. It was a calendar richer than ours, with its grey insistent days, and it is strange to think that it died without a conservationist's whimper. Aul' Eel had been its anchor-point and it was still, in the 1930s, one of the festivals from which the old crofter man dated events. His speak would be reflectively punctuated with "Just afore Lammas, that would have been..." or "That would have been about Aul' Eel".

Hogmanay, like Halloween, had once been a festival to older and darker gods, all of them now long forgotten; the last day and night of the year, it drew to it in the old landscape much of the spirit of modern Christmas (then a normal working period); its goodwill and good fellowship certainly, if none of its religious observance. As the year drew to an end straw would be *fordeled*, stored ready, so that none need put a hand to the flail all the days of the holiday. Willie Gavin, in his time, put on his small mill and threshed beforehand: his beasts would share in the season's goodwill. If, as in his father's boyhood, the *clyack* sheaf, that totem to future fertility, no longer came down from the barn's rafters as a treat for the *shelt*, the mason man would make sure, all the same, that his *bloo coos* had a turnip or two extra in their troughs on New Year's morning.

As the last night of the year drew in and all work stopped on the land and in the farmtouns of that far countryside, visiting bairns would hang their stockings from Grannie Gavin's mantelshelf and become increasingly anxious as the evening wore on: had Santa been notified of their temporary change of address? With endless patience, their old crofter grandfather reassured them. In the night outside, older children came to ring the croft-house door, swinging leering *neep* lanterns (a ring of toothy faces, when you opened the door), and cry the old orisons that linked that night with the guiser's past and an earlier, unChristian time:

> Rise up, gudewife, an' shak' yer feathers,
> Dinna think that we are beggars.
> We're only bairnies come tae play—
> Rise up and gie's oor Hogmanay.

On a night of storm the pleas would be torn from their lips and lost on the howl of the wind. That, or the failure to stir the *gudewife*'s heart at first, would lead to a further supplicatory chorus, chanted with urgency. Often enough on such a night it had a literal truth that gave it point, and at times maybe poignancy:

> Wir feet's caul', oor sheen's thin.
> Gie's a *piece*, an' lat's rin.

A *piece* it seldom was, for the *gudewife* of the croft or farmtoun, frantically preparing for the holiday, would not have time to make them one. But apples and oranges were as well-received, or a slice of seedcake that could clog your jaws for days after, and with them, perhaps, pennies would be handed round with the old salutation: "A happy Hogmanay tae ye". Few were refused on that night of nights, though folk should go begging in the morning. Yet by the 1920s and 1930s, as Willie Gavin came near to the end of his crofting days, the *neep* lanterns and the old chants were almost part of the past; they would largely die out round the countryside as the old-style cottars and crofters left it.

When their voices had faded on the night, a quiet would come down on the old croft dwelling and in that hour or two before the turn of the year, its hush was filled with the whispering of Willie Gavin's clocks in their conspiracy to end it.

Though he had no ill-will at a dram, it was only about the New Year, the end of *hairst* or a threshing or in the social climax to a wedding or a funeral that the old crofter man himself would take one. It was only at those times too, and maybe for the summer guest, that the croft's bottle was taken from the cupboard. But at Old Yule he bought goodwill as willingly as the next man and with a good grace received the first-footers of the year, taking a dram from their bottles and giving one from his own. The New Year was like the day of a fair or a feeing market, a kind of lighthouse in the year that men looked to from time to time as they charted their way across it. It was a point of destination, a landfall they reached when they had sometimes doubted it, and there were times, with relief in their souls, when they celebrated it with all the gratitude of folk who had just survived shipwreck. Poor though the croft folk were, the bottles went round with abandon, for theirs was a hardy voyage and the wind never with them.

Cottared sons-in-law (on a spree by themselves or bringing the old man's daughters with them), neighbours and folk whose degree of relationship was tenuous but would not that night of the year be inquired into (even if it could have been determined) came in from the dark for their glass and to give seasonal greeting and stayed to make fools of themselves by forgetfully trying to tell the coarse kind of story that would put them clean out of countenance for years to come. Old soldiers whose only battle-ground now was their small croft *shifts* stepped in off the road worsened by drams and drank on till the old scars of war re-opened like raw, bleedy wounds inside them and they marched Grannie Gavin's stone kitchen floor with her besom (seized from the porch) at the slope, shouting and shouldering and presenting arms as it all came mercilessly back to them, nearer to them still than the old acquaintance of the folk who sat round them; till the memory of it all shook them shivering cold sober.

More cheerful, peace-loving men wandered in on nights of *blind smorr* (just in the bygoing, they insisted, shaking the snow from their whiskers and their coats) to give the old crofter man and his wife that old salutation:

"A guid New Year, Willie. Tae yersel' an' a' yer fowk."

And, catching Grannie Gavin's eye, from some man, well-liked: "A guid New Year tae ye, Jess—you're keepin' weel?"

"A guid New Year—and many of them," Willie Gavin would wish his guests, that response as ancient, as ritually deep in the old pattern of the occasion as the greeting itself.

"Please God, she will be a better one than the last."

That, always, was the fervent wish, the glimmer of hope: that next year's crop and next year's *stirks* might bring better prices and some relief if not comparative prosperity (which was too much to ask for). With the last harvest now well behind them they could look back, stoically.

"She was an ill-*hairst*, this year by-past."

For a moment amid the conviviality of that night, the heartbreak of it came back to them, the memory of the laid crops, the way the *stooks* had stood long and *drookled* in the farmtoun parks till they had taken root where they stood, the rain never-ending.

Other men, too, stepped in from the dark—uncertain of whose house they were in as their heads swam and the cogs of memory slipped—to spout toasts that were doggerel pure and simple and yet in a crofter's world were profoundly relevant.

> Here's tae the warld that gangs roon' on wheels,
>   Death is a thing that ilka man feels.
> If life was a thing that ane could buy
>   The rich wid live and puir wid die.

Or, from the ecological panjandrum, and parodying the poor crofter's plight:

> Here's tae the tatties
>   Far e'er they be.
> The skins feed the pigs
>   An' the pigs feed me.

Neighbouring croft men brought their womenfolk with them, their country first-footer's gift of a quarter-pound of tea, a half-pound of sugar or a jar of preserve, something they could well have done with keeping for themselves. But as they so often said: "A friend's gain is nae loss."

By the 1920s and 1930s, the old women who had taken a dram (and the smoke of a clay pipe) along with their men were long into the kirkyard and their daughters more genteelly welcomed in the New Year with circumspect sips of port or the last home-brewing of elderberry wine. All the same, there were times when they might have done better to follow the old wives' example for there were croft women in that old countryside who made home-wine more damaging than bad whisky. Innocents who supped it unguardedly might soon have to be helped home the worse for it—or so unaccustomedly flushed and chattering as to be in imminent danger of letting out in loud whispers all their family's secrets. Favourites—kin and close friends—might sit sociably through the night-long traffic. When they had swallowed their drams they would be given tea while the folk came and went: out to get home, or to go to the edge of the *midden* and be sick and get over it.

Bonnets, politely doffed, dangled from slippery serge knees and fell periodically on the floor where, as the night went on, their retrieval became increasingly perilous. Men unaccustomed to the drawing-room graces juggled tea cups in their saucers in one hand, a slice of seedcake on a delicate plate in the other, an art so diabolically difficult that only the socially gifted could manage it and the older croft and farmtoun men would wave the cake-plate away with an imperious:

"Na, na . . . I'll tak' it in my hand just."

But in time even friends went home, out into a northern night hung with stars, their cry coming out of the dark as they headed up the croft close:

"Guid nicht and Guid be wi' ye."

It would be morning, and milking-time, soon enough.

It was a night that took its toll; with such a surplus of goodwill that was inevitable. Men did a mischief to themselves and to folk who were with them, and some had the kind of luck that could only be marvelled at and made them a legend in the land. Munro, long in the *smiddy*, had a journeyman smith whose bowing of an old Scotch fiddle was second to none in that long-ago landscape. Such was his artistry that folk passing by his roadside bothy on a summer night would stop to listen to the old airs that he wrung so sweetly from the strings. But Montgomery had two other loves: the drams (like fiddlers all) and his motor-bike. There was never a New Year's morning when he was not found—slightly the worse for the one but safe in the saddle of the other—in the ditch into which he had ridden it. Sober, he was a shy man and a fine smith.

With the New Year past, the croft folk looked forward, with hope, to the spring. The mason man's thoughts would be on the work he would be starting as soon as the frosts would let him. The evenings given to his children, playing draughts and dominoes and snakes and ladders or maybe hide-the-thimble, would be taken up with the men who came to see him—building men like himself, wondering would there be work with him again that year. They would time their arrival to find Willie Gavin, the milking done, still in the byre. It was, after all, a warm place to do business and the two of them would stay out there long after Grannie Gavin had gone to the house. A man whose work the mason man regarded as competent (provided he was not a trouble-maker or addicted to bouts at the bottle) would get a fair hearing and a likely starting date; stronger favourites or other master masons, some agreement reached, would be brought to the house for a cup of cocoa and a biscuit before cycling off again into the night on the wobbly glimmer of a fitful gas lamp. For business, in that old landscape, fused strongly with friendship.

For all its hardship, it was a sociable countryside. Croft wives found time (between feeding beasts and men and hens) to go visiting and in some of the old croft kitchens indeed there was a social graciousness that would have surprised the outsider. Many of the croft wives, after all, had been in service in their younger years, like Jess MacKendrick herself—at the manse maybe, or even the Big House—and when they put away their sacking aprons for an hour or two in the middle of the afternoon the tea-tray they laid lacked little but the sheen of the laird's silver sugar-bowl.

Their dress aprons then would be black with a brightening of *broderie*. Even so, these would be removed before they answered the door. To have done less would have been impolite, and the apron could always excusably be donned again when it came time to make the tea. Given that it was almost their only recreation, the gossip was less genteel. Inevitably, it concerned the countryside and its folk; few escaped with a clean character. Like the frail, babies were visited and welcomed into the world and invariably had silver coins thrust into their small clutching fists, not in the hope that it would set them on the road to much-needed riches (though that was better than crofting) but to bring luck to the donor, who might have more immediate need of it.

Still summer nights were enlivened by the occasional feet-washing, that ancient pre-nuptial rite that took on, at times, all the character of a human steeplechase as the victims were run down and plastered from head to toe by black-lead, black axle-grease (whatever might cause the most havoc) and sprinkled with flour. It was a ritual as old in the Highlands, an indication perhaps of how close the landscapes once had been, but less vicious there than in the farming North-east Lowlands, where it stopped just short of taking life.

It was a landscape in which rank got the respect it deserved, and in which the laird, with his old house, stood at the centre of rural life, a considerably greater figure then than now. If he went from home for a time, his welcome back could be effusive—maybe in the hope he would not put the rents up, but as often with a genuine response that betrayed the interdependence of a close-knit society. Here is such a reception, described in *We Twa*, the combined memoirs of Lord and Lady Aberdeen, a well-loved pair, published in 1925 after a lifetime's lairdship. It was a chilly November evening towards the close of the 1800s, but even a monarch could hardly have made a more triumphal progress. When the laird and his party reached their home station it was ablaze with light and most of their tenantry awaited them.

As we drove home every cottage and every farm was illuminated. Bonfires blazed along the route and groups of cheering spectators and children seemed to spring up at every corner.

An arch of fairy lights had been erected at Raxton Lodge entrance, and within half a mile of the house the carriage was stopped by a party of 170 torch bearers, who insisted on taking the horses out and dislodging the coachman, replacing him by a piper. So, to the tune of "The Gordons hae the guidin' o't", our carriage was dragged along by a stalwart band and escorted by a torchlight guard of honour to Haddo House, where every window was illuminated, fireworks being let off, and a great bonfire burning.

It was an occasion, of course, that neatly stratified the estate's tenantry, and though they carried no torches, put their shoulders to no carriage or spoke any word of welcome, there were crofter men on the fringe of that vast assembly who raised their bonnets and cheered with the rest. Among them were Old John Gavin and his mason son.

Yet rank never held the monopoly in friendship and the man selling besoms, or the tinker-wife, would be "Hallo'd" on the road and as warmly greeted and given a drink of milk on the doorstep. Many of the wandering folk of the old countryside came round the crofts year after year till the people would ask after the wife's man and all her bairns. Willie Gavin all his life had a weakness for the packman who hawked his wares round the country doors. Just the sight of the pedlar turning down the croft close was enough to make him drop his hoe in the drill and come home to buy more bootlaces than he would ever have need of and more collar studs than a careful man like himself was ever likely to lose. And the sight of a good pocket knife in the old man's pack never failed to excite him like a school laddie.

The arrival of the rag-and-bone man's pony and cart, too, would take him home to the croft *biggings* in a hurry—just for a *news* of the "ragger" and maybe to see that Grannie Gavin got a fair deal for the rags she had not as yet hooked into the heart of a rug. The deals with the rag-and-bone man were about the last bastion of barter in the old landscape for coin never came into it. Old John's grandson remembers the visits of Raggie in the early years of the century as well as the disability that had first turned him to his trade:

> He used to go round all over the countryside, picking up old bottles, rags—anything that would be regarded by the average person as scrap. He picked up all this sort of stuff. In exchange for a fair-sized bag of rags he would give the housewife a couple of bowls or a cup and a saucer or a few plates, or something like that—it was all china that he carried.
>
> He was a kindly old soul, well-liked by the children and adults alike. But he had only one arm. He must have lost his left arm some time early in life—I never heard how. But he was quite adept at using his one arm; he would grab a bag of rags and toss it on the hook-scale without bother. He was a noted character all over the countryside.

That the croft folk's welcome should be so cordial is little to be wondered at, for their own circumstances in life were little better. Old John Gavin, with his own *shelt* and cart, was on the road almost as often as any rag-and-bone man and frequently with less errand. He had been a sociable man, the old farmtoun horseman, easing himself through life without worry and occasionally with the help of the whisky bottle, and in his old age especially he had been most ably abetted by his sociable *shelt*. Whenever the croft work grew sore on him, he would yoke Meggie into the cart—his rig no different from the "ragger's"—and find a need to go somewhere: to deliver honey to the railhead shop; to fetch hens' feed; cow's oilcake; netting wire for a new hen's *cruive; backs* (those first bark off-cuts of the tree-trunk) from the sawmill.

In the little kirktoun he had many convivial friends, notably the innkeeper, who liked nothing better than a dram with cronies about the middle of the day (it was trade, after all). The two of them would sit well into the afternoon till the *shelt*, with more sense than its master, would come to the inn window to look in on them, knowing it was time they should be home. There were times when Old John was so low he would have to go to the sawmill several days in succession and years, as a result, when he had so many *backs* about the croft that he could have built the OK corral. As for the *shelt*, its behaviour was a disgrace and an embarrassment to the abstemious son when the old man had gone, for it stopped always at every inn they came to.

In that old landscape entertainment had been rustically simple, a pattern of ease, centuries old, that slotted neatly into the farming calendar: a once-a-year visit from the travelling circus about the end of *hairst* (in its small tent, lit by flares, a man walked tall on stilts stealing the sad clown's laughter); concerts of sorts later on in the deep of winter that brought faded sopranos out from retirement in Aberdeen (most did not travel well); the Oddfellows' Ball (and for that a lass, the maid at the manse or the merchant's, had to be asked for and went only with the kind of lad who could be relied on to return her in the condition he found her). It was a calendar that fitted its gatherings and its shows into that lull before the *hairst*.

The games had been the delight of Old John Gavin's year. If he could not travel like his laird to see the world it was this yearly event—in the grounds of the laird's Big House—that brought some of a changing world's wonders to him, for a day. The old crofter attended them until he had almost to be carried there. His grandson, who would read the programme to him to whet his excitement, recalls the wonder of that country occasion:

> The games were on a big scale and they had something really outstanding every year . . . Something really significant to draw the crowds. One year they had a lady go up in a balloon . . . after a considerable time had elapsed she came down again.
>
> The next year they had an aviator—this was in the infancy of aviation—an aviator of considerable repute, one of the pioneers, and he flew round the park where the games were being held in his aircraft, barely above the treetops. And that was something sensational to see in those days.
>
> That would draw a big crowd: they would come by the thousands and there were no motor cars in those days—they were all horse-drawn vehicles that used to be identified as charabancs; they could accommodate anything from twenty to fifty passengers on board and they would be drawn by anything from six to a dozen horses . . .

For all the wonders of that day though, the daily round of that far countryside was still one which was read for sign and portent;

where the tea-leaf circling your cup brought a stranger to the door, as did the knife that fell to the floor; where a blue gleam in the fire-flame foreshadowed the storm to come, like the ring round the moon; and the spark flying out from the fire to you meant a letter in the post ("Yer gaun tae get news"). If belief at times was thin, it mattered little, for those were merely the things that added dimension to the days.

It was a society—that of the old crofting hillside—in which friendship knitted deeply with the social hour, much more than in our own time, and understandably enough. Though suburban man can ignore his neighbour (and usually does), the croft man could hardly afford to; the time came soon enough when he had to rely on him. If the crofter men at the end of their hard *hairsts* held no meal-and-ales, those orgiastic harvest suppers of the big farm-touns, that is not to say that they did not invite near-neighbours for a dram and their supper when they all had "winter". To end such an evening, Willie Gavin liked the *cairds*, the cards, an un-expected weakness that must have come down in his father's rakish blood; there were few things he liked more—having trounced a few folk at the *dambrods*—than a hand or two of whist with worthy adversaries. But the play was for pleasure alone: no-body played for stakes at Willie Gavin's table, no more than they played on the Sabbath.

Like the land itself, friendship had its rituals. In all but the most savage weather, visitors to the Gavin croft were *convoyit*, accompanied a little of the way home, when it came time for them to leave; that was the custom, anciently observed, and departure with less ceremony would have told the thickest-skinned guest that he had over-stayed his welcome and to be in no hurry back. Willie Gavin himself *convoyit* the menfolk (it was the moment for the quiet confidence, the private word, something they had not been able to exchange at table); Grannie Gavin accompanied the women at about a fifty-yards distance, out of earshot, taking stock of such female affairs as could not be mentioned in mixed com-pany. It would have been insult pure and simple not to have been *convoyit* past McPhee's on the one side or McCaskill's on the other, and on a summer night the custom could be extended for so long that a man wanting home to feed beasts would think he was never going to get away.

For all its poverty it was a society in which care was deep and rooted; unlike our own, it cared for its old and kept them in the bosom of the family even if it sometimes tired of their opinions. The heat of a summer's day would bring the aged patriarchs of the croft hills and colonies from their winter ingles to look over the landscape and the burgeoning fields their sweat had created. Frailer still, they would be brought to the croft doors in their chairs to sit heavily-jacketed in the sun as their last days slipped from them. What saw they then, you would wonder whiles, as they sat looking out on that countryside that stirred with the shades of Dane and Highlandman, Royalist and Covenanter, Jacobite and Redcoat, that unquiet land where the old gods stalked and the past was not still.

And there was yet another side to friendship: the sorrow shared. Grannie Gavin was no stranger to it: death, like birth or disaster, could bring a knock to her door. When tragedy struck or an old person eased out of this world, whether in the crofts community or among the encircling farmtouns, it was often to the Gavin croft that folk came, sad-faced, to seek after her to wash and dress the corpse and lay it out for the coffin. It was something she would do without question, as a matter of duty, never refusing however tenuous the friendship or family connection and whatever her own health at the time. Frail though she seemed whiles as the years came on her, she would sit with the dying through the dark regions of the night (so that their folk might get sleep) and be in her own byre for the milking in the morning. In the death-room so strong was her faith that she bore up others in their grief; weighed down with its indignities, she scrupulously kept its secrets. Afterwards she would stay a night or two with a new widow till she got used to the terrible silence of her house and never the scrape of her man's foot on the door-flag.

Providence was Jess MacKendrick's staff and her consolation and she advised everyone to put their faith in it; it was her own caution in the everyday affairs of life, so strongly felt that even an invitation accepted would immediately bring its proviso: "Gin we all be spared", or "Gin Providence spare us". A merry woman, it seemed whiles that her life was hedged round with the knowledge of death; its shadow brushed her, saddening her for a day or two. In condolence she wrote letters expressive of a loss deeply shared, her penmanship (even into her nineties) in the scrawny Gothic of her day such that it was impossible to believe that her schooling had ended at the age of ten; her sentences never offended against the rigid tenets of the dominie's grammar and often caught deep and poignant truths in their simple grace. Equally, as unstintingly, she counselled mothers in their new-found maternity, comforted occasionally lasses facing confinements without being sure of the father and doubtless, in the bygoing, asked God to forgive them. For the greatest sin in Jess MacKendrick's book—as it had been since she had seen the backsliders cast out of the Scotch Girls' Friendly Society—was a meanness of spirit. That alone could kindle her eyes with anger.

XVIII

The Sabbath Road

THE GAVINS WERE kirk folk and always had been: the psalms
were their rod and had sustained them through many a bad *hairst*
and the kind of crofting catastrophe that two or three sick beasts
could bring. The Sabbath was holy and they kept it. Boots that
were going to the kirk in the morning would have to be cleaned the
night before; broth was made, ready for re-heating; potatoes, pre-
peeled, were potted and set down at the side of the fire ready for
salting and setting on to boil the moment the croft's folk came in
from the sermon. Not a needle stirred from its case, not a darn was
done, and if you were too late in discovering it you went to the
kirk with a hole in the heel of your sock uncomplaining rather than
break the Lord's Commandment. Bairns were kept in their best
suits all day to discourage the temptation to play; no newspapers
were glanced at (for fear of eternal damnation) and the only book
read was the Bible. About that old countryside, it was said, there
were small places where uncompromising men, well up to the turn
of the century (and maybe beyond it), carried the *neeps* to their byre
beasts that day in muddy armfuls in their best suits (and sometimes in their best patent boots) rather than turn a barrow wheel
and defile the Sabbath, though on any other day they would bow
to nobody.

On Saturday nights Willie Gavin shaved the frail grey stubble
from his chin, a week's growth that would be unless there was
an Oddfellows' meeting or a funeral intervening. It was a pre-
Sabbath ritual. His cut-throat came out of its thick cardboard case
in the *closet* drawer to be stropped sharp on the strap that hung
between Spurgeon and the kitchen mirror and had, it was hinted
darkly, been put to other uses. Latterly, when the years had shaken
his hand, there was hardly a time when the old man did not nick
the thin skin of his cheek, or his chin, and on winter nights he
would need the *closet* mirror on the table, and the small paraffin
lamp beside it, to see his work. Unless he was bedded with illness,

Willie Gavin went unswervingly to the kirk, and unless you were at death's door you were expected to go with him. For when he took the kirk road he carried his brood with him: as many of his kin and cottared daughters as could be conveniently assembled at the croft beforehand—and as many of their bairns as were reasonably presentable and could be relied on not to disgrace him.

For long after coming to the croft the Gavins had kept faith with the Free Kirk, the crofter's kirk, in the small quarrytoun. It had been Old John Gavin's kirk and likely his mother's kirk before him. Each Sabbath the Gavins had walked up through Laverockhill's fields to cross the old ridge track and strike on to the Cadger's Road that led all the way to the sea and brought the herring from it still, creeled on a lass's back. In Willie Gavin's grandmother's time—she had been forty at the Disruption—the Free Kirk had been strong in the land. Its fiery and demanding God had been taken round the countryside like a beacon and even Old John, strong though he was in the faith, had been later discomfited whiles, as he sat in his pew, by the unexpected announcement:

"Brethren, there will be a service this afternoon in Mister Gavin's barn, at three."

Old John had gone home in high dudgeon, ill-pleased at not even being consulted and as ill-suited at having to gulp his kail dinner to get out and make the barn presentable. The old crofter had not been sorry when they found a new man for the Free Kirk pulpit, an easier man with his own kind of indolence. But those days that had divided a countryside and its folk were bye with now; dogma had diluted to allow the men of the breakaway kirk to come again, all rancour stilled, under the roof of the laird's church and with that Willie Gavin had taken God at his nearest point, the kirktoun's Congregational.

The crofter man had paid a half-crown in the year for his Free Kirk pew and never counted it money ill-spent: it did a man no harm to hear the Word whiles, he said. But the Congregational was good for his credit and kept him in the laird's eye (which was another form of insurance). He was never more the patriarchal figure than when he turned out at the end of his croft close on to the road with his best walking stick (taken down from behind the kitchen door) and his tribe trailing him. Willie Gavin had always walked to the kirk: that was the custom—maybe it would have been unseemly to approach Him on a bicycle. For all his years, he stepped the road in style, setting the pace, discussing the close-lying parks with those of his cottared sons-in-law who had seen nothing for it but to accompany him. On a fine summer day, heady with the smell of clover, or with the hedges hanging in hawthorn or the verges clouded with wild parsley, it was like an outing almost. Though the rest of his folk might be ignored, Willie Gavin himself would be saluted from every passing gig and "Hallo'd" and "Fine morning'd" from every bicycle, and if the old man had his own reservations he showed no ill-will towards them, raising his staff in acknowledgement of the greetings. It was possible to say whether he was early or late on the road by taking note of the point at which Laverockhill's phaeton passed them for Laverocks was a grand time-keeper and folk that day would set their watches by him for the week following.

Unless the party caught up with a slower assembly and had to adjust its progress (for to nod and pass on would have been un-thinkable) Willie Gavin would have allowed time for them all to get their breath back and for a turn round the kirkyard. There, indeed, was a whole history of the countryside ("Their folk were long in Braeside," as you passed one stone; "Your cousin's folk," at another). There, also, was an ancestral past that haunted the present and family scandals long buried but not forgotten.

It was Willie Gavin's inviolable rule to go in at the kirkyard door and there, unless it was a day of storm or driving rain, there would be a word with old neighbours, exchanges with other sprigs of the family. Among the immediate gravestones, where the grass was always well trampled and unlikely to wet your ankles, Willie Gavin usually met his sister Mary and her husband who had almost overnight become a man of substance and some celebrity. His rise was a byword about the parish and Willie Gavin was never sorry to be seen in his company. From farmtoun strapper, driving the phaeton of a considerable cattle-breeder, he had risen on the unstayable tide of his master's success (and wealth) to be his chauffeur and the driver of almost the first motor-vehicle in the district. Folk without family connection thought it an honour just to say "Hallo" to him and he had come to enjoy as much esteem as the Great Man himself. In fact, Johnny Gordon had so far come up in the world that on a weekday as he took past at the wheel of the Great Man's Model T he had to avoid nods to the lesser placed of his relatives and they in their turn soon forgot to salute him and so save him the embarrassment of their acquaintance. Wherever the Great Man went, Johnny Gordon went; together they went south to the sales where, it was said, the Great Man even took Johnny into the exhibitors' tent for his lunch with the result that Johnny found it increasingly hard to call common folk his equal. His master, it was hinted, had become so dependent upon his man during their ceaseless travels that he would hardly dare buy a bull-calf without Johnny's good opinion. Out of the sober grey of his weekday livery and the official severity of his chauffeur's cheese-cutter hat, Johnny Gordon had lately succumbed to the flamboyance of crotal tweeds and almost peach-coloured boots, polished till they matched his roseate complexion. He was an affable man at a kirk door.

In the gallery pew the Gavins filled each Sabbath there was social as well as tactical advantage: you were, so to speak, up there for all the folk to see and at the same time looking down on them, the minister included, for his pulpit was just below you. For an ageing man Old McCaid was still in vigorous command of the Word, much given to exhortation and the fistic utterance. There was never a Sabbath when he did not beat hell out of the Book in front of him. Indeed, a shrewd mind might have thought Willie Gavin had selected his pew with unusual care for it was, as it were, also behind the old preacher's back and one got peace to sit there out of range of his watchful eye—except when he swung suddenly round, his face uncomfortably close, as though demanding your personal indictment for some sin or slip of behaviour. Willie Gavin was less discomfited usually than his folk, for he sat at the far end of the pew, a sentinel against all escape and handy for the collection plate when it came round. For all that, his interest was not deeply engaged; before long he would have slipped into that gently comatose doze that is ill to define and harder still to detect, and would rouse himself only to pass his bag of pandrops along the pew now and then with a glower that said "Choke on that, gin ye dare!" In fact, there was not one of his grandchildren who, having lined a small cheek with the big sweet, would not have spluttered quietly and died in silence rather than risk his wrath. It is probable that, unlike the rest of his brood, Willie Gavin, with his dour and scrupulous integrity, had little need of God's correction.

If Daft Sandy came in you were bidden not to stare at him for he might catch your eye and call your name, shaming both of you. Poor Sandy was a terrible affliction, too, to his own folk for he would sweep a wild and piercing eye round the pews, fixing his gaze savagely at times where he felt he was being too studiously ignored. Once, to relieve the tension his irregular appearances invariably caused, his mother had remonstrated with him:

"Why d'ye keep lookin' roon' ye—annoying folk?"

Sandy had looked at her straight and unsmiling.

"I was wondering gin God had come in."

Folk that day had not known whether to laugh or pretend not to have heard him. And nobody knew what to tell him.

As the kirk filled the levity of the kirkyard was forgotten; nods were circumspect, the greeting *sotto voce*. Inside there was a holiness, a sanctity; maybe there gathered there still all the long forgotten souls of that countryside. The first notes of the organ sprang resonant and deep from the pipes ranged behind the pulpit, a prelude to plain worship amid the bare brown pews and within plain, white-washed walls. Hymn and psalm were sung with solemn faces; prayer penetrated the simple heart; few there would be that day who were not moved, who did not have someone to think of, some private grief they could not tell. In the kirk on the Sabbath you felt the long continuity of God in that hard landscape that broke men whiles and sometimes inspired them; it passed down like a cloak, the spirit of those long-forgotten folk and the dreams of men whose names were outside on the tombstones—with old Grace in her lair, shrouded in secrets. The organ-notes filled your throat, bringing a lump that refused to go away. Through a veil of tears you saw for a moment that long and painful past: the surprised cry of the Covenanter as the Royalist's steel ran through him; the witch's shrieks on her burning scaffold; the swollen belly of the weeping lass on the penitence stool. What had come over folk then, you would wonder; what fear gripped them that made sweet reason a stranger?

Always the kirk had been there, for good or for ill. The pull had been strong. From all corners of the old countryside folk had flocked to the great kirkings and conventicles of the past—to the five-day Sacraments when first the Free Kirk was born—in their threadbare plaids and their poor shoes, and likely Grace among them. A plurality of preachers had wrestled in relays for souls on the bare hillside and the psalms, precentor-led, had been sung line by painful line. Folk then had not needed the Book for many could not read. At the end, and in their excesses, the big preachings had left folk weeping and unstable, prostrated at times among the gravestones. For all that, the kirk had been good to the crofter folk, with the seed corn from its girnal, the *siller* for a milk cow from its session funds. Folk did not forget: that lived long in the memory of the crofter men.

There was a continuity, too, as they came out from the Benediction to linger at the kirk gate and get the *news* of folk they had missed going in; that was the tail-end of a tradition that stretched back to the days of the *scries boord*, the notice-board, at the kirk gate. It had carried the news of the parish and its projected events like a wall-newspaper, though now it carried nothing but the name of the minister and where that man of kirk business, the session clerk, could be found.

Cut-throat commerce had once flourished at the kirk gate, to the wrath of the session for all the damage it did to men's souls, and even in Willie Gavin's day inquiries were still discreetly made— for this or that kind of work. If you were on the lookout for a *hairst* man or two or hands for the threshing-mill there wasn't a better place to find them. And still, coming out from the psalms, there was the occasional deal quietly done. His soul succoured, a man might take care of his earthly needs. A farmer-man, looking for *stirks* to fatten and bring on for the mart, would watch his chance among the crofter men, waiting till he saw that the coast was clear.

"Ye will have naething for me i' the noo, Willie?"

The negative, back-handed inquiry was a part of the bare Northeast Lowlands landscape, at the centre of its lifestyle; its negligent off-handedness avoided any bruising of egos; the bad refusal; obligation of one to another—and, totally, anything that smacked of outright commitment. It was the careful weapon of men who were maybe the finest cattle-dealers the whole breadth of the country, a disinterest at times so studied that it profoundly shook a man's belief in his own beasts and invariably took a pound or two off the price of them.

Willie Gavin though was a careful man.

"Naething much i' the noo, Charlie. Unless ——"

Men baited and laid verbal traps for each other with quiet guile.

"I could look in-bye." The response would be suitably guarded.

"Aye, surely then, gin ye happen to be on the road."

Willie Gavin, the old crofter man, loved the gambits, the careful nuances, and hardy old card-player that he was, he could play his hand as well as any. He would set away home from the kirk well-pleased with himself, stepping out in silence as he worked out in his mind the price he would be asking—and the one he expected to get.

On the Sabbath grace was said at the Gavins' dinner-table with all the meaning and added solemnity that day gave it, for hard though things were there was a memory of those earlier times when the crofter folk had been at their wits' end to provide. That was something else they did not forget in a hurry; and if they did, the next bad *hairst* would be a salutary reminder to them. There would be a hush and Willie Gavin, at the head of his table that day and with his folk around him, would wait for its silence before he bent his head into his hand.

"For that we are about to receive, O Lord, make us truly thankful, Amen."

The simple words were written deep in the hearts of many of the old crofter folk, and though the fashion for saying grace was fading by the 1930s the Gavins held to the past that they knew. The only time the old crofter man would give up his duty was when the minister, maybe after a christening, was bidden to stay for his supper. Then he would ask his guest to say a few words. And so he would, fine words to be sure, graciously said and pleasing to God no doubt if He had a feeling for the felicitous phrases a fine education could bring. Still and all, it was the grace of a man (honest soul though he was) who had never himself faced want or wondered where the rent was to come from. For all the unctuous concern he gave it, it seemed that it never equalled the old crofter's plain words or the dignity he gave them.

When Willie Gavin straightened, it was to reach to the table behind him, where his huge Paisley-patterned red napkin lay on top of the family Bible. He knotted the napkin round his neck for every meal, though table-napkins were as much strangers to the Gavins as to the tables of any of the croft folk. (When you were old enough to do without a bib, you were grown enough to do without a napkin.) That napkin was the most colourful thing in Willie Gavin's life. Its brilliance—brighter even than the faces of the playing cards he favoured so much—in the high noon of his masoning days had enclosed his *piece* dinner: his oatcakes and cheese and the penny Abernethy biscuit (or the apple) that would be his dessert. Lying, its dazzling colour on the black cover of the Gavin Bible, it was as though the two of them held the key to some point of tension in the old man's days. Maybe they did. Or maybe they were no more than the totems of Willie Gavin's life: the spirit and the toil.

Grace said, however, the Sabbath dinner got into its stride, noisy with the sound of quarrelling bairns. It was the family highlight of the crofting week when sons *fee*'d away to the farmtouns or apprenticed to some trade came home with their *news* and daughters cottared and decently married brought their children. On a busy day Grannie Gavin might have as many as three sittings, with the men and children first so that the womenfolk could linger over the dirty dishes and have out their speak. Only family or special friends would be invited for their Sabbath dinner; where the acquaintance was anything less than warm intimacy, folk came to their supper.

There would be talk round the Sabbath table—*news* of family, for it was here that the Gavins took a look at their dirty linen and washed it. There was referral and cross-referral, a reporting back on previous problems: pleas might be made and listened to, backing sought for this or that course of action and quiet blackmail levied where one felt a majority sympathy among others round the table. Willie Gavin listened and gave his opinion against which there was no appeal unless you had Grannie Gavin's ear. Then the table divided: among the men at its head there would be talk of beasts and mart prices, crops and out-going sales; at the other end, *news* of births and deaths and marriages and the whispered aside (that the bairns could not understand) about what some women (they understood) had to put up with. Giggles would get the better of well-feigned astonishment as the women bobbed up and down to refill the potato dish or re-stock the oatcake trencher.

When the cold pudding had gone down and been given time to settle on top of the boiled beef, Willie Gavin would produce his pipe and tobacco mull and rise from the table, and if you were a man or a man-child you did the same; only the womenfolk got leave to sit on. In summer the men would step out to take their smoke and take a turn in the sunshine through the cornyard where those in need, and sometimes the entire company, would relieve themselves against the blind side of a corn rick without ever interrupting their flow of conversation. Wind would be broken (permissible in all-male company) and when everyone was comfortable again Willie Gavin would lead them through his *shifts* to get their views about this or that *stirk*, the progress of his ripening oats or the condition of his grass. He was a great man for asking advice was Willie Gavin, but as his counsellors constantly complained, in the end of the day he was just as damned likely to please himself —which was true. He had never been a man to hand down his responsibilities.

For the chill of a cheerless winter afternoon, the ben-end fire would be lit the moment the Sunday meal was ended. Even before the men had put down their pudding spoons Grannie Gavin would have risen from her seat at the end of the table and, with the tongs, begun piling glowing red coals from the kitchen grate on to the ash shovel. Thus prepared, she set sail for the parlour with her smoking cargo. Having deposited the hot coals in the ben-the-house grate and piled logs on top, she would return to announce, in what had also long been a Sabbath ritual:

"Well sirs, gin ye wid like tae gang throo and tak' yer smoke."

They went, as they were told, out of the way, taking out their pipes as they walked through. Ploughman's twist as thick as liquorice sticks, bought from the grocer and made in an up-country town, was rubbed and rolled in work-calloused palms ready for the pipe-bowl, an art so ingrained in that countryside that long after you could pick out a man on a London bus and know he was raised there from the way he did it. But if it took strong hands to make the twist suitable for the pipe, it took even stronger lungs to get it alight. This indeed was so difficult that seasoned, wizened smokers who lived on practically nothing else had perfected a special technique. A little of the *aise*, the ash, would be saved from the previous smoke and balanced on one edge of the palm while fresh tobacco was rubbed on the other—a trick so fiendishly difficult that you could be an old man before you had mastered it. The ash was then sprinkled over the fresh tobacco to help to kindle it.

It was a tobacco for strong men but even so, the most fearless, with a cast-iron stomach, would have shortened his life by swallowing its juices. The result was that most of the hard-smoking crofter and farmtoun men had cultivated yet another ancillary art: that of spitting. It is fair to say that Willie Gavin was always very good: on weekdays he could hit the heart of the kitchen fire without ever touching the grate-bars. In the ben-end and on the Sabbath, though, such behaviour would not have been seemly and there the big white-enamel spitoon was beside his chair. For his guests, however, the problem was unrelenting; its positioning was less favourable for others seated round the parlour fire so that a pipe-smoker beginner of but a few years' experience faced an awkward dilemma: whether to go for the fire with safety, but with social loss, or to try for the spitoon and risk getting the shiny toecap of his host's boot.

It would have to be an afternoon of *blind smorr* or lashing rain to keep Willie Gavin happily by the fire and even then he would spend the greater part of it wandering to the window, looking for some break in the clouds.

"A coorse nicht," he would tell his guests huddled at the fire. "I doubt gin it will fair the nicht."

He would hardly be able to wait till it came time to put on his oilskin jacket and go out to the byre. For the Sabbath night, like every other of the week, brought its evening milking and in winter the mucking-out of beasts.

When he followed Grannie Gavin in from the byre, it was time to pick up the big Bible lying with his bright napkin. Riffling its pages, the crofter man would select the chapter he would read aloud to his family and as many as were in its circle and round his croft fire that night. For all his complexities and contradictions, they said, he could give them the Word deeply and movingly, so that it made a mark on all of their lives. When he had finished, the young men who had come courting his available daughters and been bidden to stay for their supper took the hint and went home.

XIX

The Old Speak

THE CROFT FOLK of the North-east Lowlands had the old speak, the language of an older Scotland. Not just the homely diminutives of later time that softened the impact of a harsh landscape and the guttural tongue that grew out of it, but a host of the words that old Jamieson had so assiduously harvested for his dictionary in the early-1800s but which languish now for want of the men who can speak them, far less understand them. Their meanings are as lost to us now as the words themselves. More's the pity, for the old speak had nuances that revealed the sin but spared the sinner, subtleties and inflexions that were inexpressible in the precise English that would replace them. And we could have done with them now, for often they were quiet words with guile in them that could slip round the outright confrontation. The croft folk, with the farmtoun cottars, were their last repository and the old speak died with them and took with it some of the dignity of that countryside.

There died then, too, much of the old culture. Like the old balladry of the landscape, it could not continue without the medium that gave it colour and life. The old words would fall silent on the lips that once had sung them to remain enshrined only on the fading page where the ear imperfectly attuned to the past could pick up again a little of their music, the shades of their old enchantment. Now that audience, too, has largely been lost; the old voices are stilled.

It would be impossible in any work that deals with the old landscape not to lament them. What was lost was a strong link with the land, for the two were closely related. The countryman's culture grew out of the soil and the seasons; many of the words in his rural society had agricultural connotations and came out of the dark past of the farmtoun hamlets, the early farmtouns. They had, some of them, a relevance to the work of the old run-rigs in those days before the hedgerow and the margined field; yet most were still in everyday use among the North-east crofter folk of the mid-1800s and a great many would remain on the lips of old men right up to the 1930s.

Sadly, the old speak of the crofter's Lowland landscape was without the strong roots of the Gaelic, that would sustain and nourish it; its words, expressive and telling though they were, were regional. Refined and sifted into an art form, they would delight the knowledgeable ear—and at once narrow the performer's appeal; if they travelled on the folk singer's lips it was as much on the strength of a ballad's vigorous, earthy beat as from any understanding of the words themselves. This was the dilemma: though the words were nurtured in an area that sent a large number of its young folk out into the world, they could not carry the old words with them. They might hold a pub audience captive for a moment or two but a sophisticated society had no use for such words; no more than it had for the crofter men who used them. Their day was over and done with, their homely sound made redundant by the catch-phrases of a glib society where the spectrum of communication was narrowed and channelled and where the brief and precise shades of response were increasingly rehearsed.

It is not difficult now to see why. It has to be admitted: Doric, the dialect of the North-east Lowlands, with its dementia for diminutives, its contortion and distortion—of the French and the English (and the tampering with the Gaelic)—and its guttural explosions, is not a genteel language. It was graceless in the drawing-room and no doubt damnably alarming at times in the English boudoir. It was—as, in its remnants, it still is—a language of the land and its folk: brusque at times and rough round the edges. Yet few now, even if they feel little grief at its loss, would doubt its relevance in a hard countryside. It had a quality the old speak, an aptness, that the words of pure English could not encapsulate, even at times a tenderness in the affairs of life that not even the gentlest Southern tongue could convey. It had, withal, a richness, that slow speak of the farm and crofting men that could surprise you. And given the nature of such men—and the bitterness, sometimes, of their days—it was a language full of cautionary aphorisms that drew their images from the land:

A drappy May mak's the hay. (Rain in May makes good hay.)
He that lippens till a lent ploo will hae his land lang in leys. (He

who depends on the loan of a plough will have his land long in grass.)

Ye've the wrang soo by the lug. (You have the wrong sow by the ear—meaning: you are indicting or criticising the wrong person.)

Ye've ca'ed yer hogs till an ill-market. (You've driven your pigs to a bad market—meaning: you have not got a good bargain.)

It was a language as full of instruction for the landsman as any in the length and breadth of Britain:

> *Fin the meen's on her back*
> *Men' yer sheen an' strap yer thack.*
>
> (When the moon's on her back,
> Mend your shoes and prepare your thatch.)

There was news of what a community itself could expect from the seasons, not exclusive to crofting society or even to the region but never more pithily expressed: *A green E'el mak's a fat kirk-yard.* (A green Yule makes for a full cemetery.)

There were saws that took care of social occasions and came into their own about the New Year especially. A man needing a drop of water with his dram (when his stomach that night had already taken enough) would stay the water-jug and his host's hand with the injunction: *Dinna droon the mullart.* (Don't drown the miller.)

Wrongdoers that night or any night, for whom retribution seemed imminent, would be advised to *Mak' yer feet yer freen'* (Make your feet your friends).

With its underlying belief in salvation through work, it was a a landscape—and a language—strong on incentives to personal industry: *A gangin' fit is aye gettin'.* (A going foot is always acquiring goods.)

There were maxims that ring down to our own time, redolent of the hardiness of life in the crofter colonies and of the need for the contents of the broth pot and the porridge pan to go round: *Pairt sma' and sair a'.* (Part small and serve all.)

Warnings abounded, most likely to lasses: *Dae naething through the day that'll mak' ye greet at nicht.* (Do nothing through the day that will make you cry at night.) More than a few embodied that most important of considerations, the need for good health: *Better tae weir oot sheen than sheets.* (Better to wear out shoes than sheets.)

There was an abundance of advice for folk who never had

enough *siller*, and that was most of them: *Short accounts mak' lang
freen's wi' the merchant.* (Brief accounts make friendship with the
grocer easier.) And there was in a chauvinistic society scant sympathy for the woman who was a dedicated follower of fashion: *If
yer warm eneuch, yer braw eneuch.* (If you are warm enough, you
are fashionable enough.)

It was a landscape with humour as dry as the proverbial Mar-
tini, one in which droll stories (sometimes with a sexual undertow)
circulated without unforgivable offence. They reflected only the
astringent wit of Willie Gavin's spare countryside and the deep
layer of human awareness that lay just under the skin of its hard-
bargaining consciousness. It was a humour, often, that allowed the
slow-spoken countryman to score slyly off his neighbour or folk
who might have considered themselves as intellectually superior.
Above all, it had a wryness to be found rarely in any other landscape.

In a community of good masons, so many of whom went to
America for a season of work, it was dryly said of one who had
hardly arrived there before becoming homesick and returning:
"He gaed owre and lookit the time and cam' hame." An old millwright of that same countryside, a craftsman who could turn wood
to any purpose under the sun and had the kind of engineering
skills that further enhanced his reputation round the parish—
maybe because he had spent so much of his time acquiring such
skills—reached middle age a bachelor still, one of the best catches
of several parishes but without even a house-keeper's bed to climb
into. One day, when all hope had gone, he was invited in by a
neighbour for his Hogmanay dram and to see the new baby that
had arrived just in time to see the old year out. His host, the father,
was understandably a man well-pleased with himself.

"I'll bet yon's something ye'd like fine tae make, eh Sandy?" he
said, with a wink to his wife and a nod in the direction of the
bundle in the cradle.

Sandy considered for a moment only. "I doubt," he said, quiet
and unsmiling, "that it is oot o' the question. As ye ken, I hae nae
wife and am therefore withoot the material."

The man's wit, like the reputation of the fine threshing-
machines he built, would pass down in the folk memory of the
countryside to be remembered and repeated (whenever the bottles
came out) long after he had left all drams and "mulls" behind him.
He took it all very well (since he had little chance to do otherwise)

and even into old age would be nudged gently as a bonnie lass flew past on her bicycle and asked: "What think ye o' yon bit o' material, Sandy? Could ye dae onything wi' that?"

That such drollery lived on, perpetuating itself, implied no paucity of humour. It was simply that life itself, like the land, turned to a pattern and in a close-knit society had a rhythm to its days. For twenty years, it is said, the Free Kirk minister of one parish met daily in the street one of his flock, a mason man whose leg had been crushed by a stone, and for all of those twenty years had daily inquired:

"And how's the leg, the day, John?"

And as regularly and as unvaryingly for the same twenty years, the reply had come back: "It's jist aboot the same, minister. I am jist aye hauding it forrit."

Neither had considered the exchanges remarkable and though sympathy undoubtedly prompted the concern, it is as likely that the droll response it occasioned had a deeper therapeutic purpose: it hardened the scars and healed the bitterness.

In many ways, it was a speak of surprising kindnesses. A man near the end of his days, did not decline into senility but got just "a little bit raivelled", that softness of phrase taking all the indignity out of the muddle his mind had become. And death itself was as gently approached and prepared for:

"Old Gordon is nae verra weel, I doot."

Or:

"Willie is a gey puir cratur, I hear."

In such announcements there was a studied avoidance of anything that might come near to the categorical, a concern that kept open a man's option on life even as he slipped out of it. Death when it came brought regret as softly expressed, as gently voiced:

"Puir man, he didna lie lang."

Or:

"Puir man, he was taken away in a hurry"—an indication that the deceased had not been expected to succumb so quickly or perhaps that he had not been allowed a fullness of years. And even then there could be the subtler nuances that only a native ear would register:

"It's a pity yon man was taken away in such a hurry"—a regret that obliquely recorded the fact that a man's passing left something unaccomplished or a promise unfulfilled.

Understandably it was a landscape in which appeals to the Almighty were not infrequent, though with its horror of blasphemy, they had to be couched in the careful terms that avoided taking His name in vain. Surprise and astonishment were accordingly muted, exclamation watered down to: "Dyod be here . . ." or "Guid be here . . ." or even "Guid fegs!" though the heedless spirit might come close to vain usage with the explosion of "Michty be here . . .!" an utterance that never failed to darken Grannie Gavin's brows. Strangely, there were no problems about disbelief; then, amazement or the kind of consternation that would not call a man an outright liar to his face might be expressed by summoning a more appropriate Being: "De'il be here . . ."

God's name, however, might be invoked on matters of some moment ("God hae pity . . .") or in qualification of some serious compact ("God willing . . .").

And there were other sly words of doubt in that old countryside that avoided the direct confrontation yet as surely indicated the strain of a statement on belief. "Dammit" was often a prelude to doubt that could be transmuted to "Daggit" in delicate company. It introduced the merest *soupçon* of suspicion. "Dag the bit . . ." was a stronger doubt that could be strengthened by inflexion to the level of outright disbelief without ever so much as saying so. Such careful phrasing had a further advantage: in bellicose company it left you a path of retreat.

Always the speak of the old croft folk was ruminative; opinion emerged, it was never jumped at. Inevitably, it wildly eschewed anything that seemed remotely to ring of commitment. Question, as often as not, took the form of statement, to the confusion of the outsider, with only the note of curiosity rising in the tail of it to tell the experienced listener that it was in the interrogative.

"You will be going to the meeting the morn's nicht, Andra?"

"Likely," would be the rejoinder, its meaning as near to certainty short of flood or disaster you were ever likely to get but still and all, this side of definite, categorical commitment. A man did not parade his intentions.

Nor was endorsement given lightly. The most ordinary and sociable of greetings, civil to all whether it was the laird or the passing tink on the road, could verge on the careful hesitancy of high diplomacy.

"Fine day," a ploughman might cry over the dyke to the croft wife passing on the road to the kirktoun. "But cauld ——"

"Aye—caulder nor yesterday."

"Aye—but better nor last week."

Nearly all the old landscape's responses were as finely measured, as cautiously hedged.

If it was a society with its fair share of rude rhymes (at the expense of bald men and cripples), it had others that had long been a part of that landscape, traditional and fit even for the ben-end on a bad Sabbath. They were the repertoire of the crofter's and the cottar's wisdom, the couplets that related to crops and to weather, their belief often ill-founded. Though Willie Gavin in his keen mind must have known otherwise, he gave credence still to their warnings, as had his father before him. Some, indeed, were as important to the mason man as they were relevant to the crofter he also was:

> Gin Can'lemas Day be dry an' fair
> Half the winter's tae come an' mair.
> Gin Can'lemas Day be weet an' foul
> The half o' winter's gaen at Yule.

The crofter man knew their old words and their portents as well as he knew the old psalms and as the days came on him—St Swithin's for instance—he would turn them over on his tongue as earnestly as a sinner counting his beads. There were other couplets that prophesied what each day would bring:

> The evening reid an' the mornin' grey
> Is aye the sign o' a bonnie day.

The landmark of Willie Gavin's countryside was the lonely hill of Bennachie, where some of the bitterest chapters of the Northeast's crofting history had been written. From the very start of his days, from his first wetted *hippen* in the old croft dwelling, it had been a factor in his life, and in his old age it was to the blue saddle of the hill that he looked each morning to see whether it was hidden by cloud or whether its peak was raised proudly in the clear air.

> When Bennachie pits on her tap
> The Garioch lads will get a drap.

If the old crofter man had the lore of the countryside on his lips, his speak was rich too in the old words that described the human condition. Obscure though their origins now are, their guttural sound gave colour and texture to the daily round and expressively recorded its calumnies and disasters. The folk of Willie Gavin's countryside rose in the morning to their *bickers* (wooden dishes) of brose, to *trauchle* (toil) through the day until they became *foisonless* (tired) and came home *girning* (complaining) with *teem* (empty) stomachs. Folk did not tinker with things, they *fichered*; they did not delay for an instant, they *dauchled*; they did not fall headlong, they *gaed clyte*; they did not go head-over-heels but went *heelsterheid* or maybe *heelstergowdie*; they did not deafen each other with gossip, just *deaved* one another. Ungainly persons with a capacity also for the eccentric were *halyrackit;* add to that anything further in the way of outrageous behaviour and they could be called *glaikit*, or, pushed to extremes, go *clean gyte* (demented).

And there were the words that signified and marked distress: *feuch!* for the unsavoury smell that assailed the nostrils; *fich!* for the anguish of stinging your fingers on a hot pot-handle, the nuance so slight that no stranger would hear it.

It was a society whose menfolk were inclined to go on the *splore* (on the spree) and with drams in them took to *stravaiging* (wandering) where they shouldn't, or *stoitering* (staggering) and even likely to *tummle doon* (fall down) before eventually reaching home, no doubt to be upbraided for their lack of *rumgumption* (good sense). There were old words that described a man in somewhat better shape: in his prime and dignity, for instance, or his *potestatur*; or in a more affable and amiable mood, as a *furthy cheil*. There were words equally old and just as enchanting that grouped folk in their gatherings for ball, kirk or market: a *boorich* (a confused assembly and a small crowd); a *hantle* (smaller, but still a fair number): and a *pickle* (a small cluster), all of them words, like so many more, that would never make a liar of you.

A man, like as not, would take the terminology of his fields into the croft or cottar-house kitchen as the hunger gnawed at him and ask, in the middle of the afternoon, for a *sheave o' loaf* (a slice of bread) to stay him till it came suppertime. It was indoors, too, that such French as had once filtered into the language came to grief on the rocks of guttural corruption and threw up such offshoots as *aumery* and *ashet*. Both had a home still in Grannie Gavin's kitchen in the late-1930s, along with such native survivors as *thieval* and *spurtle* (the stick that stirred the porridge) and *tattie-chapper* (potato masher).

Old words would linger on old lips as descriptive of the fashions as of the contents of the kitchens. The scarf the old crofter man wound round his neck on a cold morning before going to the field to pull turnips for his stock was his *gravat* (the early Scots spelling of cravat); a jersey or pullover when he wore one, which was seldom, was his *mauzie* or *gansey*, words more from the fisherman's world than the crofter man's though they had percolated inland and into the speak of farmtoun and small-holding.

When a man of that old landscape had to replace his Sabbath suit, something of a major investment, he kept the old one as a *scuddler*—to wear on less important occasions till he had finally had the last thread of wear from it. In speaking of their tweeds, crofter men would refer to their *shute*, a word not exclusively of the Northeast for it was known in the Border country in 1802, when Susan Sibbald wrote her *Memoirs* and used it to distinguish a coachman's rig.

In any discussion of *claes* (clothes) the old words surface like bubbles in a porridge pan: *worsit* was worsted; *gartens* were garters (a fine word indeed for those bands of thick black elastic); and *breeks*, for all its couthie sound, came down from a grander past than one commonly supposed—from the days of the courtier and doublet, when it early described the breeches that kept the rest of the grandee warm and decent. History would give the word a terrible down-come—to describe a mere crofter man's trousers. *Shank*, though it had latterly designated the knitting that leapt like a kitten into a croft wife's hand every time she sat down, came surprisingly out of a similar and illustrious past: in that time of doublet and hose, the shank had been the lower part of the attire. It was natural that in the land of the factory stocking-knitter it had descended in the dialect to describe the piece of work itself. *Hose* was as reluctant to fade from the scene and endured among the lonely farmtouns and the crofts right up to World War II and the lure of nylon to describe the stockings the womenfolk wore, whether woollen, lisle or sinfully silk.

And if it held history, that old speak, it could also spring its surprises. Who now would believe that in the mid-1800s in that bare landscape there might be such modern-sounding sayings as "I'll bet ma beets (boots)" or "Like me, like ma dog"? Yet there were. Or that the crofter folk, Grannie Gavin among them, would speak regularly of getting "a terrible aggravation" long before television filtered that expression from the dark corridors of villainy into the staid suburban sitting-room?

There were delightful words that survived not only from their everyday use for the things they described but for the sheer flavour they could give to a conversation; like rare birds they fluttered into the talk of men whiles as they met in old age, in the mid-afternoon, to speak of earlier times. They rang in the mind, defiantly in the face of their English usurpers, their past as much a mystery as the dark side of Hogmanay: *forhooiet* (deserted, forsaken); *tootie-mootie* (whispering); *disjasket* (worn out); *galshich* (a tasty titbit). There were many more. Odd were their sounds and strangely they fell on the ear; but anything that followed them in the years to come, you knew, would be poor counterfeit. And so it would prove.

One might suppose that the packaged American TV serial—if not the increasing oil industrialism of the landscape that Willie Gavin trod—might be bringing an entirely new speak to the old crofting countryside. That assumption would be less than correct. Long, long before the oilmen came and even before John Logie Baird was born, one crofter man might ask another: "Foo are ye makin' oot?" ("How are you making out?"). The same men, indeed, would be as likely to complain to one another about the *on-gang* of work or the *on-ding* of rain—years before the parlance of the space age gave a kind of lugubrious respectability to such grammatical leap-frogging. Had the New World, you would wonder whiles, plucked its phrases from the lips of some emigrant Scots ploughman?

Standing now, at a distance of years, one hears in the mind the language of a lost landscape and of a lost people, piquant and love-able words that fell once so easily on the ear, the old chants that took the croft folk through the seasons. Sometimes one hears the poetry unintentional in them. Is there anything now that holds the haunting melancholy of the *fa' o' the year*, that season that brought down the curtain on all green and growing things? Certainly not the English of "autumn". Is there any other phrase that proclaims so exuberantly that prelude to summer, the *gab o' May*, the interlude that as surely lifts it? Both were part of the calendar that Willie Gavin lived his days by. Sadly they no longer spring spontaneously to the lips and their loss diminishes a landscape (and maybe a nation).

But perhaps, after all, that was inevitable: the schoolroom with its dementia for the English took the old words out of a croft bairn's mouth before he had time to savour them—and almost rendered him speechless in the bygoing, for in his educational years he dwelt in a divided kingdom, going home from his desk (surreptitiously vandalised) to a home where the slow Doric described the day, the work, the seasons, in turn a refugee from both.

There were other factors, also, that would put the old words out of common usage, not least the rapid changes in the countryside in which they were nourished and had their roots; the increasing urbanisation of society; and the encroachment of alien cultures. In the 1920s and 1930s, as society settled itself again and resharpened the old class distinctions, those young folk taking the old words with them to become part of it soon thought the better of it, for they were neither the words of commerce nor social advancement. Their utterance would have been as dreadful as being caught in the fraudulence of passing bad currency. Even in their home-land, tradesmen's wives who took to the sophistication of wearing French knickers and making coffee, became guarded with a language so steeped in the past, so certain to betray a provincialism in its homely phrases.

So the old speak faded from the land like the folk who used it. Few would regret it, still fewer make a fuss about it. Yet it would have its champions: a dour northern newspaper editor or two loth to let the past slip so easily away, an occasional poet, a writer or two working determinedly and with a persistent integrity in the clay of childhood, an inner ear forever tuned to its old rhythms and and cadences, striving to sustain the old patterns of speech that synthesised soul and landscape. There would be Jamieson's old dictionary, a *hairst* of fine words that his successor, the diligent Dr Longmuir after him had bound and *stooked* anew. Now and then, in the time to come, folk might turn to mull and mourn over the treasures that lie buried there and wonder that something so rich in its texture—so near to a separate language—should have died so quickly. Hearing the old words—a thin crackle perhaps on the recordist's tape—they might turn, to see how they fitted in the old landscape, to Helen Beaton's *At the Back o' Benachie*, where they are spread like a feast. Yet already her sentences would need a translator to unlock their secrets for the young. And that would be nonsensical, an act of literary vandalism, for like the old ballads of the farmtouns, sung in the stables and bothies of that old Northeast Lowlands countryside, it is only in the old speak that they come truly alive.

XX

Willie Gavin's last "Hairst"

WILLIE GAVIN WAS struck down between the haytime and harvest, while he was giving his turnips their second hoeing with the
old Highland *croman* he had long kept for the work. Laverockhill
would have been willing enough to send down a man with a horse
and a *shim* for the half-*yoking* that was all it would have taken. But
he knew the old crofter man would not hear of it, for Willie Gavin
had long lived with the belief that the horse-hoe tore down the
drills too savagely, leaving not enough soil for his *neeps* to *boddam
oot* and get fat in the row. He was seventy-five and had been frail
for some time. A decision had been made: he would be out at
Martinmas, the end-of-year term for the hiring of men and the
ending of things, a time (like Whitsunday) when men shut the
book on long and eventful tenancies and broke finally with the soil.
It was a decision Willie Gavin had made with a sore heart; and
since making it he had become quiet and withdrawn.

It was Grannie Gavin, going out to cry him in when he did not
come home for his dinner, who found him: sprawled helpless
between the drills, his old steel-rimmed spectacles splintered where
he had fallen on the shaft of the old implement. He was not dead,
but neither could he move nor speak to tell her what had come
over him. Only his eyes could appeal to her. She would remember
them, like the gaze of a sick beast that had lost its reason for living.
She took off her apron to make a pillow for his head and then ran
for Lang Andra McCaskill, never more glad of him. Together they
took Willie Gavin home to his croft *biggings* for the last time, in his
own barrow, his legs lifeless over its end-shelving. Lang Andra, a
resolute man, wheeled the barrow indoors unthinking, negotiating
the turn of the porch with some difficulty, but then into the kitchen
and finally the *closet*, where they lifted Willie Gavin gently into his
bed.

He would not rise again. He lay through the harvest and the
stooking, rallying a little to turn his head on the pillow to see the

sheaves come home past the *closet* window and into the cornyard—
led in by one of Laverockhill's horsemen—before the second
stroke killed him. It was a fine *hairst*, the best he had ever had, for
he had finally let himself be persuaded and changed his seed corn.
Still and all, it did not take the horseman that long, and when he
had finished he stepped into the croft house to see the old man. It
was a fine end-of-*hairst* day with a strong sun and a light breeze
that siftered round the corners of the croft *biggings*.

"We will have gotten winter?" Willie Gavin said to him, the
words slow and no more than a whisper, as though he had
husbanded his strength just to ask him the question.

"Aye, yer hairst is in, man," the young horseman had said
quietly, taking his bonnet off, ill at ease in the sickroom and sad to
see the old man so sorely come-at at that time of year when men
stood for once in the benign shadow of nature, the one at peace
with the other.

Tears were shed for Willie Gavin, hard man though he was, and
his family mourned him. The croft folk came to see him in his
coffin, laid out in the ben-end in his best nightshirt, his face new-
shaved and strangely serene as though his eyes beheld still the
bounty of that last harvest, his long moustache spruced up. It was
the custom. Simple folk, they put their regrets into stumbling
words and walked through to see him.

"It was the worry of leaving the croft."

"It was the way he would have wantit it," they said one to
another, knowing the man. "He would not have wantit to be long
an invalid-body, not able to step round his parks whenever he had
a mind to."

They spoke too for themselves.

On the day of the funeral folk came from farther afield, not only
from the crofts but from the farmtouns far round where they
remembered him still as a good mason-man. His family and its
immediate friends, the McCaskills and the McPhees, gathered in
the ben-end for the service round the coffin; outside in the end-of-
hairst sun the men of the crofts and the countryside broke their
news and took off their bonnets and stood bare-headed as the
words carried out to them through the widely-opened windows.
By and by, when the lid of the coffin had been screwed down, they
stood back to let it come out through the ben-end window to be
loaded into the motor-hearse. With that special stealth that is the

art of undertakers, it had eased down the croft close during the service, the purr of its engine all but inaudible.

It was all of it now a far cry from that cold wintry day when Willie Gavin's father had made the same journey. Then the *shelts* yoked in the horse-hearse, fretful in the cold, had stood and champed on the bit and scraped their hooves, anxious to be home again and into the warmth of their stable. Mettlesome black *shelts* they had been, high-steppers, jingling their bright harness. They took some holding on the rein as the cortège moved off, tossing the black plumes of death in their hames; who can say now but that they gave death a greater dignity. It was a grand rig; in life Old John had never ridden in such style. Great-grannie Gavin (for it was not then the custom for the womenfolk to go to the graveside) had set her foot on a chair by the kitchen's back window and her chin into her hand, to watch the hearse go ben the road, trailing its black ribbon of men. Old John had gotten a good turn-out, though it had not been respect that brought them that day but honest friendship, for they had all of them known him for the crofter he was. Dry-eyed she had watched their solemn dignity as they *convoyit* her man and straggled from her sight round the corner of the Pairtrick Wood behind his glass coach.

"God, Johnny," she had said—her last words to the little, likeable man who had slept so long in her bed—"you micht well think something o' yersel' this day, wi' sae mony fowk trailing ahint ye."

Old John, certainly had been a different man from his son, a different man entirely. He had been a man putting his days past easily. Willie Gavin had been a man with a dream and it would be hard, now, to give meaning to it. He had believed that his croft acres would be his kingdom, supporting him and his folk, bearing his crops, rearing his stock in a harmony of man with the seasons. It was a fragile dream, an impossible dream, and it had been old long before Willie Gavin's time. But he had invested in it—good money after bad, every penny he had earned from his craft skill that could be scrimped from feeding his bairns and buying their clothes. His croft *biggings*, built by his own hands, were better by far than those of most of the estate's farmtouns. But what good had that been, when the soil had betrayed him? It is likely that each poor *hairst* fed the roots of Willie Gavin's disillusionment; that in his soul he knew the heartbreak of it. Quietly, he had come to bury that dream, telling nobody, not even Grannie Gavin—

though maybe she guessed it—for even with her there would be times when he was austere and distant. But then, Willie Gavin had never had the gift for sweet words, not even when they were young.

Jess MacKendrick took her man to the little kirktoun's cemetery to lie with his own folk in the family lair, as she herself would do when the time came. There had been no rain and the grass was dry; nobody slipped as they walked him slow down from the kirkyard gate into the shadows where the manse trees overhung the wall. The stone would be cleaned before Willie Gavin's name was chiselled to join those of his ancestors: his father and mother, his old grandmother Grace, husbandless still in her last sleep.

Slowly the kirkyard would gather his children.

XXI

A Break with the Land

OLD JESS MACKENDRICK auctioned herself out of the croft at
Martinmas that year, for it had been clear enough that none of her
family—neither the sons long away and settled in a different way
of life nor the cottared men of her daughters—wanted it. The
croft line would be broken, but she could not blame them for that:
for as long as she had known it, it had been a millstone round the
necks of her menfolk. It had taken the best of her married years
and though she had never complained she never had liked it; without her man she had no stomach for the life.

Not all the folk who came to see Willie Gavin sold up had known
him for the *roup*, the auction, had been widely advertised in the
newspapers—in the slender columns, beside the mart prices, that
the farmtoun eye reaped daily about dinner-time like the bouts of
harvest, gleaning event and time and place. Nor were all of them
croft folk. Far from it, for it was deep into the depression days that
hit the farmtouns and not a few of their poorer tenants were there
for the bargain or two that might come their way: a barn fork or
two or a byre *graip* would be easier bought there than new from
the merchant.

It was a dry and sunny day for the middle of November but
with a chill in the wind that sent the first-comers into their coat
collars and eventually into the shelter of the byre and the barn.
Mistress McPhee and Mistress McCaskill came shawled for comfort, to be with their neighbour. The three of them watched from
the kitchen back window as the waiting folk re-grouped in the cornyard. Suddenly they were attentive: the auctioneer was up on his
rostrum, Jess MacKendrick's old kitchen table. He was the man of
the moment, on whom everything depended; his quick tongue
would give repartee and riposte where it was wanted, his guile
bring a guinea where only a pound was expected. For Jess Mac-
Kendrick (and the future of the mart company) he would bleed
them for every penny.

That day they sold all that remained of Willie Gavin, all his long past and his hopes, lock, stock and barrel: his milk cows and his *stirks*, the stacks newly into his cornyard and his hay-rick with them (after all the lean years his oats would thresh-out at twelve quarters to the acre); his picks and shovels and his shaving-mirror; his old oil engine and his small barn-mill; the muck of his byre *midden* and his yellow turnips still sitting in the drill. A young mason's apprentice inspected his hammers and trowels and chisels, turning them over carefully on their frayed canvas bag before bidding for them, as though he had known their reputation, bringing a tear to Jess MacKendrick's eye.

The bidding was brisk (as it was always on a fresh afternoon) and the sell-up hindered nobody long. Soon the folk with the farthest to go were putting on their bicycle clips, keen to be home before night came on them, and the auctioneer came down from his pulpit (sold from under him) in the shelter of the corn ricks to walk the croft *shifts* and value the grass and the fences where they stood for the in-going tenant—if ever they should find one.

"Willie would not have made muckle siller oot o' the croft," folk said, cycling home round the bend of the Pairtrick Wood in groups till such time as their roads diverged and their separate croft and farmtoun tracks claimed them.

"Verra little . . ."

"She was always poor grun."

Only the old crofter man himself would have known for sure for like most of his kind he did not keep books. His accounts were in his head, where no one could see them.

"Aye, she was always poor grun," a lone voice would say, the words torn away on the wind, an epitaph for the crofting dream.

Though he never admitted it, Willie Gavin's croft was more loss than profit. In the depressed 1930s lockjaw could clear the *stirk* stalls of his small byre in advance of the hard-bargaining farmer, losing him £30 in one swift, savage blow. It was the kind of loss a crofter man could never afford—or absorb. He grew poor in the life and his folk will tell you so. Arguably, his crofting returns were poorer than his father's had been for Old John's economy had been more strongly based on stock—those *stravaiging* turkeys and wandering guinea fowl (that were as often feeding on his neighbours' *shifts* as his own), pigs and *stirks*, to say nothing of the honey from twenty hives. With his *shelt*, and the borrowing of someone else's, the old horseman saved himself the cost of contract ploughing as well. And in the years up to 1880 he would have shared in the general prosperity of the farming countryside before the bubble burst. How else could he have afforded a harmonium with which to pace the Free Kirk's psalms?

It is unlikely that his son could have done so. When the auctioneer finished his work that day, there would be enough for Jess MacKendrick to rent a house in the little quarrytoun she had come from those long years ago. The irony of it could not have escaped her.

That end-of-year too, Puir Angus McPhee, with a resolve unexpected and never shown before, put his head in the calfies' trough and almost managed to drown himself before they found him. Poor man, he would have no more sheep to herd, no more lambing ewes to keep him awake in the long reaches of the night while other folk slept. Two men, sternly overalled, came in a blue van disquietingly anonymous and Angus went with them. Thus and forever was he taken out of the crofting life to dwell in a world of lucid fantasy and high conversation. He was happy, folk said, when they went to see him, as though his soul had found release from the utter loneliness of his life. His wife would continue in the croft house, letting Laverockhill rent the ground to graze a few *stirks*.

The Gavin croft sat empty for long enough, till finally the estate lost hope and let Lang Andra McCaskill take in its land with his own, realising his age-old ambition. But even for Lang Andra it was too late. Suddenly, like an old horse, he had gone wrong in the legs. He would not be able to work the *grun* after all. He put it all down to grass, breaking its old rhythms and rotations, running sheep through the war years and turning a fine penny or two. Then Lang Andra too would pass from the crofting landscape—to a street in the city and the trim little house that Mistress McCaskill always had wanted. It had a low stone wall that drew Andra up short every time he stepped on to his own doorstep and sharply demarcated the end of his interests and the point where the corporation's commitment began. He had only a small back garden and he had filled it with gooseberry bushes and very little else. From time to time, at the end of a mart afternoon, or between buses on his days of hospital treatment, an old crofter man might still go to see him: he looked lost, folk said, and sad and bewildered.

For long the old Gavin house stood lonely as a ghost beside its still acres, empty of life, its land undisturbed by the plough and so sadly unadorned by the *stooks* of harvest; silent now of all the voices that once had filled it. In time, maybe on a bad winter's night, some wanderer of the roads broke down its door to claim the shelter it could afford him in an uncomfortable countryside. Soon, too, the sheep found their way in and out, unfrightened by its presences, leaving their droppings in the kitchen, in the ben-end where the Gavin men had smoked their thick twist on a wet Sabbath and taken the affairs of the farmtouns through-hand— even upstairs in the garrets where the grandchildren slept on ball nights, and in the back *closet*-room where Willie Gavin had lain long a-dying. When its window-frames rotted and its loose slates became a danger to adventurous bairns; when it was little more than a shell and had begun to smell like a sheep fank, a townsman bought it. With grant and government subsidy he ripped down the walls of Willie Gavin's old dwelling and built in its place a pretty little house with picture windows and an integral garage where the old crofter man had once had his byre.

It was a fine house, no doubt. But it had no business there. It was a trespasser in that bare cloud-capped landscape. He was a fine enough man who built it, for all that, a quiet man who brought his worries home in a briefcase; a man with a crisp city walk and a crisp city suit. His children ran sandalled all summer long.

XXII

The End of the Old Croft Folk

IN THAT DOUR landscape they have forgotten Willie Gavin's dream and the hopes of the men just like him. It is long years since the old crofter man went slow past the gold of the autumn stack-yards to meet his implacable God, and it is all of it bye and done with now. The old croft folk have gone from the land and their old ways with them. A few here and there might endure for a time, too stubborn to change, too proud to admit defeat, but it was un-reasonable to suppose that their small and pitifully unprofitable holdings could survive the revolution of the machine-farming age. With them (though something of the kind would remain, unchanging, in the Gaelic kingdom) there closed an era and a lifestyle that endured against the odds. Theirs was already an ancient landscape; their qualities and their agriculture those of a vanished time. For the croft on the bare hillside or the lonely moor had been out-dated from the moment of its inception. It geared the crofter man to that old subsistence agriculture that the laird's improvements were set in supplanting. That was the irony, the tragedy, of the crofts. The question, still, is: were they ever meant to be viable, self-sufficient; intended to succeed? Or were they, in the land-owning mind—since his few acres could give the crofter so little— a way of allowing an illusory freedom while effectively trapping a pool of pliable labour for light industry, estate or farmtoun? It would be sinister to suppose so and their rise may simply have been a spontaneous thing that coincidentally gave the laird some advantages. In the North-east Lowlands, certainly, there was never anything approaching the cynical and calculated exploitation that marked, say, the kelp-gathering communities of the Western Highlands and Hebrides.

The old crofts would largely die out with World War II, but even before the end of the 1930s their lifestyle had lost its appeal, like that of the farmtouns that ringed them. Indeed, their decline during the depression years was in tune with that of the farmtouns though their story, by comparison, was one of failure, of a long betrayal by the land. It could hardly have been otherwise. Its span of development may have been fractionally longer than that of the farmtouns, but certainly from the late-1880s, if not before, the crofter's world was hit by the same forces and beginning its long slide into extinction. His *stirks*, those young beasts in his byre that paid the rent, were fetching poorer prices. His economy, if one can invoke such a grand word for such a basic agriculture, was on the ebb; no longer was there a clamour for crofting ground.

For a time it had seemed that the self-sufficiency that was at the very heart of his simple lifestyle might protect the crofter man, and isolate him from the grip of the factors—fluctuating prices being perhaps the most important—that were beginning to have their disastrous impact on the countryside. But gradually, by the 1920s if not earlier, the old croft folk started to lose that self-sufficiency. The traditional life began to break down and in that came the old crofter's undoing. Ready-mades ousted the croft wife's shirts; the draper's van, where the road was anything reasonable, brought *breeks* that were a feeble imitation of the trousers the country tailor made, but were part, nonetheless, of the disposable lifestyle that would make his old moleskins redundant. The basic diet could now be varied with the visits of the grocer's van—even the occasional odyssey of the fruiterer's cart round the countryside. But at a cost. And again, the self-sustaining life of the crofts took a further knock as it became more convenient for the harassed croft wife to buy a loaf from the baker's passing van than put on the *girdle* for the making of oatcakes, that earlier *breid*. Hawkers on a summer night even brought linoleum squares round the croft doors that lessened the need for a scattering of *clickit* rugs.

None of these factors helped to keep the old crofting way of life alive. And there were others that would speed the crofting decline and the demise of an intriguing lifestyle. One was that general decline of the old countryside itself. Willie Gavin was living in a region that had passed its population peak somewhere about 1880, the last tide of the farmtouns' prosperity; thereafter, as machinery came increasingly into the fields, the numbers needed (even on a casual or seasonal basis) for the running of the big touns diminished and the country folk began their migration—to the towns and a different pattern of labour, even to other continents and new lives. Their ranks were swelled by the drain from the old crofting communities. Even the kind of folk who were the backbone of the old crofting society became fewer as machines began to push out the Clydesdale and the factory-made implement closed the village *smiddy* as surely as the ready-made suit shut down the tailor.

So, sadly beaten by progress—or rushing to embrace it—the folk who had taken in a piece of land, with or without the laird's grace initially, and tamed it, began to drift away from the hill and the edge of the moss into lives unrelated to the soil. As they moved away, the heather and the rushes that had thatched their stackyards repossessed their fields and gradually the old stones of their dwellings tumbled into decay. Who but a crank could want them?

There was something else that hastened the end of the old crofting life in the North-east Lowlands: the reluctance of its womenfolk to toil all the long hours that its way of life demanded, for the hardy old pioneers in their lace mutches had long passed from the scene. The crofter lad likely to ascend his father's Throne began to be shunned matrimonially, however handsome. And where it was not the work that frightened a lass, it was the isolation—on the edge of some broad moor far from any centre of civilisation, any cinema or place of entertainment; and with nothing remotely approaching travel facilities and only the most basic sanitation. A crofter man, poor in cash terms but geared to the old style of self-sufficiency, might indeed be richer than he thought. It was the lack of cultural and social contact that often engendered the feeling of poverty.

True, in the latter days of the old crofting there were shrewd and speculative men who forsook the old patterns and traditional ways entirely to keep hens or pigs under an intensive system and managed to leave the stench of both behind for the headier heights of a farmtoun tenancy, or even ownership. The times were always right for such men: they were the entrepreneurs who saw the chance of a penny long before it became apparent to others, and knew how to turn it. But they were not men of Willie Gavin's kind: they took no soil into trust to be deceived by it. And in any case, their success had no relevance in a wider context and offered no hopes for a revival. The drift from the crofting life would go on.

Where the old crofts stood cheek by jowl with the farming land —where they existed in the niches of the landscape rather than as colonies—the future was simple enough. As their folk moved out the dividing fence was flattened by the bulldozer and the old *shifts* surrendered to the machine age and the multi-furrow plough. It is all of it now a far cry from the old days. Today the machine-harvester, the leviathan of farming's increasing technology, encompasses the long days of anguish of Willie Gavin's *hairst* and those of his near neighbours, McPhee and McCaskill (their *shifts* now into the convenience of one modest 24-acre field), into one swift operation and the space of a brief afternoon. Willie Gavin, so adamant against letting the ungentle binder on to his land, would not have liked it and maybe it is as well that he did not live to see it. The "combine" cares nothing for compaction of soil; and it has made the whole operation so void of meaning—compared with those long days of the *heuk* and the scythe—that the old crofter man would have felt it a kind of betrayal.

Even now, perhaps because of the excesses of the Clearances of the West, crofting is still an emotional subject. Lairds have been blamed for their lack of sympathy with the crofting dream. Their attitude is understandable: from the land-owner's point of view it was always more economically sound to hitch the land of a dilapidated croft, if not to its neighbour's, to that of an adjoining farmtoun than to put money that could never be recouped into rebuilding the croft's *biggings*. Yet this was not the only factor that came into such a decision and lairds were not always blind to that. Recalling his fifty years of lairdship in 1925, in *We Twa*, Lord Aberdeen, a former Governor-General of Canada, came nicely to the nub of the problem as it affected not only the crofter's fragile economy at that time but the laird's own:

> On the one hand it is admitted that the crofters have, in the past, formed in large measure the backbone of the population. On the other hand, there has been a steadily increasing difficulty in placing small holdings on a satisfactory footing, except when the tenant has also a trade. In that case it is plain sailing; otherwise the question of erecting and maintaining the buildings presents serious difficulty.

Alas, even where the crofter man did have a trade or the kind of regular work that gave his economy some stability, his way of life was on the wane.

Those early squatters of Bennachie, moved on by legal might and the lairds unless they paid rent, penned a song to that loss of crofter freedom:

Oh ye were once a monarch hill,
To freedom's footsteps free,
But now unless their honours will,
We daurna tread on thee.
Alas, the heather on thy broo
Will bloom nae mair for me:
The lairds aroon' hae ta'en ye noo,
Ye're nae oor Bennachie.

If that was the first defeat for the crofter men, there were many more to come. All that would remain of that enterprising, "outlaw" community on the old commonty was a patch of green in the heather and the unbroken sound of the wind. Its last resident, a mason and dyker, left the hill in 1939, in his coffin, having grown strange in his loneliness. For all the oddity of his later years though, his was the true crofter's creed: "I beg and bow to no man and no man begs and bows to me." It was a proud dictum, bizarre in its independence, for in their vulnerability few of the croft folk could live up to it.

Yet still for many people the croft and its simple way of life represents a dream, an escape route from the disenchantment of city streets and (worse still) the de-personalisation of a complex industrial society. At a distance it seems a life of enviable freedom, a model for the self-sufficient existence far from the tensions of ordinary life. It isn't. Nothing has changed: the crofting drop-out (discounting the assistance of social aid) still needs a secondary source of income to make anything meaningful of the life. What the croft does hold is the challenge of raw reality and an environment that re-establishes elemental values. Few folk now are fitted to cope with either.

When we look back, it is into a different landscape. What, one wonders, did the old crofts and the crofter folk accomplish? What did they add to the sum of farming knowledge? What was their contribution to the structure of the farming landscape beyond filling in its odd corners and, for a time, the high marginal land of its hillsides? The answer is: very little. For the croft was never a farming unit; what it produced was folk, hard men and sometimes hardier women, resilient and dour; determined folk whose children were scattered by life like *windlestraes* to the ends of the world, taking with them their uncompromising creed of thrift and hard work and the expectancy of little.

The grandson of that laird who had come home in gilded youth all those long years ago to refashion the landscape in which the Gavins had lived their crofting years, in recognising that, would display yet another awareness not always shown by his kind, and with it, in *We Twa*, reveal the reason why he had persisted in retaining so many of the crofter-homes of his estate:

> . . . the type of person who seems to be produced by such homes as these is something that may well be described as a national asset. I am sure that any schoolmaster in Scotland would say that his most promising pupils, and those who have been the greatest successes in after life, have been those who have had the advantage of having been brought up not only in a home but a homestead, amongst all the surroundings of rural life . . .

The old crofts, certainly, were always more than the sum of their sour acres. Sometimes their names can be picked out, even now, on the Ordnance Survey map: isolated outposts where the meal-mill once stood or the *smiddy* forge or the old country *souter*'s *bigging* so far from the centre of trade but once in the middle of the farm-touns with their teams of men. (He too had put away his awl and his last as the population of that old landscape dwindled.) But as many—and maybe more—of the old names have been lost from the map as well as from memory. In 1936, as the old crofter days drew to a close, in uplands Lumsden—born of the moor and cradled in the hills between Strathdon and Strathbogie—a local historian would stop to take stock of the past. In one small area of just three square miles, sixty of the old holdings had gone. Such had been the congestion in crofting's high noon. Their names were redolent of a time and of a wiry folk who had once embarked on a dream but without illusions: Bogmore, Murchybrae, Staneyslack, Littlemill, Birkenbrowe, Linthaugh, Willowbush . . . In some there is a poetry that shows the affection of the folk who named them.

Mostly though the old crofts are forgotten now, except maybe by those who once had connection there. In their later generations they return yearly (taking a hired car from Inverness or Aberdeen or Montrose) to a green patch of the hill or the site of some ruined dwelling to plant co-respondent's shoes in the heather and ponder the lie of the land and absorb its contours—carried long in the mind and passed down, once, from the lips of an old man in a house at the prairie's edge or in the snow fastnesses of some trapper's wilderness. It is a strange fealty that draws them: a need to identify with an older culture perhaps, a quest for simple kinship far from the air-conditioned world and the concrete canyon. It may be difficult for them to relate to the past as they pick out again the outline of the small fields and the site of the old croft *bigging*. It matters little; that they come at all is testimonial enough to the old crofter folk and their bare lifestyle. Poor and driven though they were, they had a kind of dignity.

SELECT GLOSSARY

SELECT GLOSSARY

ablins: perhaps; if able
aboot: about
ahint: behind
airn: iron
aise: ash
ane: one
ashet: assiette (F)
aumery: armoire (F)
aye: always

bade: stayed
ben: along; ben-end, best room
bere: barley
bicker: large wooden bowl; large quantity
biggings: buildings; biggit, built
binks: fireside hobs
birns: heaps
birsle: to burn; birsled, well-browned
blatter: downpour (or rain)
blind smorr: thick blizzard
bloo coo: blue cow, a slatey-grey animal much favoured by crofter
    folk in North-east at one time
boddam oot: bottom out, grow fat
bourtree: elderberry
bowie: cut-down barrel
bree: liquid, juice
breeks: trousers
breid: oatcakes
brock: fragments, usually of potato
byordinar: extraordinary

ca-canny: take it easy
cairds: cards

caul': cold; caulder, colder
caup: wooden bowl from which brose was traditionally supped
cheil: young man; gey cheil, a young man worth taking notice of
claes: clothes, attire
claith: cloth
clay biggings: dwellings built with stones and clay
clickit: hooked; clickit rug, made by hooking rags through sacking
clippit cloots: cut-up rags
closet: small room, traditionally formed by backs of box-beds in but-and-ben dwelling
clyack sheaf: last-cut sheaf of harvest
coggit: weaned
coles: haycocks
convoyit: conducted, accompanied
coorse: coarse, dirty-minded
couthie: homely, cosy
creeshy: greasy
croman: Gaelic hoe
crook: hook
cruive: hen's pen

dae: do
dambrods: game of draughts
dinging: lashing
dinna: don't
disnae: does not
drogs: drugs
drookled: sodden
dyke: stone wall margining field

een: eyes

fairmer: farmer
farl: a quarter-portion of oatcake circle
fechts: fights
fee: engagement of an employee, agreed term of employment; fee'd, hired
feering: first furrow of plough-rig
foons: foundations
fordel: cache, store; to fordel, to store

forrit: forward
fowk: folk
frae: from
furls: whirls

gae: go
galluses: braces
gang: go; gaun, going; gangs, goes
gin: if
girdle: griddle
girn: complain, whine
girnal: oatmeal store-chest
girss: grass
graips: farmtoun forks
gravat: scarf; from cravat
growth: weeds
grun: ground; bit grun, bit of land
gudeman: crofter, farmer, head of the house
guid: good
gurr: growl

hae: have
hairst: harvest
hakes: hayracks
hasher: turnip slicer
haud: hold; hauding, holding
heuk: sickle
hinging lum: hanging chimney; canopy structure over fireplace,
    jutting out into room
hippen: nappy
hiv: have
hoast: cough
horn-eyn: best room, croft ben-end
hough: calf, leg
hyowing: hoeing or singling of turnips

ilka: every

jaud: knowing lady; a tease
John Gunn: privvy

kens: knows
kist: chest

lang: long
lat's: let's
leading: taking sheaves home from field by cart or barrow
leys: leas; grass
limmer: troublesome lass
littlin: little one; child
lookit: looked
loups: jumps
lowse: loosen

mair: more
mak's: makes
marriet: married
mart: weekly livestock auction
meenit: minute
midden: dung-heap
morn (the): tomorrow
muckit: mucked-out

nae: not
nane: none
neeps: turnips
news: gossip, conversation; to news, to chat
nip: tot of whisky, a dram
noo: now

on-ding: downfall
orra-loon: youngest member of farmtoun crew
o't: of it
owre: over

piece: snack; packed lunch
pig: earthenware jar; sometimes stone hot-water bottle
pikit: piked; spiked
pish: piss
press: cupboard
puir: poor

puirman: candelabrum for bog-fir taper

quarter (of oatcake): farl or quarter portion of original griddle
    round of oatcake

raivelled: confused
rantle-tree: crossbar built into either side of the chimney from
    which cooking pots were hung
rattons: rats
ree: hens' cruive
reeshle: rustle
reesin: reason
richt: right
riggin', rigging: couples, rafters
rimrax: ample sufficiency
rin: run
rodden: rowan
roup: auction sale
rowth: a plenty, a frenzy
rushen cords: rope made from rushes

sark: shirt; flannel sark, flannel undershirt
saut backet: salt bucket; old-time container for salt
sedge: rushes
semmit: undervest, singlet
shak': shake
shank: knitting
sharny: shitty
sheelin': winnowing; removing chaff from grain
sheen: shoes
shelt: light horse
shifts: small croft fields
shim: horse-hoe
sids: oat-husks from miller, steeped in sowens bowie
siller: silver; money generally
skirlie: oatmeal-based concoction eaten to keep boiled (or mashed)
    potatoes company
smiddy: smithy
smiler: hayrake
smoor, smorr: suffocate; to smoor fire, to "rest" it overnight

sned: wooden frame of scythe
snibbit: latched
sookit: sucked, drank
souter: shoemaker
sowens: a gruel of water and oatmeal, sweetened for human consumption
spence: best room, croft parlour
sprots: rushes
spurtle: stick for stirring porridge
stirk: steer; young cattle beast
stook: shock; to arrange sheaves in shock
stooking: work of setting harvest sheaves into shocks
stoorum: a gruel of oatmeal and water
stovies: potato-based dish for which the Scots have always been truly thankful
strae: straw
straiked: sharpened
stravaiging: wandering
swey: swee-frame on fireplace

tae: to
tattie: potato; tattie corn, potato corn
tattie chapper: wooden utensil for mashing potatoes in the pot
thacking: thatching
thigging: begging
thrash: thresh
thraw: wring, twist, strangle
threid: thread
tow: string
traviss: partition between beasts' stalls
trochs: troughs
trump: tramp
truncher: trencher

vrapper: female jacket-style garment

warld: world
wha: who
whiles: sometimes, occasionally
wi': with

windlestraes: straws blown in the wind
wir: our

yard: vegetable garden; presumably from ancient kailyard
yavil: second crop
yoaming: foaming
yoking: harnessing; period of work, morning or afternoon